MW00825368

HIRE MANAGE & RETAIN

EMPLOYEES FOR YOUR SMALL BUSINESS

A *CCH Business Owner's Toolkit* Publication

Edited by Joel Handelsman, J.D.

CCH INCORPORATED
Chicago

Cover designed by Steve Blatt, Staff Designer

Books may be purchased at quantity discounts for educational, business or sales promotion use. For more information please contact:

Small Office Home Office Group
CCH INCORPORATED
2700 Lake Cook Road
Riverwoods, Illinois 60015

ISBN 0-8080-0175-2

Printed in the United States of America

THE CCH BUSINESS OWNER'S TOOLKIT TEAM

Joel Handelsman has almost 20 years of experience writing about business, tax, and financial topics. He has experience with multiple new product and business ventures in the publishing industry and has held a variety of management positions. Joel is an attorney and holds degrees from Northwestern University and DePaul University.

Susan Jacksack is a frequently quoted small business expert in national publications like *The Wall Street Journal*, *The New York Times* and *Worth*. She has 12 years of experience advising and writing for small business owners and consumers on tax, personal finance and other legal topics. Susan is an attorney and a graduate of the University of Illinois.

Alice Magos has over 35 years of experience running the operations of numerous small businesses. She is the author of the *CCH Business Owner's Toolkit* online advice column "Ask Alice," and serves as a member of *Home Office Computing's* expert team of advisors. Alice is an accountant, Certified Financial Planner and holds degrees from Washington University in St. Louis and Northwestern University.

Bob Barnett is a regular columnist for *Dividends* magazine, a publication for small business owners with a circulation of over 300,000. He has 12 years of experience representing small and medium sized businesses in their legal matters and covering a variety of topics for business and legal publications. Bob is an attorney and holds degrees from the University of Alabama and Northwestern University.

Martin Bush has 15 years of experience providing legal, financial and tax advice to small and large businesses in various industries. He is a frequently quoted small business expert and has appeared on CNBC and National Public Radio. Martin is an attorney, CPA, and holds degrees from Indiana University and DePaul University.

We would also like to acknowledge the significant efforts of others who contributed to this book: Tom Blazek, Jim Fortmann, Catherine Gordon, Ron Hirasawa, Janet McCabe, Kathleen Larrison, Richard Larson, Tom Lauletta, Todd Mata, Erich Schuttauf, John Siegel, and Richard Yamamoto.

In addition, we would also like to thank the following individuals for their contributions in the production of this book: Donna Bacidore, Steve Blatt, LaVerne Dellinger, and Geoff Huckleberry.

FOREWORD

There are many ways to invest in your business to make it a success. Equipment can make you more productive. More capital can help you expand. Successful business owners also know that employees can be good investments, too. They can add needed expertise and, with more resources, you will be able to develop new business opportunities.

When you hire an employee, you invest your time, money, and trust. However, if you don't select employees with care, nurture them, and oversee them, you can lose them. You also risk being the target of legal actions that can cost you much more. Claims of discrimination, sexual harassment, and violation of worker's privacy are just a few examples.

So with peril at every turn, why have employees? Because the benefits are still often greater than the risks. However, you must be able to identify, manage, or avoid these risks and, at the same time, get your employees to perform their best. Sound impossible? Not if you read this book!

Written by a special team of small business experts, attorneys, and accountants, *Hire, Manage & Retain Employees for Your Small Business* will help you handle common, yet difficult, employee issues. Learn how to recruit well, how to keep good employees, and how to fire bad ones. Using this book, you will be able to do all of this with confidence and, most importantly, without legal liability.

Why should you turn to us? **CCH INCORPORATED** is a leading provider of information and software to the business and professional community. More than four generations of business advisors have trusted our products, and now you can too.

A caution and an invitation — the discussions of the laws contained in this book are current as of the date of publication. But remember, things change. To keep abreast of the latest news affecting your business, visit *CCH Business Owner's Toolkit* on the Internet (www.toolkit.cch.com) or on America Online (keyword: CCH). While you're there, take a look at the other interactive information and tools we offer to assist you in running your business. You can also ask follow-up questions of our team of small business experts. We welcome and look forward to your questions and comments.

Martin Bush

Publisher

Table of Contents

Part I

The Decision To Hire

Hiring your first employee can be one of the most difficult things that you do as a business owner. Up until now, you've probably done it all yourself. Bringing in another person is an admission that that there's more to do than you can handle alone. On the bright side, deciding that you need help probably also establishes that your business is growing and successful.

When you hire, you want to get the most benefit at the least cost. To increase your chances of finding the right person for the right price, approach your hiring decision in an organized and methodical fashion. Take some time to decide exactly what you want someone to do for your business. Then, consider the ways you can fill that need. For example, you may not need full-time help at first, just someone to help out a few days a week or a few hours a day.

How you choose to fill your need for assistance will have a substantial impact on the types of obligations you'll assume as an employer. Some businesses choose to avoid some of the responsibilities traditionally associated with having employees by working with employee leasing firms or temporary help agencies.

However, it's not possible to insulate yourself completely from the responsibilities and risks associated with having people work for you. Thus, it's in your best interest to do your best to carefully define the job you want done and to take the time needed to find the right person for the job.

In this part, our discussion will focus on the steps you'll take to implement your decision to hire.

Chapter 1: So You Need Some Help discusses how to determine exactly what it is that you want an employee to do for you. It also highlights the risks and potential liabilities that you'll bear as an employer.

Chapter 2: Consider Your Options introduces a number of staffing alternatives that can help you get just the right type of help.

Chapter 3: Find the Right Person explains how to attract qualified job applicants and determine what it will cost you to hire one.

Chapter 1

So You Need Some Help

When the work gets to be too much, you may find yourself toying with the idea of adding someone to help out. But do you really need help? Or do you just need to get better organized? If that's the problem, consider a time management course. Make sure you can effectively manage your own time before you take on the management of someone else's time.

Can you afford an employee? Do you have sufficient cash flow, or some other source of funds, from which you can pay an employee? Will you recover the amounts you pay out through increased income? Remember that you'll have to pay at least the minimum wage. In addition, there will be payroll taxes and legally mandated employee benefits, like workers' compensation.

Well, if you're paying your bills, taking a reasonable draw, and still have money left over, you probably can afford to hire an employee. Or you might have a line of credit, a contingency fund, or other source to pay a salary, at least to begin with. Most new employees take some time to come up to speed. So, at first, the income they produce for your business may not cover the cost of paying them.

Will the cost of paying the employee *ever* be recovered? That is, will the increase in your business's income that results from having an employee exceed the expense of the employee? If an employee is going to sell your product or services, it's easy to estimate the sales volume required to cover the cost. However, where an employee isn't going to directly contribute to income, such as clerical or accounting help, the answer is less clear. Consider whether adding an employee will free up some of your time, which can result in increased income as you increase production or take on more clients.

If you're fairly sure that the extra business would amount to more than the expense of taking on an employee, then you're in a good position to hire someone. If the added business won't cover the cost, look for alternatives to hiring a permanent employee. Don't forget to include the impact of the time you'll spend on the hiring process.

How Much More Than Salary Will You Pay?

An employee will cost you more than the actual compensation that you pay. Your responsibility for payroll taxes and any benefits you choose to provide increases you out-of-pocket costs by as much as 30 to 40%. This excludes the investment of your time, both as a supervisor, and as an employer required to keep employment records, withhold and remit payroll taxes, etc.

DEFINE YOUR NEEDS

Once you've decided you need some help, it's time to define exactly what you want someone else to do for you. This might be easy. For example, you may want to provide delivery service and need a driver. On the other hand, if you're a one-person shop and you need a little help with almost everything you do, take a step back and figure out exactly what duties you'd like an employee to perform.

Attitude Counts

Remember, you'd like an employee to act the same way you would in any given situation. But it's unlikely that another person will have exactly the same skills, outlook, and personality that you have. Be sure to effectively include your "philosophy" in defining your needs, particularly with regard to dealing with customers or clients.

Doing Job Analysis

The process of defining your needs begins with job analysis. This means taking a critical and objective look at how you do business now. Exactly what do you do each day, and how much time do you spend doing it? Most employees are hired to perform a subset of the employer's activities. What's included in that set of activities is shaped in large part by what you're willing to trust to someone else.

Employees also may do things that you didn't do before. The fact that you're adding an employee probably means your business is growing, so your business may be able to provide additional goods or services. How will this affect the job that you'll expect an employee to perform?

Once you've defined the job through job analysis, you'll have the information you need to determine the skills and abilities a person needs to effectively perform the work you want done (see Chapter 3). Planning is the key to successful, efficient, and cost-effective hiring. The better you know what you need in an employee, the more likely you are to find the right candidate.

Hiring Your First Employee

If you're hiring for the first time, job analysis will involve more than determining what set of tasks you want someone else to do. It also means figuring out how your life is going to change by having someone else working with you. Questions to ask yourself include:

- **What work will I let someone else do?** What are the tasks that you want, or are willing, to give up? Many owners have a hard time bringing in someone, especially a stranger, to help them work. You don't want to delegate a task to an employee and then wind up micromanaging their work.

- **What decision-making authority am I comfortable delegating?** Being in business means making decisions all of the time. Consider whether you want to give an employee the discretion to handle customer complaints, negotiate prices, receive inventory shipments, etc. Will you let an employee bind you to contracts? How about signing privileges on your bank account?

- **What type of personal relationship do I want to have with my employees?** The answer to this question may not impact your job analysis, but it's critical to the employee selection process. Small business owners frequently spend a lot of time with employees. A good relationship is important, so selecting someone you can get along with is essential.

Hiring an Additional or Replacement Employee

Job analysis is a bit easier if you're hiring to replace an employee who's leaving, or adding a position similar to an existing one. Although you probably have a pretty good idea of what your employees do, use this opportunity to gain additional insight into exactly what's involved on a day-to-day basis. You may be surprised at how existing positions evolve over time. If you have only one or two other employees, just sit down with each and discuss what they're doing and how they do it.

Historically, simply observing employees has been one of the more commonly used job analysis techniques. In most small businesses, the owner is the only supervisor, so to some extent you'll already be observing employees. Observation can complement an interview by assuring that nothing was left out. However, you also have to run your business, so you might not be able to observe a complete job cycle. And it isn't so easy to observe certain types of employees, such as an administrative assistant, service provider, or salesperson. Make sure that you're assessing what the job is, and not the performance of the person who's doing it.

Need more help? There are plenty of resources that can provide some direction in analyzing jobs and duties:

- **In a hurry?** The best source for information is to ask around. Call your colleagues; call people who do the job that you're thinking of creating. You might get some help from the Small Business Administration or your local chamber of commerce.

- **Have some time?** There are some helpful government publications that you can find at the library or purchase. The *Dictionary of Occupational Titles*, prepared by the U.S. Department of Labor, contains comprehensive descriptions of job duties for nearly 20,000 jobs and occupations. The *Occupational Outlook Handbook*, published by the Bureau of Labor Statistics, describes the education and training necessary for the listed jobs and the tasks involved in a variety of jobs. If you can't find these books, look at the BLS website at http://www.stats.bls.gov.

Job Analysis Checklist

One way to organize information regarding a position is to make a list of all the tasks that you want the employee to perform. Each job will involve a different mix of duties and responsibilities. When you compile a list, include every activity essential to the job being done well. For example, identify the types of equipment or other tools that the employee will use, such as computers and particular software packages, cash registers, scanners, production equipment, etc. Also decide on a reasonable measure for the relative importance of each task. For example, you might indicate the percentage of time that the employee would spend on each task, or how frequently the task must be performed.

Even a "simple" job can involve quite a lot. But, if you have a solid understanding of what you expect an employee to do, you greatly increase the chance of finding someone right for the job. Capture everything that you want done in sufficient detail so that you can compare each applicant's abilities to the work to be done. The following checklist illustrates the work that might be performed by a clerical worker.

Routine Clerical Responsibilities

Activity	Time Commitment
Type all correspondence, labels, envelopes, invoices, contracts, reports, etc.	
Pay routine bills; track and ensure payment of larger invoices.	
Receive and welcome visitors; refer to appropriate people.	
Maintain daily ledger and petty cash account.	
Process and file business records, including confidential materials.	
Order and stock office supplies.	
Schedule equipment maintenance and repair.	
Maintain financial information and generate reports using Microsoft Excel.	
Open, sort, and distribute mail.	
Answer telephones, screen and direct calls.	
Take dictation and transcribe from voice recordings.	
Record, type, and distribute meeting minutes.	
Respond to routine correspondence.	
Schedule appointments, meetings, conferences, travel arrangements, etc.	
Prepare meeting and conference rooms.	
Monitor and follow up on voice mail and e-mail.	
Maintain and update mailing lists.	
Data entry into PC-based project and time management software.	
Provide support to other computer users.	
Process payroll records.	
Keep and distribute keys for secure areas and records.	
Orient and train new employees.	
Handle cash and negotiable instruments.	
Act as resource for others as to staff and locations.	
Maintain records of cash receipts and disbursements, expense account activity.	
Maintain vacation and time off records.	
Serve as key operator for photocopy machine.	
Date and log in documents.	
Maintain written procedures and information manuals.	
Create routine, periodic, or special reports as required.	
Balance bank accounts and reconcile statements.	

CONSIDER THE LIABILITIES AND RISKS

If you decide to get help, it's extremely important to be aware of the numerous federal and state laws that can affect the employment relationship. These laws cover topics as diverse as minimum wages, discrimination, required leave, and smoking. Whether or not your business is subject to specific employment laws depends on how many employees you have and how long they've worked for you. In some states, you're subject to certain employment laws if you have even a single employee.

Take your responsibility to comply with laws against employment discrimination very seriously. These laws are intended to prevent the rights of people in identified segments of the population from being treated unfairly.

Protected Groups

Protected groups are groups of people that are distinguished by special characteristics such as their race, color, ethnicity, national origin, religion, gender, age (over 40), disability or veteran status. People in these groups can't be discriminated against in any facet of employment, including hiring, promotion, training, discipline, pay, and termination. State laws may protect other groups, such as individuals in different age groups, people who smoke, and individuals with a particular sexual orientation.

Antidiscrimination laws aren't unreasonable or inflexible: they recognize that there are situations in which it's necessary to exclude certain people from consideration for employment. Foremost among these exceptions is the concept of "*bona fide* occupational qualifications."

Bona Fide Occupational Qualification (BFOQ)

Some federal and state employment laws permit employers to select employees based on religion, gender, or national origin where those factors are "reasonably necessary to the normal operation of that particular business or enterprise." For example, a religious school may require its teachers to be practicing members of the religion being taught.

Your legal liability as an employer involves three elements:

- understanding who will be treated as an employee
- knowing your obligations under federal employment laws
- knowing your obligations under state employment laws

In addition, if you have workers who aren't employees, try to structure contracts with independent contractors so that you minimize your liability.

Work Smart

The U.S. Supreme Court ruled in 1997 that federal antidiscrimination rules apply even after an employee has been terminated. People who no longer work for you can file suits charging you with a violation of their employment rights.

Who Is an Employee?

Anyone who performs services for pay is an "employee" if the one for whom services are performed can direct and control what will be done *and how it will be done.* For purposes of most laws affecting the employment relationship, a worker is generally considered an employee if the person for whom the work is performed has the right to direct and control both the final results and the details of when, where, and how the work is performed.

Example

People who worked for a construction contractor were his employees since he supervised and controlled the workers, supplied major tools and equipment, sometimes dictated the manner in which a job was accomplished, and had the power to hire and fire. However, even had he not actually exercised that control, the fact that he had the right to do so is sufficient to establish an employer-employee relationship.

Your Federal Responsibilities

The following table provides a broad overview of the major federal fair employment laws that apply to most employers. Normally, these laws become applicable when the hiring process starts, and continues through the termination of the employment relationship.

Federal Law	What It Does	Who Has To Comply
Fair Labor Standards Act (FLSA)	Requires you to pay minimum wage and overtime pay to nonexempt workers.	All employers of employees engaged in interstate commerce[1].
Occupational Safety and Health Act (OSHA)	Requires you to maintain a safe workplace and comply with specific safety standards and recordkeeping rules.	All employers, except that in states where a federally certified plan has been adopted, the state plan governs.

Federal Law	What It Does	Who Has To Comply
Federal Insurance Contributions Act (FICA)	Requires you to pay Social Security and Medicare taxes, and withhold such taxes from workers' pay.	All employers.
Federal Unemployment Tax Act (FUTA)	Requires you to pay federal unemployment payroll taxes.	All employers.
Equal Pay Act	Requires equal pay for men and women who perform the same work.	All employers.
National Labor Relations Act	Prevents discrimination against employees who engage in or refuse to engage in union activity. Protects nonunion employees who act together in an effort to improve or protest working conditions that affect them on the job.	Employers whose business has a significant impact on interstate commerce.
Employee Retirement Income Security Act (ERISA)	Prevents employees from being discharged solely to prevent vesting or qualifying for benefits under qualified pension plans.	Employers who maintain qualified pension plans for their employees' benefit.
Immigration Reform and Control Act	Prevents discrimination against employees on the basis of national origin or citizenship.	Employers having at least 4 employees.
Americans with Disabilities Act (ADA)	Prevents discrimination against disabled employees.	Employers having at least 15 employees.
Civil Rights Act, Title VII	Prevents discrimination against employees on the basis of race, color, religion, sex, or national origin.	Employers having at least 15 employees.
Age Discrimination in Employment Act (ADEA)	Prevents age-based discrimination against employees who are over 40 years old.	Employers having at least 20 employees.
Family and Medical Leave Act (FMLA)	Requires employers to grant up to 12 weeks' unpaid leave per year for certain medical conditions of a worker or family member, or for new births or adoptions.	Employers having at least 50 employees.

[1]Note that courts routinely find that virtually all businesses have an impact on interstate commerce. Shipping goods to, or acquiring materials from, another state is frequently sufficient to satisfy that requirement.

Your federal responsibilities for temporary or leased employees. In almost all temporary or leasing situations, your business and the staffing agency are likely to be considered joint employers. That means that *both of you* will have some legal responsibility under federal and state employment laws that apply to your employees. For example, your business *always* retains liability for the safety of employees in the workplace under OSHA, and for compliance with antidiscrimination laws.

Independent contractors. A person who works for you who isn't an employee is usually classified as an independent contractor (see page 25). Many of the laws that apply to employees don't apply to independent contractors. However, it isn't always easy to determine whether a particular worker is an independent contractor or an employee. In an annual poll, small business owners repeatedly identify the independent contractor rules as the ones that they would most like to see clarified and improved.

Example

The owner of a pet grooming business hired some workers to groom animals, and she had them sign contracts stating that they are independent contractors. An IRS investigation was initiated when one of the groomers filed an unemployment claim. The IRS determined that the groomers were employees, not independent contractors. As a result, the owner had to pay employment taxes on the amounts she paid to the groomers.

Your State Responsibilities

Other than state tax laws, state employment discrimination laws have the biggest potential impact on small businesses. Only employers who have 15 or more employees are subject to the most complex and comprehensive *federal* antidiscrimination laws. However, in some states, employers with just one employee are subject to *state* antidiscrimination laws. You can be exempt from federal laws, yet still be subject to your state's civil rights laws. And some state laws are broader in scope and coverage than similar federal laws.

Every state except *Alabama* has enacted various laws pertaining to employment discrimination. Your state's laws *may* not apply to you, depending on the size of your business, and occasionally, on other factors as well. But if they do, take the steps to comply with the rules and consult a lawyer, if necessary.

Warning

Almost every state bars employers from retaliating against employees who oppose or report improper employment practices ("whistleblowers"). They also prohibit employers from discriminating against employees whose wages are garnished for child support, alimony, or other debts.

The laws of each state regarding employment discrimination, as they relate to small businesses, are summarized below. Rules relating to non-profit organizations, governmental entities, domestic service, labor unions, political office holders, etc., have been excluded. Details are provided regarding who is an employer subject to discrimination rules and what types of discrimination are prohibited. Many states exempt the employment of immediate family members from application of their employment discrimination rules.

State Laws on Employment Discrimination

State	Employer and Employee Defined; Discrimination Prohibited
AK	*Employer:* A person who has one or more employees in the state. *Discrimination Prohibited:* Race, religion, color, and national origin (including ancestry), age, physical or mental disability, marital status, changes in marital status, pregnancy, or parenthood.
AZ	*Employer:* A person who has 15 or more employees for each working day in each of 20 or more calendar weeks in the current or preceding calendar year. *Discrimination Prohibited:* Race, color, religion, sex, age (at least 40 but less than 70), handicap, or national origin.
AR	*Employer:* A person who employs nine or more employees in Arkansas in each of 20 or more calendar weeks in the current or preceding calendar year. *Discrimination Prohibited:* Race, religion, color, ancestry or national origin, gender (includes pregnancy, childbirth and related medical conditions), sensory, mental, or physical disability, or medical condition.
CA	*Employer:* Any person regularly employing five or more individuals (15 or more for purposes of the prohibition against discrimination on the basis of physical or mental disability). *Discrimination Prohibited:* Race, religion, color, national origin, age (over 40), ancestry, physical or mental disability, medical condition, marital status or sex (sex includes pregnancy, childbirth and related medical conditions), actual or perceived sexual orientation.
CO	*Employer:* Any person employing persons within the state. *Discrimination Prohibited:* Race, creed, color, sex, age, national origin, and ancestry. Disability, except where the employer can't reasonably accommodate the disability, the disability actually disqualified the person, and the disability has a significant impact on the job.
CT	*Employer:* Any person employing three or more workers. *Discrimination Prohibited:* Race, color, religious creed, age, sex, marital status, national origin, ancestry, present or past history or mental disorder, mental retardation or physical disability, sexual orientation, and smoking preference outside the course of employment.
DE	*Employer:* Any person employing four or more persons within the state. For purposes of the law prohibiting discrimination based on disability, includes any person employing at least 15 employees for each working day in each of 20 or more calendar weeks in the current or preceding calendar year. *Discrimination Prohibited:* Race, marital status, color, disability, age (only persons between the ages of 40 and 70), religion, sex, or national origin.
DC	*Employer:* A person who, for compensation, employs an individual, except for the employer's parent, spouse, children.

State	Employer and Employee Defined; Discrimination Prohibited
DC (cont.)	*Discrimination Prohibited:* Race (both the employee and individuals with whom the employee has a relationship), color, religion, national origin, sex (includes subsets of a sex, such as a pregnant female), age (between 18 and 65), marital status, personal appearance, sexual orientation, family responsibilities, physical handicap, educational activities, or political affiliation. Also, use of tobacco or tobacco products, although employers may restrict smoking in the workplace based on a BFOQ.
FL	*Employer:* Any person employing 15 or more employees for each working day in each of 20 or more calendar weeks in the current or preceding calendar year. *Discrimination Prohibited:* Race, color, religion, sex, national origin, age, handicap, sickle-cell trait, or marital status. Also, knowledge or belief that an individual has taken an HIV test or the results or perceived results of such a test, unless the absence of HIV infection is a BFOQ of the job.
GA	*Employer:* Persons employing at least 10 workers are prohibited from giving unequal pay for equal work based on sex. Employers with at least 15 employees are prohibited from discrimination against people with disabilities. *Discrimination Prohibited:* Sex, age (between 40 and 70), and disability.
HI	*Employer:* Anyone employing one or more employees. *Discrimination Prohibited:* Race, sex, sexual orientation, age, religion, color, ancestry, disability, marital status, and arrest and court records. Hawaii's House of Representatives has requested that employers respect the legal lifestyle activities of their employees and refrain from discriminating in employment practices based on such activities.
ID	*Employer:* One that hires five or more employees for each working day in each of 20 or more calendar weeks in the current or preceding calendar year whose services are to be partially or wholly performed in Idaho. Includes contractors or subcontractors that furnish material or perform work for the state. *Discrimination Prohibited:* Race, color, religion, sex, national origin, age (between 40 and 70 years), physical handicap, or disability.
IL	*Employer:* Any person employing at least 15 employees in Illinois during 20 or more calendar weeks within the calendar year or preceding year and any party to a public contract without regard to the number of employees. For purposes of discrimination based on physical or mental handicap unrelated to ability, includes any person employing one or more employees. *Discrimination Prohibited:* Race, color, religion, sex, national origin, ancestry, age, marital status, parental status, physical or mental handicap, use of lawful products, including tobacco or alcohol, outside the workplace during nonworking hours, military status, or unfavorable discharge from military service. Additional protections are afforded that prohibit employers from inquiring about certain criminal records.
IN	*Employer:* Any person employing six or more persons in Indiana (one or more for purposes of the law against discrimination on account of age). *Discrimination Prohibited:* Race, religion, color, sex, disability, national origin or ancestry, and age (at least 40, but not yet 70). Employers can't require, as a condition of employment that employees refrain from using tobacco products off premises during nonworking hours.
IA	*Employer:* Any person employing four or more workers within Iowa. *Discrimination Prohibited:* Age, race, creed, color, sex, national origin, religion, or disability.
KS	*Employer:* Any person in Kansas employing four or more persons. *Discrimination Prohibited:* Race, religion, color, sex, disability, national origin or ancestry, and age (over 18 years).

State	Employer and Employee Defined; Discrimination Prohibited
KY	*Employer:* A person who has eight or more employees within the state in each of 20 or more calendar weeks in the current or preceding calendar year. For purposes of disability-based discrimination, employer means a person engaged in an industry affecting commerce who has at least 15 employees for each working day in each of 20 or more calendar weeks in the current or preceding calendar year. Persons employing two or more workers are subject to provisions prohibiting unequal pay for equal work based on sex. *Discrimination Prohibited:* Race, color, religion, national origin, sex, age (between 40 and 70), disability, or smoking preference outside the workplace.
LA	*Employer:* A person employing more than 15 employees receiving services from an individual in exchange for compensation. For purposes of discrimination based on age or sickle cell trait, a person engaged in an industry affecting commerce who has 20 or more employees for each working day in each of 20 or more calendar weeks in the current or preceding calendar year. For purposes of Human Rights Commission enforcement of age discrimination rules, anyone employing at least eight workers. *Discrimination Prohibited:* Race, color, religion, sex, age (40 to 70 years), disability, national origin, sickle cell trait, parental status, assertion of a claim for worker's compensation, or use of tobacco outside the workplace.
ME	*Employer:* Any person in Maine employing any number of employees and any person outside the state employing any number of employees in the state. *Discrimination Prohibited:* Race, color, sex (including pregnancy and related medical conditions), physical or mental disability, religion, age, ancestry or national origin, asserting a workers' compensation claim, or use of tobacco products outside the course of employment.
MD	*Employer:* A person engaged in industry or business who has at least 15 employees for each working day in each of 20 or more calendar weeks in the current or preceding calendar year. *Discrimination Prohibited:* Race, color, religion, sex, age, national origin, marital status, or physical or mental disability. Also, applicants can't be required to disclose information regarding criminal charges that have been expunged.
MA	*Employer:* Excludes employers with fewer than six employees. *Discrimination Prohibited:* Race, color, religious creed, national origin, sex, sexual orientation (except when it involves minor children as the sex object), ancestry, age, disability, failure to furnish an arrest record for which no conviction resulted, having a criminal record for a first offense or misdemeanor over five years old, marital status, military service, or having been admitted to a mental health facility.
MI	*Employer:* A person who has one or more employees, and a person working as a contractor or subcontractor, furnishing material or performing work for the state or a governmental agency of the state. *Discrimination Prohibited:* Disability, religion, race, color, national origin, age, sex, height, weight, marital status, or refusal to provide records of an arrest that didn't result in a conviction.
MN	*Employer:* A person with one or more employees. *Discrimination Prohibited:* Race, color, creed, religion, national origin, sex, marital status, status with regard to public assistance, disability, sexual orientation, or age (under 70). Also, AIDS and off-premises use of lawful consumable products during nonworking hours.
MS	*Discrimination Prohibited:* Use or non-use of tobacco products outside the course of employment.

State	Employer and Employee Defined; Discrimination Prohibited
MO	*Employer:* Any person employing six or more persons within Missouri. For purposes of the law barring employment discrimination based on refusal to participate in an abortion, employer means a person with two or more employees in Missouri. *Discrimination Prohibited:* Race, color, religion, national origin, sex, ancestry, age, disability, or use of lawful alcohol or tobacco products off the business premises during nonworking hours. Also, AIDS, unless the individual would pose a threat to the health and safety of others or is unable to perform the job because of the currently contagious disease or infection. Also, refusal to assist in an abortion.
MT	*Employer:* An employer of one or more persons. *Discrimination Prohibited:* Race, creed, religion, color, national origin, age, physical or mental disability, marital status, or sex. Also, off-premises use of lawful products during nonworking hours.
NE	*Employer:* A person engaged in an industry who has at least 15 employees for each working day in each of 20 or more calendar weeks in the current or preceding calendar year, and any party whose business is financed, in whole or in part, under the Nebraska Investment Finance Authority, regardless of the number of employees. *Discrimination Prohibited:* Age, race, color, religion, sex, disability, marital status, national origin, or because the applicant has or is suspected of having AIDS.
NV	*Employer:* Any person who has at least 15 employees for each working day in each of 20 or more calendar weeks in the current or preceding calendar year. *Discrimination Prohibited:* Race, color, religion, sex, age, disability, national origin, or use of a lawful product outside of the workplace during nonworking hours.
NH	*Employer:* Excludes any employer with fewer than six persons in its employ. *Discrimination Prohibited:* Age, sex (includes height and weight requirements), race, color, marital status, physical or mental disability, use of tobacco products outside the course of employment, religious creed, or national origin.
NJ	*Employer:* All business entities. *Discrimination Prohibited:* Race, creed, color, national origin, ancestry, age, marital status, affectional or sexual orientation, sex, disability or atypical hereditary cellular or blood trait, military service, or smoking preference outside the course of business. New Jersey guidelines on pre-employment inquiries indicate that questions about education, arrest records, and economic considerations are potentially discriminatory.
NM	*Employer:* Any person employing four or more persons. *Discrimination Prohibited:* Race, age, religion, color, national origin, ancestry, sex, physical or mental disability, medical condition (including the results of AIDS virus tests), or smoking preference.
NY	*Employer:* Excludes any employer with fewer than four persons in its employ. *Discrimination Prohibited:* Age, race, creed, color, national origin, sex, disability, marital status, genetic disorder, AIDS, legal political and recreational activities, or legal use of consumable products outside the course of employment.
NC	*Employer:* For purposes of the ban on disability-based employment discrimination, employer means any person employing at least 15 full-time employees in North Carolina. For purposes of the law barring employment discrimination based on use of a lawful product, employer means employers of three or more workers.

State	Employer and Employee Defined; Discrimination Prohibited
NC (cont.)	*Discrimination Prohibited:* Race, religion, color, national origin, age, sex, disability, AIDS, sickle cell or hemoglobin C trait, use of lawful products outside the course of employment, military service.
ND	*Employer:* A person in North Dakota who employs one or more full-time employees for more than one quarter of the year and a person, wherever situated, who employs one or more employees whose services are partially or wholly performed in North Dakota *Discrimination Prohibited:* Race, color, religion, sex, national origin, age, mental or physical disability, marital status, receipt of public assistance, or lawful activity outside the course of employment.
OH	*Employer:* Any person employing four or more persons within Ohio. *Discrimination Prohibited:* Race, color, religion, sex, national origin, disability, age, or ancestry.
OK	*Employer:* A person who has at least 15 employees for each working day in each of 20 or more calendar weeks in the current or preceding calendar year, or a contractor or subcontractor furnishing material or performing work for the state. *Discrimination Prohibited:* Race, color, religion, sex, national origin, age, disability, or smoking preference.
OR	*Employer:* Any person who employs one or more employees in Oregon. *Discrimination Prohibited:* Race, religion, color, sex, marital status, pregnancy, childbirth, sexual orientation, AIDS, national origin, age, juvenile records that have been expunged, another family member works for the employer, filing a workers' compensation claim, or disability.
PA	*Employer:* Any person employing four or more persons within the state. *Discrimination Prohibited:* Race, color, religious creed, ancestry, age, sex, national origin, or non-job-related disability.
PR	*Employer:* All private employers in Puerto Rico. *Discrimination Prohibited:* Age, race, color, sex, disability, origin or social position, political affiliations, or religious beliefs.
RI	*Employer:* Any person in Rhode Island employing four or more individuals. *Discrimination Prohibited:* Race, color, religion, sex, sexual orientation, disability, age, national origin, use of tobacco products outside the course of employment, or a positive AIDS test or the perception of a positive AIDS test. Applicants can't be required to provide records of criminal convictions that have been expunged.
SC	*Employer:* Any person who has at least 15 employees for each working day in each of 20 or more calendar weeks in the current or preceding calendar year. *Discrimination Prohibited:* Race, religion, color, sex, age, disability, national origin, use of tobacco products outside the workplace.
SD	*Employer:* Any person within South Dakota who hires or employs any employee, without regard to location, or any person who hires an employee to perform services in the state. *Discrimination Prohibited:* Race, color, creed, religion, sex, ancestry, disability, national origin, or use of tobacco products off premises during nonworking hours.
TN	*Employer:* Persons employing eight or more persons within Tennessee. *Discrimination Prohibited:* Race, creed, color, religion, sex, age (over 40), national origin, disability, or use of tobacco or other legal agricultural products off premises during nonworking hours.

State	Employer and Employee Defined; Discrimination Prohibited
TX	*Employer:* A person who is engaged in an industry affecting commerce and who has at least15 employees for each working day in each of 20 or more calendar weeks in the current or preceding calendar year. *Discrimination Prohibited:* Race, color, disability, religion, sex, national origin, or age (over 40).
UT	*Employer:* Every person employing at least 15 employees within Utah for each working day in each of 20 calendar weeks or more in the current or preceding calendar year. *Discrimination Prohibited:* Race, color, sex, pregnancy, childbirth, pregnancy-related condition, age (over 40), religion, national origin, or disability.
VT	*Employer:* Any person employing one or more employees in Vermont. *Discrimination Prohibited:* Race, color, religion, ancestry, national origin, sex, sexual orientation, place of birth, age, disability, or positive AIDS test.
VA	*Discrimination Prohibited:* Race, color, religion, national origin, sex, age, marital status, or disability. Applicants can't be required to tell whether or not they smoke.
WA	*Employer:* Any person who has eight or more employees. *Discrimination Prohibited:* Age, sex, marital status, race, creed, color, national origin, arrest or conviction record, disability, or an applicant has, or is perceived to have, AIDS.
WV	*Employer:* Any person employing 12 or more persons within the state. *Discrimination Prohibited:* Race, religion, color, national origin, ancestry, sex, age, blindness or other disability, use of tobacco off premises outside working hours.
WI	*Employer:* Any person or business employing at least one individual. *Discrimination Prohibited:* Age, race, creed, color, disability, marital status, sex, sexual orientation, national origin, ancestry, arrest record, conviction record, military service, or use or nonuse of lawful products off the employer's premises during nonworking hours.
WY	*Employer:* Every person employing two or more employees in Wyoming. *Discrimination Prohibited:* Age (at least 40 but less than 70), sex, race, creed, color, national origin, ancestry, disability, or smoking preference outside the course of employment.

Other areas of employment relations that are often affected by state law include criminal record checks (see page 76), drug and alcohol tests (see page 83), and use of credit reports (see page 73).

Chapter 2

Consider Your Staffing Options

The fact that you need help doesn't establish the type and amount of help that you need. Your business may be seasonal, with short-term needs for delivery or sales help when sales peak. Or you may need help for a few hours each day to handle the rush period. Whatever your needs, consider all of the options before bringing help on board. Try to find the lowest cost approach that satisfies your needs. Here are some of the options open to you.

FULL-TIME EMPLOYEES

Many people tend to think of employment in terms of employees who work for one employer on a substantially full-time basis. As little as 20 years ago, people entered the workforce with the expectation that they would work for a single employer for their entire careers. Employees were rewarded for their longevity.

Those days are gone. Changes in technology and business philosophy have had a dramatic impact on how and where people work. Nevertheless, many businesses still require employees who work on a continuing and regular basis. A full-time employee is often the right choice. However, you can be quite creative about what constitutes full-time employment. And the law can be equally creative in classifying workers as full-time employees.

Don't assume that an employee must work a 40-hour week to qualify as full-time. The definition of "full-time" varies, depending on which law you're looking at. However, in many cases, a person who works at least 30 hours a week (1,500 hours a year) will be considered full-time. In some cases, a person who works at least 75 percent of the average number of hours that are customary for an employee in that particular position must be considered "full time."

Example

ABC Corporation hires Joe Sloan. It is customary for bookkeepers who are employed by ABC to perform services 35 hours per week or 1,820 hours per year. During the next consecutive 12-month period, Joe performs 1,450 hours of services for ABC. Joe doesn't meet the first leg of the test for being employed on a substantially full-time basis because he didn't perform 1,500 hours of service.

However, Joe does meet the second test for full-time service because he performed services for a number of hours equal to at least 75 percent of the number of hours that are customarily worked by an employee in that particular position (0.75 x 1,820 hours = 1,365 hours customarily performed). Therefore, Joe is a full-time employee of ABC. This is especially significant if you have other full-time employees who receive benefits. Because Joe qualifies as a full-time employee, he may become entitled to benefits also.

Pros and cons of full-time employees. There are several advantages to hiring full-time staff. Because most people work only one full-time job, you are more likely to have control over the employee's time and to get increased employee loyalty from a full-time worker. You may have the peace of mind that there will be someone around to "mind the store" in your absence. You may also be looking ahead to the day when you want to sell your business, and full-time employees who already know the ropes make excellent buyers.

For some, however, the disadvantages far outweigh the advantages. Consider the burden of computing payroll taxes and staying on top the federal, state, and local employment laws. Often, full-time employees receive benefits such as health insurance and paid vacation. Will you have to provide these types of benefits to be competitive? Who will do your employees' work while they're away?

But, if you're convinced that you need or want a full-time employee, your next step will be to formulate a clear picture of what you need done. If you aren't sold on the idea of a full-time employee, check out other options such as part-time employees, leased workers, temporary help, hiring your children, or independent contractors.

PART-TIME EMPLOYEES

Part-time employees are an option to consider even if you believe you need full-time help. Hiring two or more part-time employees instead of a single full-time employee can have advantages. For

---

example, if one of the part-timers is ill, you already have someone you can ask to fill in.

Pros and cons. Part-time employees can be a great compromise between full-time employees and non-employee staffing solutions. They give you control over the employees' work, but generally cost less because they work fewer hours and usually don't get as many benefits as full-time employees. In some cases, you can hire part-time hourly workers and ask them to work more or fewer hours in any given week, depending on how much work you happen to have.

Of course, part-time employees may have full-time jobs elsewhere, so employee loyalty may be sacrificed. Part-time employees may also tend to leave your business if an offer of full-time employment comes along, so you may end up with an employee turnover problem. Part-time employees are still counted as employees for purposes of determining liability under antidiscrimination laws.

Sources of part-time workers. An advantage of offering part-time employment is that it may create a larger pool of possible employees to choose from. Students and retirees are two groups that are more likely to be able to work for you if you offer part-time employment. If you can arrange flexible hours, you may also attract individuals with children and others who need to work on an irregular schedule. If you have children, you may be able to hire them as part-time help and get special tax breaks.

If you think that a part-time employee is the solution for you, the next step is to figure out what work you want done. If an employee/employer relationship isn't what you want, there are alternative staffing options, such as independent contractors, temporary help, or leased workers.

LEASED EMPLOYEES

Leasing employees is different from using temporary workers in that it generally refers to a situation where a third-party business "employs" your staff. This business takes care of payroll withholding, administering benefits, etc., and you pay it a fee plus expenses. You may decide to work with an employee leasing firm before you hire your first employee. Or you can have a leasing agency take over your existing staff of permanent employees. If you're considering the latter course, be sure that your employees are comfortable with the arrangement.

In any case, don't forget that you'll have less control over your workers in exchange for a certain degree of protection from liability. If you aren't comfortable giving up this much control, leasing isn't for you.

Leasing is usually also not an option for the one- or two-person shop, since most employee leasing companies aren't interested in such "small fry." But if you have at least a dozen employees and don't have the time or expertise to be a human resources manager, leasing might work for you.

Leasing isn't an "out." In many cases, a temporary worker or leased worker will be considered an employee for purposes of employment laws and benefits requirements. It may not make sense to lease employees if your intent is to avoid or circumvent these requirements. Usually, if you have a great degree of control over a worker's work and how and when it is performed, you'll be considered the worker's common law employer.

However, because a leasing company aggregates the employees of many companies in negotiating for health insurance, pensions, etc., you can sometimes provide more benefits at a much lower cost. Also, the leasing company can achieve economies of scale in hiring, doing the payroll, and keeping records on all these workers, so their fees for performing these services might be lower than what you'd pay to do it yourself.

Successful employee leasing. If there are employee leasing firms in your area that provide the type of help you need, take a little time to prepare before you start shopping around. It's helpful to put together a brief document explaining what you need done. This job description will be quite similar to what you'd have to put together in order to hire workers on your own. You'll have to address the nature of the work, the skills required, and the hours of the job. But you'll also need to estimate how long you will need help.

We strongly suggest that you seek legal counsel before deciding that leasing is for you. Legal advice is crucial for determining the implications of the leasing arrangement on your legal liabilities. Use the same care in picking a leasing firm that you would use in establishing any long-term business relationship. Consider whether what you'll have to pay is reasonable for the services that the agency will provide. Make certain that you're comfortable with how the agency does business. For example, what happens if a particular employee isn't working out?

A quality agency can provide references to satisfied customers, either current or former. A good agency will also provide insurance coverage that may include employee bonding, workers' compensation, general liability, professional liability, and fiduciary responsibility. Have your insurance agent review the firm's coverage to make sure that you're adequately protected in the event of a problem. Also verify that the leasing firm will pay all required employment taxes and all employee benefit contributions specified in the agreement. Leasing firms that are members of the National Staff Leasing Association or the National Staff Network are already required to do this under their bylaws.

TEMPORARY EMPLOYEES

Many businesses use temporary employees for special projects or when a full-time employee is absent for an extended period. But temporary help can also fill your long-term needs. A temporary help agency can cut the time it takes to get from the decision to hire to having a productive employee. When you deal with a temporary employment agency, be prepared to provide the same information that you would if you were hiring or leasing employees. Describe the job, establish what skills are required, specify work hours, and estimate how long the temporary employees will be needed.

By doing this in advance, you'll be able to quickly and effectively communicate your needs to an employment agency. In many larger markets, you'll find that there are numerous temporary help agencies. Many of these will specialize in providing specific types of help (accounting help, secretarial help, day labor, etc.). If you live in an area with a lot of agencies, find one that's experienced in providing the type of help that you need. Again, choose an agency with the same care you use when you enter into any long-term business relationship. Consider the cost and whether the agency provides appropriate insurance coverage and complies with all applicable tax and benefit laws.

Pros and cons. The trend toward using temporary employees is growing, with good reason. You may save on payroll administration and fringe benefit costs. The employment agency recruits the employees and sends you people with the qualifications you specify. Some agencies may even train workers. If you're not sure whether you have enough work to keep a full-time employee busy, you can try a temp and find out. You may feel uncomfortable being dependent on non-employees if much of your business is farmed out to independent contractors, and temps may cost less than contractors. With a temp, you have the power to directly supervise the employee's work. If a particular temporary worker seems to fit well into your business, you can always offer to hire him or her as a permanent employee. In this case, you avoid the risks of a probationary period you'd normally have with a new hire.

While temporary employees can be a good option, they aren't without their disadvantages. Some business owners may think that hiring temporaries means avoiding employment laws. That's not always the case. There have been instances where temporary help agencies and the businesses where the temporary help worked were involved in discrimination cases. In many cases, you'll have to offer a temporary employee the same benefits you offer your regular employees after the temp has worked for you for one year. Many businesses encounter morale problems when so-called temps work 40 hours per week alongside permanent employees who receive the benefits associated with full-time employment. Not all jobs and businesses lend themselves to using temporary workers. The job may require special expertise or skills, or a personal relationship with clients or customers. In rare cases, there may be union constraints.

Getting temporary help. You can either hire temporary workers on your own, or you can use a temporary help agency. Either way, target people who want temporary work and not those who really want full-time work but who take a short-term position hoping that they will develop into full-time employment. If you use a temporary help agency, you're going to pay more for the convenience of having someone else do the legwork. For example, you may have to pay a temporary help agency $10.00 to $12.00 an hour for a worker who gets $8.00 per hour in pay from the agency. Nevertheless, for short-term projects or situations where the worker will need a lot of supervision (for example, receptionists, secretaries, administrative assistants), temp agencies are a great alternative. Consider other options (such as independent contractors or part-time employees) for long-term projects — it may end up being cheaper.

Warning

If you decide to use either leased or temporary workers, remember that you will always have to assume certain risks. The idea is to avoid taking the responsibility for any of the potential liabilities that may legally be placed on the agency by the terms of your contract with the agency. Therefore, negotiate the contract as you would any legal contract and be sure to seek legal guidance *before you sign* to be properly protected.

In any event, a contract with a leasing or temporary help agency should clearly delineate the rights and responsibilities of each party with respect to such issues as hiring, firing, training, assigning work, etc. The contract should also make it clear who will be responsible for payroll withholding and complying with workers' compensation and other employee benefit rules. To the extent possible, you or your lawyer should negotiate a contract that places as much responsibility on the agency as you can.

The increasing responsibilities of employment agencies have led the National Association of Personnel Consultants, the professional organization of employment agency personnel, to establish a Certified Personnel Consultant program. The CPC designation is granted, upon payment of a fee, to agencies whose representatives pass a written examination. Look for this certification.

HIRING YOUR CHILDREN

If you hire your children to work in your business, either full-time or part-time, you could be eligible for special tax breaks. The tax break is an exemption from FICA, or Social Security taxes. A business ordinarily pays 7.65 percent of each employee's salary in Social Security and Medicare taxes and withholds another 7.65 percent from pay for the employee's share of those taxes. By not paying or withholding FICA from your child's paycheck, you save 15.3 percent.

Child labor restrictions may not apply. There are both federal and state laws that pertain to employing children. Generally, employing a child under the age of 16 is a violation of federal law although there are certain exceptions carved out for employing children aged 14 and 15. However, the general rule that no child under the age of 16 years may be employed in any nonagricultural occupation *does not apply to the employment of a child by a parent* as long as the job isn't in manufacturing, mining, or any other hazardous occupation as defined by the Department of Labor.

INDEPENDENT CONTRACTORS

Independent contractors make it possible to get some help without becoming subject to payroll taxes or to many state and federal employment laws. The practice of using independent contractors isn't uncommon and is growing more popular each year. Many consultants advise businesses to contract out any function not directly related to the production of core products or services. For example, many "white collar" businesses contract out their building maintenance work or food service functions. Independent contractors are particularly useful when you need a specific skill or technical knowledge for a special project that's expected to last a relatively short length of time.

What Is an Independent Contractor?

Independent contractors run their own business. You don't employ them, you enter into contractual relationships with them. Thus, you aren't the employer of an independent contractor, and you aren't liable for payroll taxes or for providing benefits for them. Nor are they protected by workers' compensation or most labor laws.

Independent contractors differ from employees in that they control *how and when* the work is performed, based on their experience, license, or special education or training. Independent contractors are frequently paid based on their results (i.e., a flat rate per job, or a per-unit-completed rate) rather than the amount of time they put in.

Independent contractors and the tax laws. The IRS carefully examines arrangements that involve use of independent contractors, in part because they are responsible for paying their own payroll taxes and it's much more difficult to ensure that they're doing so. As previously noted, the key question for tax purposes is the degree of control you can exercise over the worker. A worker will be treated as an employee if you have the right to determine not just what the employee does, but when, where, or how the work is performed. The following table summarizes how the IRS will apply the 20-factor test it uses to evaluate whether a worker is an employee or an independent contractor.

IRS 20-Factor Test for Independent Contractor Status	
Test	*Favors independent contractor status if*
Instructions	Business has no right to control how work results are achieved.
Training	Worker uses own methods and receives no training.
Integration	Worker's services aren't integrated into business's ongoing processes.
Services performed personally	Worker has the right to substitute others to perform services.
Hiring assistants	Worker is responsible for results only and can hire and pay others.
Ongoing relationship	There is no continuing relationship between worker and business.
Set work hours	Worker is free to select own work hours.
Full-time required	Worker can select when and for whom to work.
Work on premises	Business has no right to designate where work is performed.
Order or sequence set	Worker is free to establish order in which work will be performed.
Reports	Worker isn't required to furnish reports to the business.
Payments	Worker is paid by the job or on a straight commission basis.
Expenses	Worker is responsible for own business and travel expenses.
Tools and materials	Worker provides tools, materials, and supplies at own expense.
Investment	Worker has significant investment in facilities used to perform services.
Profit or loss	Worker can realize either a profit or loss.
Multiple jobs	Worker may provide services to one or more unrelated businesses.
Services offered to public	Worker makes services available to the general public.
Right to fire	Worker can't be fired if work is performed according to contract terms.
Right to quit	Worker must complete job according to contract terms.

You can request a determination from the IRS regarding how you should treat particular workers on IRS Form SS-8. Don't file this form yourself because the way you complete the form is the largest single factor in how your workers will be classified. Get help from an attorney, accountant, or other tax advisor.

Work Smart

If you're waiting for an IRS determination, treat workers as employees until the determination is made by deducting and paying all applicable taxes. You can seek a refund if the workers turn out to be independent contractors after all.

Independent contractors under the Fair Labor Standards Act (FLSA). The FLSA is another important federal law governing your treatment of workers. Unfortunately, it has its own definition of independent contractor that is slightly different from the IRS's definition. In order to be truly sure that you're safe in treating workers as independent contractors, you must meet *both* definitions.

Independent contractors are not employees under the FLSA. Thus, they aren't entitled to the protection afforded by minimum wage and overtime laws. For purposes of the FLSA, six factors are used to determine if a worker is an employee or an independent contractor:

- the extent of the worker's right to control the manner in which the work is performed

- the worker's opportunity for profit or loss depending upon managerial skill

- the worker's investment in required equipment or materials

- whether the services rendered require special skills

- the degree of permanence of the working relationship

- whether the service rendered by the worker is an integral part of the alleged employer's business

No single factor is controlling in determining independent contractor status. When the issue comes up in courts, the judge must consider whether, as a matter of economic reality, a worker is *dependent on the business for continued employment*. A worker who signs an independent contractor agreement will be treated as an employee for purposes of the FLSA if the six-part test isn't satisfied.

Workers employed by an independent contractor are employees of the contractor, and not of the business that the contractor is serving.

Work Smart

Develop a written contract that relinquishes the right to control how the work will be done, and specifies that the worker won't be treated as an employee for federal tax purposes. You should also file information returns (Form 1099-MISC) for independent contractors.

A contract with an independent contractor should also include terms addressing the termination of the relationship. Independent contractors aren't employees, so "termination" would be done according to the provisions of the contract. Because the relationship between a business and an independent contractor is a contractual relationship, not an employment relationship, any misunderstandings about job performance or termination of the relationship are governed by contract law.

Other laws defining employment status. Each of the other federal and state laws that impose a payroll tax has its own general provision that defines the classes of workers to which the tax applies. (See Chapter 12 for a discussion of the other payroll taxes you'll have to become familiar with.) However, the basic standard is whether an individual who performs services for you is properly characterized as an employee as opposed to an independent contractor under so-called common law rules. (The term "common law" is used in legal circles to refer to principles that have evolved primarily through court decisions rather than through legislative enactments.) In general, your workers are common law employees if you have the right to direct and control the way they do their work.

Pros and Cons of Using Contractors

Using independent contractors offers significant tax and nontax advantages. Since employers are required to pay certain benefits and taxes on behalf of their employees, the financial benefits of having a large independent contractor work force can be significant.

For example, by using independent contractors, a business owner may be able to avoid responsibility under:

- the Federal Insurance Contribution Act (FICA) or Social Security and Medicare taxes
- the Federal Unemployment Tax Act (FUTA)
- the Consolidated Omnibus Budget Reconciliation Act (COBRA)
- workers' compensation laws
- retirement plans

All payroll taxes and benefits are handled by the individual contractor, who doesn't participate in any company-offered fringe benefit plans.

Also, your own exemption from many federal, state, and local laws is based on how many employees you have working for you.

Independent contractors aren't counted as employees. Thus, if you contract with independent contractors instead of hiring regular full-time employees, you may not be subject to some of these laws. These laws include: state and local smoking laws and some state family leave laws, and the federal ADA, ADEA, and Title VII of the Civil Rights Act of 1964 (see page 9).

Disadvantages of independent contractors. The main disadvantage to using independent contractors is that you must keep on top of exactly what qualifies someone as an independent contractor. If you misclassify someone as an independent contractor who isn't, the penalties can be extremely costly. And don't forget that there are two different sets of "tests" for independent contractors — the IRS test and the FLSA test.

Another disadvantage is that independent contractors, by definition, are permitted to work for a number of different companies at a time. You won't have as much control over the worker's time, efforts, and loyalty as you would with a permanent employee. Furthermore, most contracts permit the independent contractor to substitute another individual on any job, so you may not even be sure who's ultimately going to do the work for you. Finally, independent contractors make a commitment to work for you for the length of the contract, and that's it. If you like their work and want to continue the relationship, you may have to renegotiate the agreement (including their payment rate).

Establishing Independent Contractor Status

Here are some things you can do to help ensure that those who work for you qualify for independent contractor status, and that you can win any challenges to your arrangements:

- Be careful, when advertising for independent contractors, not to place newspaper ads in the "Help Wanted" sections and to avoid using words or phrases such as "wages" or "steady work." Instead, look for independent contractors who have placed their own ads under "Situations Wanted" or "Trade Services."

- When establishing the relationship, avoid setting a regular pattern of daily or weekly hours. Self-employed individuals presumably have the opportunity to select when and where to work in relation to all their customers.

- Allow or require contractors to supply their own tools, supplies, and equipment wherever possible in the performance of the services required. This will demonstrate that there is a risk of loss as well as an opportunity for profit.

- Use contractors who normally advertise their services in some manner. Keep on file any business cards, circulars, or even telephone directory ads.

- Allow contractors to hire their own assistants, if necessary. Insist that the contractor pay the payroll taxes normally required for such employees.

- Don't include contractors under the insurance coverage for workers' compensation, health insurance, or other benefits that are provided for employees.

- If possible, compensate independent contractors on a per-job basis rather than by the hour or week.

- Always ask for an invoice or statement before paying for any work that has been performed. If possible, make checks payable to a company rather than to an individual.

- Don't directly reimburse contractors for any expenses they might have, such as gasoline, meals, etc. Such expenses should stand as part of the contractor's set fees. However, from a cost perspective, you may get a better price if you agree to reimburse certain expenses. Since the amount of expenses may not be certain at the start of the job, independent contractors must estimate the expenses they'll incur, and the estimate may exceed the actual expenses.

- Remember that, in theory, you cannot discharge an independent contractor from employment. If dissatisfied with a contractor's performance, look to your contract for a remedy. If there is no contract, sever relations by offering no more work.

It is best, of course, in examining these relationships, to have a contract in writing with an independent contractor. This can be used on behalf of the employer to demonstrate the validity of an independent contractor relationship. In fact, in many states, it is *required* in order to establish an independent contractor relationship.

Contracting With an Independent Contractor

In contracting with an independent contractor, you should attempt to structure an agreement around the IRS 20-factor test. You can help ensure that your contracts pass that test by:

- structuring the agreement between your business and the other business, rather than between your business and an individual, if the independent contractor has incorporated or formed a limited liability company

- specifying the fee and the due date for the work

- calling the work "a project" and saying that it can be done whenever the contractor wants to work

- indicating that the person is free to work on other things (even though your project may require a full-time commitment)

- doing nothing that makes the person appear to be your employee, e.g., don't pay benefits or employment taxes, keep a personnel file, or prepare I-9 forms

- requiring that the contractor invoice you for all services

Here's a sample contract between a business and an independent contractor. This contract envisions a relationship in which the independent contractor will primarily perform services. If you're structuring a contract where the contractor will also provide materials, supplies, equipment, etc., specific contract terms should spell out the agreement between the contracting parties with respect to those items as well. Check with your attorney.

Sample Independent Contractor Agreement

This Agreement is entered into as of the [   ] day of [   ], 199[ ], between [company name] ("the Company") and [service provider's name] ("the Contractor").

1. Independent Contractor. Subject to the terms and conditions of this Agreement, the Company hereby engages the Contractor as an independent contractor to perform the services set forth herein, and the Contractor hereby accepts such engagement.

2. Duties, Term, and Compensation. The Contractor's duties, term of engagement, compensation and provisions for payment thereof shall be as set forth in the estimate previously provided to the Company by the Contractor and which is attached as Exhibit A, which may be amended in writing from time to time, or supplemented with subsequent estimates for services to be rendered by the Contractor and agreed to by the Company, and which collectively are hereby incorporated by reference.

3. Expenses. During the term of this Agreement, the Contractor shall bill and the Company shall reimburse [him or her] for all reasonable and approved out-of-pocket expenses which are incurred in connection with the performance of the duties hereunder. Notwithstanding the foregoing, expenses for the time spend by Consultant in traveling to and from Company facilities shall not be reimbursable.

4. Written Reports. The Company may request that project plans, progress reports and a final results report be provided by Consultant on a monthly basis. A final results report shall be due at the conclusion of the project and shall be submitted to the Company in a confidential

written report at such time. The results report shall be in such form and setting forth such information and data as is reasonably requested by the Company.

5. <u>Inventions.</u> Any and all inventions, discoveries, developments and innovations conceived by the Contractor during this engagement relative to the duties under this Agreement shall be the exclusive property of the Company; and the Contractor hereby assigns all right, title, and interest in the same to the Company. Any and all inventions, discoveries, developments and innovations conceived by the Contractor prior to the term of this Agreement and utilized by [him or her] in rendering duties to the Company are hereby licensed to the Company for use in its operations and for an infinite duration. This license is non-exclusive, and may be assigned without the Contractor's prior written approval by the Company to a wholly owned subsidiary of the Company.

6. <u>Confidentiality.</u> The Contractor acknowledges that during the engagement [he or she] will have access to and become acquainted with various trade secrets, inventions, innovations, processes, information, records and specifications owned or licensed by the Company and/or used by the Company in connection with the operation of its business including, without limitation, the Company's business and product processes, methods, customer lists, accounts and procedures. The Contractor agrees that [he or she] will not disclose any of the aforesaid, directly or indirectly, or use any of them in any manner, either during the term of this Agreement or at any time thereafter, except as required in the course of this engagement with the Company. All files, records, documents, blueprints, specifications, information, letters, notes, media lists, original artwork/creative, notebooks, and similar items relating to the business of the Company, whether prepared by the Contractor or otherwise coming into [his or her] possession, shall remain the exclusive property of the Company. The Contractor shall not retain any copies of the foregoing without the Company's prior written permission. Upon the expiration or earlier termination of this Agreement, or whenever requested by the Company, the Contractor shall immediately deliver to the Company all such files, records, documents, specifications, information, and other items in [his or her] possession or under [his or her] control. The Contractor further agrees that [he or she] will not disclose [his or her] retention as an independent contractor or the terms of this Agreement to any person without the prior written consent of the Company and shall at all times preserve the confidential nature of [his or her] relationship to the Company and of the services hereunder.

7. <u>Conflicts of Interest; No-hire Provision.</u> The Contractor represents that [he or she] is free to enter into this Agreement, and that this engagement does not violate the terms of any agreement between the Contractor and any third party. Further, the Contractor, in rendering [his or her] duties shall not utilize any invention, discovery, development, improvement, innovation, or trade secret in which [he or she] does not have a proprietary interest. During the term of this agreement, the Contractor shall devote as much of [his or her] productive time, energy, and abilities to the performance of [his or her] duties hereunder as is necessary to perform the required duties in a timely and productive manner. The Contractor is expressly free to perform services for other parties while performing services for the Company. For a period of six months following any termination, the Contractor shall not, directly or indirectly hire, solicit, or encourage to leave the Company's employment, any

employee, consultant, or contractor of the Company or hire any such employee, consultant, or contractor who has left the Company's employment or contractual engagement within one year of such employment or engagement.

8. <u>Right to Injunction.</u> The parties hereto acknowledge that the services to be rendered by the Contractor under this Agreement and the rights and privileges granted to the Company under the Agreement are of a special, unique, unusual, and extraordinary character which gives them a peculiar value, the loss of which cannot be reasonably or adequately compensated by damages in any action at law, and the breach by the Contractor of any of the provisions of this Agreement will cause the Company irreparable injury and damage. The Contractor expressly agrees that the Company shall be entitled to injunctive and other equitable relief in the event of, or to prevent, a breach of any provision of this Agreement by the Contractor. Resort to such equitable relief, however, shall not be construed to be a waiver of any other rights or remedies that the Company may have for damages or otherwise. The various rights and remedies of the Company under this Agreement or otherwise shall be construed to be cumulative, and no one of them shall be exclusive of any other or of any right or remedy allowed by law.

9. <u>Merger.</u> This Agreement shall not be terminated by the merger or consolidation of the Company into or with any other entity.

10. <u>Termination.</u> The Company may terminate this Agreement at any time by 10 working days' written notice to the Contractor. In addition, if the Contractor is convicted of any crime or offense, fails or refuses to comply with the written policies or reasonable directive of the Company, is guilty of serious misconduct in connection with performance hereunder, or materially breaches provisions of this Agreement, the Company at any time may terminate the engagement of the Contractor immediately and without prior written notice to the Contractor.

11. <u>Independent Contractor.</u> This Agreement shall not render the Contractor an employee, partner, agent of, or joint venturer with the Company for any purpose. The Contractor is and will remain an independent contractor in [his or her] relationship to the Company. The Company shall not be responsible for withholding taxes with respect to the Contractor's compensation hereunder. The Contractor shall have no claim against the Company hereunder or otherwise for vacation pay, sick leave, retirement benefits, Social Security, worker's compensation, health or disability benefits, unemployment insurance benefits, or employee benefits of any kind.

12. <u>Insurance.</u> The Contractor will carry liability insurance (including malpractice or errors and omissions insurance, if warranted) relative to any service that [he or she] performs for the Company.

13. <u>Successors and Assigns.</u> All of the provisions of this Agreement shall be binding upon and inure to the benefit of the parties hereto and their heirs, if any, successors, and assigns.

14. <u>Choice of Law.</u> The laws of the state of [   ] shall govern the validity of this Agreement, the construction of its terms, and the interpretation of the rights and duties of the parties hereto.

15. <u>Arbitration.</u> Any controversies arising out of the terms of this Agreement or its interpretation shall be settled in [   ] in accordance with the rules of the American Arbitration Association, and the judgment upon award may be entered in any court having jurisdiction thereof.

16. <u>Headings.</u> Section headings are not to be considered a part of this Agreement and are not intended to be a full and accurate description of the contents hereof.

17. <u>Waiver.</u> Waiver by one party hereto of breach of any provision of this Agreement by the other shall not operate or be construed as a continuing waiver.

18. <u>Assignment.</u> The Contractor shall not assign any of [his or her] rights under this Agreement, or delegate the performance of any of [his or her] duties hereunder, without the prior written consent of the Company.

19. <u>Notices.</u> Any and all notices, demands, or other communications required or desired to be given hereunder by any party shall be in writing and shall be validly given or made to another party if personally served, or if deposited in the United States mail, certified or registered, postage prepaid, return receipt requested. If such notice or demand is served personally, notice shall be deemed constructively made at the time of such personal service. If such notice, demand or other communication is given by mail, such notice shall be conclusively deemed given five days after deposit thereof in the United States mail addressed to the party to whom such notice, demand or other communication is to be given as follows:

> If to the Contractor: [name]
>
> [street address]
>
> [city, state, zip]
>
> If to the Company: [name]
>
> [street address]
>
> [city, state, zip]

Any party hereto may change its address for purposes of this paragraph by written notice given in the manner provided above.

19. <u>Modification or Amendment.</u> No amendment, change or modification of this Agreement shall be valid unless in writing signed by the parties hereto.

20. <u>Entire Understanding.</u> This document and any exhibit attached constitute the entire understanding and agreement of the parties, and any and all prior agreements, understandings, and representations are hereby terminated and canceled in their entirety and are of no further force and effect.

21. <u>Unenforceability of Provisions.</u> If any provision of this Agreement, or any portion thereof, is held to be invalid and unenforceable, then the remainder of this Agreement shall nevertheless remain in full force and effect.

IN WITNESS WHEREOF the undersigned have executed this Agreement as of the day and year first written above. The parties agree that facsimile signatures shall be as effective as if originals.

[company name]   [contractor's name]

By:_____   By:_____

Its: [title or position]   Its: [title or position]

SCHEDULE A

DUTIES, TERM, AND COMPENSATION

DUTIES: The Contractor will [describe here the work or service to be performed]. [He or she] will report directly to [name] and to any other party designated by [name] in connection with the performance of the duties under this Agreement and shall fulfill any other duties reasonably requested by the Company and agreed to by the Contractor.

TERM: This engagement shall commence upon execution of this Agreement and shall continue in full force and effect through [date] or earlier upon completion of the Contractor's duties under this Agreement. The Agreement may only be extended thereafter by mutual agreement, unless terminated earlier by operation of and in accordance with this Agreement.

COMPENSATION: (Choose A or B)

A. As full compensation for the services rendered pursuant to this Agreement, the Company shall pay the Contractor at the hourly rate of [dollar amount] per hour, with total payment not to exceed [dollar amount] without prior written approval by an authorized representative of the Company. Such compensation shall be payable within 30 days of receipt of Contractor's monthly invoice for services rendered supported by reasonable documentation.

B. As full compensation for the services rendered pursuant to this Agreement, the Company shall pay the Contractor the sum of [dollar amount], to be paid [time and conditions of payment].

NO-COST STAFFING OPTIONS

Believe it or not, there are places to get some help at no, or at very little, cost. These options may involve a little more work and creativity on your part than hiring a full-fledged employee, but cost a fraction of the dollars.

Barter. Bartering organizations will allow you to trade your goods and services for those of other businesses. It can be an economical alternative if you're strapped for cash and need some work done. It doesn't relieve you of responsibility for income tax on amounts you receive in exchange for your goods or services.

Bartering won't work for everyone. If you need someone to be in your office eight hours a day to answer the telephone, it's going to be tough for someone to trade with you for that type of work. On the other hand, if you need some help marketing your new product or service, for example, you may be able to barter with a marketing consultant who would be willing to help you write an advertisement or a press release in exchange for something from you.

Internships. Internships can be a great way to get workers at little or no cost, provided a local school sponsors a program. Interns expect their employment to be a learning experience, so you're unlikely to get clerical or general office help through this type of program. And, it means that you'll have to offer something of value, like teaching interns a new skill or exposing them to a certain industry.

Volunteers. Volunteers are a great way to get work done for free, but they are hard to come by and sometimes hard to rely on. If you aren't a not-for-profit organization or one that serves "glamorous" constituencies such as the arts, it will be hard to find anyone willing to work for free. However, you can get free help with marketing, finances, getting a loan, or organizing your operations by contacting your local branch of the U.S. Small Business Administration. Their SCORE program for retired executives matches up people willing to share their expertise with small businesses in need of assistance.

Occasionally, would-be entrepreneurs will volunteer to work in a business similar to one they're thinking of starting. If someone approaches you with such a plan, don't agree until you're sure that they're not planning to start up a competitive enterprise that might drive you out of business as soon as they learn all your best ideas.

Chapter 3

Find the Right Person

You've decided that you need to hire some help, and you have a good idea of what you want an employee to do for your business. The next step is to determine what skill, knowledge, talent, expertise, or education is required to perform those tasks. The job qualifications you set will form the basis for a job description and, probably, a help wanted ad. Remember that federal and state antidiscrimination laws place certain restrictions on how you define and use job qualifications in the hiring process.

EXPERIENCE

In most cases, the ideal candidate will have at least some exposure to or experience in performing the required work. Sometimes it's difficult to find individuals with just the right experience, especially if your industry is specialized or relatively new. When creating experience requirements for a position, you can demand specific experience, but that may make it more difficult to find someone to fill a position. Avoid setting your experience qualifications so strictly that you disqualify people who are capable of doing the job.

Work Smart

Draft job qualifications in broad terms, particularly for entry level positions. If you need an administrative assistant who can type, answer phones, and file, you want someone with good organizational skills. Someone who was, for example, an assistant department store manager or a server in a restaurant may have some of the same skills and abilities.

EDUCATION

Many employers require at least a high school degree or an equivalency certificate for most jobs they fill. Some jobs require more advanced thought and responsibilities and, therefore, may require more advanced education. When you determine job qualifications, focus on the applicant's ability, not just the degree. After all, there are plenty of people who have degrees but not the skills to do a specific job.

Education doesn't just mean school. Education doesn't always occur in a traditional academic setting. Training that a person may have received during an internship or prior employment is also a form of education. People also acquire knowledge outside the scope of employment in pursuit of hobbies and other interests.

For employers of 15 or more. There are some lawyers and consultants in the field of employment discrimination who will advise you to drop all degree requirements, relevant or not, because they invite discrimination claims. However, the EEOC says only that employers can't set educational requirements so high that they tend to restrict certain protected groups of people from getting hired or promoted. Be prepared to justify why any degree you require is itself a necessity to job performance.

Example

High school graduation requirements for applicants are discriminatory when applied to positions that don't require that level of education. A person without a high school diploma may still read well enough or have the other skills necessary to perform the reading required by a certain job.

ABILITY

When you consider what is needed to perform a job, distinguish between abilities (what someone can do) and education (what they have learned). In some instances, ability *is* related to education, and only after a certain amount of education does a person have the ability to perform certain tasks. Consider doctors, lawyers, and accountants who, generally, must have a degree and be licensed by the state. However, the abilities required to perform many jobs well are skills that weren't necessarily acquired through formal education.

Language Fluency

As with all skills and abilities, you can't require language fluency unless it's related to the performance of the job. This means that fluency must be an *important part* of doing the job. If a person can do the job without having the language skills you demand, then your language requirement is discriminatory.

Example

A policy of refusing to hire applicants with "poor grammar" as computer programmers was determined by one court to be unlawful bias. The employer was unable to show a business reason for requiring programmers to have good grammar skills. Another court reached a similar result when faced with an employer who conditioned employment on passing a written examination, in English. The test was biased because members of some ethnic groups who were qualified welders had difficulty passing the test. There was no relationship between English language skills and the work to be performed.

However, a hotel's failure to promote a room attendant to front office cashier was justified because greater English proficiency was necessary for successful job performance.

If you have at least 15 employees and you require language fluency, you must be able to prove that it is an important and *necessary* part of the job. Federal law prevents you from discriminating against any protected groups, including groups whose ethnicity, national origin, or race may prevent them from speaking English.

Physical Effort

Some jobs require certain physical abilities or strength. These requirements should be included in your defined job qualifications. Making sure that employees are physically able to perform the necessary duties of the job will help them do the job better and more efficiently, and help avoid injuries, safety problems, and worker's compensation claims.

Americans With Disabilities Act

If you're an employer of 15 or more employees, you're subject to the Americans with Disabilities Act (ADA). The ADA is a federal law that protects people with disabilities from employment discrimination. An employer may not refuse to hire a disabled person if that person can do the *essential functions* of a job with *reasonable accommodation*.

"Essential functions" refers to the outcome of a job, not to how it is performed. "Reasonable accommodation" is a technical concept defined by the ADA. If you suspect you may need to provide reasonable accommodation to an applicant with disabilities, check with your professional legal advisor.

Example

A warehouse job requires moving 50-pound sacks from the loading dock to storage. This can be done by hand, or by using a dolly, hand truck, or cart. Therefore, the ability to lift and carry 50 pounds isn't an essential function. The essential function is moving 50 pounds from the loading dock to the storage area. Providing a hand truck to an employee who can't carry 50 pounds the distance required may be a reasonable accommodation.

Where safety is a concern. You may refuse to hire applicants who pose a direct threat to their own safety or the safety of others if there's no reasonable accommodation that would either eliminate or reduce the significant risk. See page 45 below, for a listing of the types of activities that might require employees to possess particular physical or mental abilities. Broad categories to consider include:

- **Physical demand.** What mix of physical activities does the job require? Will the employee be sitting, walking, climbing, lifting, or carrying objects?

- **Physical conditions.** What kind of environment will employees be working in? Inside? Outside? Will there be chemicals present, or temperature or humidity extremes? Are there particular hazards that are specific to the position?

- **Mental requirements.** Will the employee have to read and act on various types of documents? Does the job involve working with equipment where the employee must monitor operating conditions or perform discretionary repairs? Are there required skills, such as reading blueprints?

- **Communication and social skills.** What kind of contact will the employee have with others? Will they be the voice of your business, answering your phone and providing customer service? Do they need to understand terminology that is specific to your business or industry?

Example

If you run a construction company and you're hiring a person to answer phones, keep the books, and run the office, the physical requirements are far different than if you're hiring a drywall or flooring installer. A person perfectly well suited to work in your office might not be up to lifting drywall or kneeling all day while installing floors.

RESTRICTIONS ON JOB QUALIFICATIONS

If you have 15 or more employees, or are planning on hiring your 15th employee, you're subject to federal employment laws barring discrimination. In that case, requirements you impose must be *business-related* and can't discriminate against any protected group. For example, you can't require that applicants be of a certain race or color, unless you have a justifiable business reason for this requirement. Few business have ever demonstrated such a necessity.

"Business necessity" has been narrowly defined by the courts. A hiring practice with discriminatory effects can be justified only if:

- It's necessary to the safe and efficient operation of the business.

- It effectively carries out the purpose it is supposed to serve.

- There are no alternative policies or practices that would better or equally serve the purpose with less discriminatory impact.

You must be able to demonstrate that any job qualification, recruitment method, or selection procedure that has a "disparate impact" on protected groups can validly predict successful performance of the job in question. Disparate impact occurs when a fair policy is applied fairly, but the result is discrimination against one or more protected classes of individuals.

Example

A movie theater operator required that all of its employees who had contact with the public speak both English and Spanish. African-American applicants alleged that the bilingual requirement had an adverse impact on African-American applicants and employees. The employer was able to defend its bilingual requirement as a business necessity since the majority of its customers spoke only Spanish.

If you can't demonstrate the business necessity, you must stop using that procedure or method or alter it in such a way that it is no longer discriminatory. Even if you can demonstrate that a procedure, requirement, or method is valid, you can't use it if there are other ways to accomplish the same goal with less of a discriminatory effect.

CREATE A JOB DESCRIPTION

If you're just hiring one person, perhaps your first employee, you don't need to write a formal job description unless you want to. Job descriptions aren't required by law for *any* employer, but they're good to have for several reasons. A job description can help when you're interviewing, explaining a job to a new employee, or evaluating an employee's performance. It also provides evidence of your hiring practices, should you ever have to defend them in court.

You've already analyzed, to the extent that you can, what the position entails. You've also identified the skills and qualifications needed to do the job effectively. A job description blends these two elements into a single document that is a blueprint for the job and a logical precursor to writing a job ad.

Creating a job description, step-by-step. Here's how to proceed.

1. Jot down a few key words for each task that might go into a job description (e.g., "greeting customers").

2. Rank the tasks in terms of importance (and frequency or time commitment, if those factors are relevant).

3. List the activities involved in doing each task. For example, to "greet customers," an employee might answer telephones, welcome customers to the office, and answer questions.

4. List the skills necessary to perform that activity. Continuing the example, skills might be "pleasant phone voice," "strong speaking skills," "good organizational skills," "tremendous patience," and "a working knowledge of the business."

Case Study — Simple Job Description

Mr. McCay runs an automobile repair business. Business is brisk and he has more customers than he can accommodate on his own. He needs to hire his first employee to help out. He wants the employee to answer the phone and greet customers, write up repair orders, perform minor repairs, and pick up shop supplies. From this list, Mr. McCay determines that he needs someone who has good communication skills, basic knowledge of automotive repair, a driver's license, and good organizational skills, to balance the variety of tasks that will be performed.

There are as many different formats for job descriptions as there are jobs, but most job descriptions include some basic pieces of information. You can use the following sample job description form to assist you in writing your own job descriptions. Following the blank sample is a completed job description.

Job Description

Job Title:	Date:
	Employment Status:
	Regular ☐
Incumbent:	Temporary ☐
	Full-time ☐
Department:	Part-time ☐
	Intern ☐
Supervisor's Name/Title:	Regular Hours: _____/wk
	Exempt ☐ Non-exempt ☐

A position description is written to describe work currently organized and performed by a fully qualified employee (who possesses knowledge, skills, and experience required by the position). One should be on file for each regular full- and part-time position. Attach a copy of the last position description prepared for this position.

When was the last time this position description was updated:

What is the overall purpose and objective of this position (why does the position exist)?

List in order of importance the major responsibilities of the job and estimate the percentage of time spent on each (the main function of the job may or may not be the one where the most time is spent).

1. _____ ____ %

2. _____ ____ %

3. _____ ____ %

4. _____ ____ %

5. _____ ____ %

6. _____ ____ %

7. Able to react to change productively and handle other essential tasks as assigned. ____ %

Total: 100 %

Is this position closely, moderately, or minimally supervised?   Please explain:

Does this position have supervisory responsibility (i.e., responsible for hiring, firing, performance appraisals, etc.)? Yes _____ No _____ If yes, list the number and title for positions that directly or indirectly report to this position (i.e., three secretaries, four programmers, etc.):

Does this position have access to confidential information? Yes _____ No _____ If yes, please explain:

Does this position have access to or handle company funds? Yes _____ No _____ If yes, please explain:

Is it important to this position that the incumbent be able to communicate fluently in English? Yes _____ No _____ If yes, please explain:

Describe required work experience (including length of time), training, and/or level of education:

List any required technical skills (typing, software, mechanical, engineering, etc.):

What other special training and/or abilities are necessary to qualify for this position?

Check any of the following factors that are important to successful performance in this position:

Problem Solving	❏	Bilingual	❏
Analytical Ability	❏	Interpersonal Skills	❏
Communication Skills	❏	Dexterity	❏

Describe the requirements of this position that make these factors important:

Working Conditions

Are there particular working conditions associated with this position that should be noted (i.e., working environment, hours of work, travel, work space, etc.)? Yes _____ No _____

If yes, please explain:

_____

_____

_____

_____

_____

Analysis of Physical Demands of Position

Check physical demands that apply.

Describe job responsibilities that require physical demands checked.

1. Strength ❑ _____ % of time _____
    a. Standing ❑ _____ % of time _____
        Walking ❑ _____ % of time _____
        Sitting ❑ _____ lbs. _____
    b. Lifting ❑ _____ lbs. _____
        Carrying ❑ _____ lbs. _____
        Pushing ❑ _____ lbs. _____
        Pulling ❑ _____ lbs. _____
2. Climbing ❑ _____
    Balancing ❑ _____
3. Stooping ❑ _____
    Kneeling ❑ _____
    Crouching ❑ _____
    Crawling ❑ _____
4. Reaching ❑ _____
    Handling ❑ _____
5. Speech ❑ _____
    Hearing ❑ _____
6. Sight ❑ _____
    Depth perception ❑ _____
    Color vision ❑ _____

SAMPLE JOB DESCRIPTION—NONEXEMPT (production)

JOB TITLE	WORK TEAM LEADER?	DIVISION	Operations
Assembler/Packer	yes no x	DEPARTMENT	Rectangle Dedicated Line

LOCATION	___ part-time: ___ hours	DATE WRITTEN	July 18, 1996
	_x_ full-time		

REPORTS TO

Fletcher Abercromie   Work Team Leader

SALARY GRADE	SALARY RANGE	SHIFT

PURPOSE (Include *primary accomplishments, products, & services, who* benefits from them and *how.*)

The purpose of an assembler/packer on the rectangle dedicated line is to complete a partially completed work surface and package it according to standards.

ESSENTIAL DUTIES (What do you have to be able to do to achieve the desired results of your job? Include management and leadership responsibilities for work team leaders.)

- Visually inspects and transfers work surfaces into boring machine.
- Assembles and attaches understructures to work surface.
- Packages completed work surfaces, instruction sheets, and correct parts.
- Knows and adheres to standards of quality.

GENERAL DESCRIPTION (How would you describe this job to someone who has never done it?)

This job has five workstations. One station has two people working together. Assemblers rotate between stations every two to four hours. Assemblers are responsible for making sure their coworkers know the correct parts that go with each work surface. Work surfaces include laminates and solid composites. Assemblers keep the work area clean, maintain tape dispensers, gather parts needed for assembly, etc. This job is done while standing and working on a work surface that is 35 inches off the floor. The tools used are stratovac (pneumatic lifter), air driven, in line screw-driver, and, infrequently, pliers. The product moves through the line at a rate of one every 1½ to 3 minutes. Work surfaces vary in size from 24" x 24" up to 30" x 96"', and in weight from 27 to 116 pounds. They are lifted with a partner off the line, into a box, and onto a pallet. The highest point it is lifted is roughly six feet.

MINIMUM REQUIREMENTS (What is required to perform the essential duties?)

- A minimum of three years of production experience.
- Ability to do essential duties.
- Ability to understand and follow English instructions.
- Ability to transfer 116 pounds, with the help of another person, a distance of six feet.

I have reviewed and determined that this job description accurately reflects the position.

Work team leader signature	Date	Employee signature	Date

FOR STAFFING USE ONLY

Posting #

EEO Job Group

Posting Date __/__/__

SET A COMPETITIVE STARTING SALARY

When you began thinking about hiring an employee, one of the first issues you faced was how much you *could* pay. How much you *should* pay is based on who you hire and the employment market in your geographic area. Pay enough to keep good employees, but not so much as to jeopardize your cash flow.

What Other Employers Are Paying

Getting salary data is the first step in determining what "competitive" pay is for the work you want done. The best way to find out what a competitive wage is in your area is to find out what others are paying for the same type of work. Other reasons to keep on top of market rates are:

- **Inflation.** Inflation decreases the buying power of your employees' salary when the dollar amount stays the same. Many employers adjust for inflation each year, so maintaining competitive pay may require you to adjust base pay levels every 12 to 18 months.

- **Workforce mobility.** Employee turnover can be a problem if employees can leave your business and earn more elsewhere.

- **Credibility.** Wage and salary data make it possible to offer pay that satisfies employees' need to feel that they are paid fairly in relation to those who work for other businesses.

- **Threat of unionization.** Competitive pay reduces the chance that your workers will consider joining a union. Some unions now target small businesses for organizing activity.

Using the Want Ads for Salary Data

The quickest and easiest way to find out the going rate for a particular kind of work is to check the classified ads in your local newspapers. Look for similar jobs that entail the same kind of work. Many classified ads will include a starting salary or approximate pay range. If you find that not enough of the ads include a pay range, you can always call the business that placed the ads and ask.

When you're looking at or calling about jobs listed in the classifieds, note job duties, location, and benefits offered, if any. Reevaluate your target salary range based on the amounts others are willing to pay, adjusting for differing duties, benefits, and other factors. Jobs listed outside your geographic area aren't comparable and probably will provide little information about your employment market.

Networking for Salary Data

In addition to using the classified ads for salary data, there are some other, more informal ways to get data, too. They tend not to be reflective of an entire industry or area, but they can give you a starting point. If you have a relatively common job opening, you can always ask:

- other small business owners, friends and business associates, suppliers, or customers

- employment agencies or temporary help agencies

- competitors (If a competitor has a job opening, call and ask how much the salary would be.)

- job applicants (they may be willing to tell you how much they were paid in their previous positions

- anyone doing that job for someone else (Who knows, maybe they can give you some leads on people you can hire.)

Public Sources for Salary Data

There are many public sources of salary data. The Bureau of Labor Statistics has Occupational Compensation Surveys for most geographical areas in the United States. The information is broken down by type of occupation as well as by various levels within that occupation. The advantage of using these surveys is that they reflect data in your geographical area so you can get an idea of what employers in your area are paying for a specific job. Go to the BLS Internet site: http://www.stats.bls.gov:80/ocsdata.htm and type in the name of your city or state. For price information on a specific survey or to order by phone, call the General Printing Office at (412) 644-2721.

Other sources. You may be able to get information from other sources, including: consulting firms, company and trade associations, professional associations, and your local chamber of commerce.

Warning

Before you use data from *any* source, make sure it's up to date, was done by a reputable source, and covers employees like yours.

PUBLICIZE YOUR JOB OPENING

Your budget is likely to be the largest factor in deciding how you let the world know you're hiring. But it's also important to keep your audience in mind. Your best choice will be the one that targets the people you want to reach within your budget.

Advertising Media for Job Ads

Advertising is the most common way to get the word out about your job. Choosing a medium for your ad is the first step in the process. Newspapers and trade journals are the most commonly used media, but you may have other options. Once you've selected a medium, you can turn your attention to writing your job advertisement.

Newspapers

In many areas, you can choose from among a variety of community and local papers. Classified ads are a good bet because, traditionally, people looking for work read the classifieds. And you can quickly and inexpensively reach a large audience to fill an immediate need. You might even get some free Internet exposure, since many newspapers also make their classified ads available online for free.

One drawback of classifieds, especially if the unemployment rate is high in your area, is that you might be swamped with more applications than you can handle. To avoid this, use well-written ads that discourage clearly unqualified persons from applying. You can also use blind ads, which don't reveal your identity. That way, you don't have to respond to every applicant or deal with those you have no interest in hiring. However, blind ads may generate fewer responses because people are suspicious of an employer that won't put its name in print.

Trade Journals

Professional and trade journals are good places to advertise when you're looking for a professional or technical employee with special skills. The *cost per reader* for advertising in these journals is relatively high but, overall, the *total cost* of the ad is generally fairly low. Balance the need to reach a specialized audience with the need to keep advertising costs at a reasonable level. Ads aimed at journal readers should emphasize those aspects of the job that appeal to professional pride: responsibility, challenge, and opportunities for advancement. A downside of choosing to advertise in this medium is the slow response time. These publications are often published monthly or quarterly. Thus, they may not be the best choice if you need some help in a hurry.

Other Options

Television and radio. With the exception of cable television systems that provide a forum for help wanted ads on a local access channel, television is just too expensive to be an option for recruiting employees. Not only does the air time cost a great deal, but there are also the production costs associated with creating your ad. Radio, on the other hand, is much cheaper than television and you can be more selective in the audience that your ad will reach. In some markets, certain radio stations air employment ads for local businesses free of charge.

Electronic posting. Posting jobs electronically is a relatively new form of advertising. Many companies advertise jobs on their Internet home pages. A large number of employment data bases exist, and employers are using these in addition to the more traditional advertising media. If you post a job on the Internet, you'll reach a broader audience than through a local newspaper and you'll enjoy quick, electronic responses (unless you specify otherwise). Electronic posting can be valuable as a recruiting tool for positions requiring advanced computer-related skills because many people with those skills are frequently online.

Finally, a "help wanted" sign in the window can also be appropriate if having applicants appear at the door won't interfere with your business operations.

CREATE YOUR JOB AD

Once you've chosen a medium for your advertising, you're ready to draft an ad. Use the job description and job qualifications that you've established to decide what to include in the ad. When you're drafting a job ad, regardless of the medium it will appear in, include the information that will draw responses from the best candidates. Avoid discriminatory language, whether it's illegal or not. It's bad PR, and many papers won't accept discriminatory ads.

Information To Include in Job Ads

A job ad should describe the position you're trying to fill, provide a salary range (if you want), and make it clear how people should respond and what information they should supply. Try to minimize the demands that screening responses will place on your time. If you want a resume, including salary history, say so. Ask for all the information you need to *decide whether to interview* an applicant, but no more than that. *Don't* gather all the information that you need to make a hiring decision.

Work Smart

Choose your response method carefully. Think twice before putting your business phone number in a job ad. You can never anticipate how many calls you'll get, or how disruptive a flood of calls can be. Just looking through a few dozen resumes and cover letters can consume hours. Whatever method you choose, realize that the hiring process represents a substantial commitment of your time.

Tell enough about the job so that those reading the ad can decide whether they are interested and qualified. Give the job title along with a brief description of duties, especially if the job title is ambiguous. List the minimum education, experience, and skill levels that are acceptable, if applicable. Note any special factors, such as extensive travel or relocation, that would immediately weed out applicants unwilling to take on those aspects of the job. Use proper grammar and punctuation so your ad will be easy to understand. Don't use abbreviations or acronyms that make it difficult to read or understand the ad. Be specific about the type of equipment, software programs, etc., that applicants should know how to use or operate.

Remember, writing it right saves you and applicants a lot of time and energy. They want to find the right job as much as you want to find the right employee. A clear, specific job ad goes a long way toward achieving both those goals.

Avoiding Discrimination in Job Ads

Federal law prohibits discrimination against individuals in any protected group by employers with 15 or more employees. Some state laws apply to even smaller employers. These laws dictate what you can and can't say in a job advertisement. A very narrow exception from federal and some state discrimination laws is available for jobs where religion, gender, or national origin factors are "reasonably necessary to the normal operation of that particular business or enterprise."

Gender-specific language. The law doesn't prohibit you from using titles that seem to specify one gender over another. We recommend that you avoid these terms if you can. Most can be changed to a gender-neutral form, anyway (e.g., salesperson). If you choose to use gender-specific terms, the EEOC won't permit you to use the phrase "Equal Opportunity Employer."

Age discrimination. You also have to be careful not to use language that will discriminate against potential applicants for your job because of their age. The EEOC gives policy guidance on how job advertisements may violate the ADEA.

Age Discrimination in Employment Act

The ADEA is the federal law that prohibits businesses with 20 or more employees from engaging in age-based employment discrimination, including discrimination in the payment of compensation for employees who are at least 40 years of age. Under the law, age cannot be the reason for paying one employee more than another one. Nor can it be a reason for giving one person a job over another. However, nothing in the ADEA makes it unlawful to observe the terms of a bona fide seniority system.

Although the prohibition against job advertisements that discriminate on the basis of age is pretty straightforward, the EEOC uses a case-by-case assessment to decide whether an advertisement, or the context in which it is used, would discourage persons in the protected age group from applying for the job. For example, the mere presence of "trigger words" (words and phrases that refer to age such as "recent college graduate," "young executive," "athletically inclined") alone doesn't violate the ADEA. An ad must be read in its entirety, taking into consideration the results of the ad on the employer's hiring practices.

To illustrate these concepts, here are several case studies from the EEOC illustrating how the EEOC determines if an ad discriminates against people who are 40 or older.

Case Studies — Age Discrimination in Ads

Case Study 1. "Applicant must be young and energetic and possess excellent customer relations skills. Applicants who are selected will be required to stand for long periods of time and to lift 20-30 pounds."

In this case, the Commission *would* find a violation. Use of the word "young," specifically indicates a preference, limitation, specification, or discrimination based on age. Such an ad would almost certainly deter many qualified older persons from applying. Note that if the word "young" was deleted, the ad would probably be acceptable.

Case Study 2. "Opening for a person seeking to supplement pension. Part-time position available for Laundromat Attendant from 9:00 a.m.-2:00 p.m., Monday-Thursday. Responsibilities include dispensing products sold on premises, maintaining washer, dryer, and vending machines. Retired persons preferred."

This ad improperly limits the applicant pool by indicating a preference based on age. Persons rarely receive pensions or attain retirement status before 55 and frequently not until age 65. Thus, the ad illegally deters younger persons within the protected age group (i.e., persons over 40 but less than 65) from applying.

Case Study 3. *"Wanted:* Individuals of all ages. Day and evening hours available. Full- and part-time positions. All inquiries welcomed. Excellent secondary source of income for retirees."

While the ad mentions "retirees," it isn't illegal. Individuals of all ages are welcomed for the employment opportunity. The reference to retirees notifies them of an opportunity and invites them to participate. The language in this ad differs from the language used in Case Study 2, which suggests that *only* retired, pension-eligible persons will be considered for employment.

OTHER METHODS OF FINDING EMPLOYEES

You have some other, less-used options for acquiring the people you need for your business. These include personal recruiting and outsourcing the search process to an employment agency.

Recruiting. Personal recruiting is just that — personally looking for, meeting with, or contacting people who you would like to work for you. If you have existing employees, you can ask them if they know anyone who might meet your needs. Colleagues, friends, and others may know people who are looking for jobs. Referrals can bring in quality recruits and can create a pleasant work environment where employees support one another and work harder. However, if working within your circle of friends and acquaintances doesn't seem likely to generate results, you have other options.

- **Local job fairs:** Governmental and social service organizations often hold job fairs to bring together employers and applicants. Watch the Sunday papers and check with local civic groups.

- **Schools:** Recruiting at schools can involve contacting a school office that arranges for employment listings to something as simple as getting permission to post a want ad on a bulletin board. Obviously, rules will vary, both by location and level (e.g., high school v. college). But in most cases, it's *free*.

Work Smart

Schools can be a particularly valuable source of temporary and seasonal (especially summer) help. Employment is short-term, students generally accept lower pay than other part-time help, and they usually don't require benefits.

A job posting should be written in the same way as a job ad. Don't use discriminatory language, and don't impose job qualifications that tend to discriminate against one protected group of individuals.

Outsourcing. Some business owners opt to outsource recruiting functions, either in part or completely, instead of doing it themselves. This can save time, although costs can add up. You also lose some control over the process. On the other hand, outsourcing relieves you of some of the more tedious functions of finding the right employee but leaves the ultimate choice — the hiring decision — to you.

In Chapter 2, we discussed how to deal with an employee leasing or temporary help agency. The same rules apply to dealing with public and private employment services.

Warning

Be sure you know how much doing business with a service will cost you. Public services are usually inexpensive or even free. Private services have fees that can be as high as 30 percent of first-year salary. You might get your money back if the employee doesn't work out, but that's not much consolation if you have to start looking for another employee.

Public employment services. There are hundreds of state employment services affiliated with the U.S. Department of Labor's Training and Employment Service, located in every large city and in every county. These agencies were originally set up to process unemployment compensation claims. Today, they provide a variety of services for job seekers and employers, including counseling, testing, training, placement, and analytical and statistical services.

These agencies can provide all types of employees for every occupation, including professional, technical, and managerial positions. They have a large pool of job seekers, not merely because they handle unemployment, but because many smart job hunters would rather use their services than deal with a private employment agency. Services are free to both employer and job hunter (except, of course, that they are financed through the taxes we pay).

Measure Your Success and Plan Ahead

If you anticipate that you'll need to hire more employees in the future, keep a file of all the ads or other recruiting methods you've tried, and make a notation as to the number of responses (and qualified applicants) you got through each recruiting channel. That way, you'll be able to recruit more quickly and effectively next time.

Part II

The Hiring Process

It's time to deal with the people who apply for your job opening, and there's no way to predict how many people will respond. This is particularly true if you're hiring for the first time. So be prepared to deal with the disappointment of receiving few or no applications *or* the panic of trying to deal with hundreds of responses.

Also recognize that you'll be diverting some time and attention from your regular business activities. Prospective employees will want to meet with you before or after regular working hours, during your regular working hours, or at lunch. Do your best to accommodate *qualified* applicants, but don't let the hiring process have a negative impact on your business.

Hiring means that you'll also be spending time verifying information provided in resumes or job applications. This may include background checks, employment and personal reference checks, and even credit checks. You may even want to test applicants, if testing will provide information you need to find the best person for the job. The steps that you take to verify that you're getting the right person will vary based on the nature of the job your trying to fill.

Example

If you're hiring someone to make deliveries, an applicant's driving record is extremely significant. You'd be less interested in the driving record of a person applying to be a cashier, who won't ever drive a company vehicle. In contrast, you'd be a lot more interested in checking references and background information relating to that person's honesty and ability to deal with numerous cash transactions.

After you've selected the person you want to hire, you'll have to make an offer and work out the terms of the person's employment. Prospective employees have become increasingly likely to want to negotiate starting pay, vacations, and other issues. In many cases, you may have to make some concessions to get the person you want. Only agree to an arrangement if you're comfortable with it. If you think a prospective employee is being unreasonable, don't offer him or her the job. Don't forget that you're likely to have a long-term relationship with this person.

Once an applicant accepts your offer, you still have some work to do to get ready for the employee's first day. There are records to create and government paperwork that must be filled out and filed. You'll also need to prepare some kind of orientation for the new employee to introduce him or her to how you do business and what your expectations are. Don't make the mistake of merely showing your new employee where to sit and assuming that the rest will be picked up by osmosis. Like it or not, for at least a little while, it's in your best interest to be a teacher as well as a business owner and an employer.

Chapter 4: Screening Job Applicants explains how to narrow down the field of candidates who apply for your job opening.

Chapter 5: Extending an Offer of Employment walks you through the process of coming to mutually agreeable terms with the applicant you've decided to hire.

Screening Job Applicants

Once you've made it public that you're hiring, set aside the time necessary to go through the responses that you get. Understand that the actions you're about to take can have serious legal consequences. Any person who responds to your ad is probably an applicant, and may be protected by state or federal antidiscrimination laws. Which types of discrimination are prohibited depend on how many employees you have and what your state laws dictate (see pages 9 and 12). So, here's how to efficiently screen job applicants and avoid discrimination at the same time.

- Determine who is an applicant.

- Respond to each applicant as appropriate.

- Verify that you have the information you need to give all applications equal consideration.

- Arrange for interviews with the most qualified applicants.

- Check employment and other references for candidates you're still considering after the interviews.

- Test qualified applicants (if required).

DETERMINING WHO IS AN APPLICANT

You can decide to excludes from applicant status all those who submit unsolicited resumes. You have a lot discretion in establishing such procedures. However, once you establish a rule or procedure, apply it fairly and consistently to *all* applicants. Try to keep the policy simple. Vague or confusing procedures invite challenges.

Work Smart

If you have 15 or more employees, federal antidiscrimination laws administered by the EEOC require you to keep records of all applicants, hired or not, for one year to ensure that you aren't excluding people in protected groups from consideration for employment.

ACKNOWLEDGING APPLICANTS

It's good practice to acknowledge everyone who applies for a job, unless you get a real flood of applicants. It creates good will, doesn't cost much, and helps avoid calls or letters from applicants who want to know if you received their application or resume. It also opens the door to contacting someone if you need more help in the future.

Work Smart

If you receive a lot of applications, indicate that you will contact the applicant *only* if you intend to arrange an interview. Give a time frame within which you will contact the applicant. That way, you don't have to follow up further with anyone who doesn't make it past the initial screening of applications or resumes. It's also easier on the applicant.

Prepare a separate letter for applicants who don't qualify, thanking them for their interest, but indicating that you won't be considering them for the opening. Be polite. Don't point to the applicant's lack of qualifications. Instead, indicate that you have received numerous applications from candidates whose qualifications better match the particular needs of the job you're try to fill.

JOB APPLICATION FORMS

If you followed our advice, your job ad clearly indicated what type of response you wanted from job applicants. Hopefully, people who answer the ad will respond in the manner that you requested. If you requested resumes, cover letters, and other information, such as work samples, you're well on your way.

But, suppose you need to gather very specific information from every applicant? Or suppose you're filling a position where people traditionally don't have resumes, such as retail sales. In that case, you'll probably want to use a job application. A wide variety of generic application forms (see page 59) are available in office supply stores. You can look at several of these and edit them as you choose. Or you can create a job application that focuses on the specific information that you need. Your form need not be fancy or lengthy. Just ask what you need to know and leave room for the answers.

Application for Employment

PERSONAL INFORMATION

LAST NAME	FIRST NAME	MIDDLE INITIAL	SOCIAL SECURITY NUMBER

STREET ADDRESS	CITY	STATE	ZIP	HOW LONG?

PRIOR ADDRESS	CITY	STATE	ZIP	HOW LONG?

HOME PHONE	BUSINESS PHONE

MILITARY SERVICE

BRANCH   DATES OF SERVICE

YES ☐   NO ☐

JOB-RELATED MILITARY EXPERIENCE

EDUCATION

HIGH SCHOOL NAME AND MAILING ADDRESS	DID YOU GRADUATE?
	YES ☐ NO ☐

STUDIES PURSUED

UNIVERSITY, COLLEGE, TRADE SCHOOL NAME AND MAILING ADDRESS	YEARS COMPLETED
	1 2 3 4 5

MAJOR	MINOR	DEGREE

GRADUATE SCHOOL NAME AND MAILING ADDRESS	YEARS COMPLETED
	1 2 3 4 5

MAJOR	MINOR	DEGREE

OTHER EDUCATION OR TRAINING

EMPLOYMENT HISTORY (LIST MOST RECENT JOB FIRST)

EMPLOYER'S NAME AND ADDRESS	STILL EMPLOYED?
	YES ❑ NO ❑

NAME AND TITLE OF IMMEDIATE SUPERVISOR	MAY WE CONTACT?
	YES ❑ NO ❑

DUTIES AND RESPONSIBILITIES

	RATE OF PAY

REASONS FOR LEAVING

EMPLOYER'S NAME AND ADDRESS

NAME AND TITLE OF IMMEDIATE SUPERVISOR	MAY WE CONTACT?
	YES ❑ NO ❑

DUTIES AND RESPONSIBILITIES

	RATE OF PAY

REASONS FOR LEAVING

PROFESSIONAL REFERENCES

NAME	RELATIONSHIP	PHONE
NAME	RELATIONSHIP	PHONE

AVAILABILITY

ANY RESTRICTIONS ON YOUR AVAILABILITY TO WORK?

SIGNATURE   **DATE**

BY SIGNING, I GRANT THE COMPANY THE RIGHT TO CHECK THE REFERENCES AND INFORMATION PROVIDED HEREIN. I ALSO ACKNOWLEDGE THAT, IF HIRED, MY EMPLOYMENT WILL BE "AT-WILL," AND SUBJECT TO TERMINATION WITH OR WITHOUT CAUSE OR NOTICE.

Decide in advance whether you'll interview job applicants when they come in to fill out an application. You'll probably save time if you ask candidates to complete the application form, then follow up only if you determine an interview is warranted. Otherwise, you might waste time talking to applicants whose applications show that they aren't qualified.

Work Smart

If you choose to use job applications, decide how and where applicants are going to get and fill out the forms. If you can arrange to monitor prospective employees as they complete the application forms, you might get some idea of how fast they work. You'll also get a chance to assess their accuracy, handwriting, etc. Particularly in an office environment, inability to spell and illegible handwriting can be problems.

What Not To Ask on Job Applications

For every question you can ask someone on an application, there's at least one that you *can't* ask. Many of these prohibitions are designed to protect applicants from discrimination. If your business is subject to federal or state antidiscrimination laws, include questions only if you need to know the answer in order to make an informed hiring decision. Have your attorney review your form before you use it.

Here are some danger areas to avoid should you choose to create your own application form:

- **Marital status.** Don't ask applicants to "circle one: Mr. Mrs. Ms. or Miss" or in any way divulge their marital status.

- **Maiden name.** Asking this can raise questions of discrimination based on marital status, gender, or even national origin.

- **Age.** Ask for age *only* if it's necessary to comply with minimum age and child labor requirements under state laws. A permissible question is, "Are you at least 18?"

- **Children.** It's permissible, but *not recommended*, to ask "Have you made arrangements to care for any children?" since that can be justified on grounds of availability and reliability.

Warning

If you feel compelled to pursue the child care issue, which can increase your exposure to charges of discrimination, do so in the interview, not on the application form, to minimize the risk. Question men as well as women and treat the answers the same.

- **Gender, race.** There are very few bona fide occupational qualifications based on gender, and so far, there are none recognized based on race. Ask *only* if you need to in order to comply with affirmative action obligations.

- **Birthplace.** Don't ask because of the possibility of national origin or immigration issues.

- **Personal references - friends, business contacts, etc.** Ask for names and current addresses, but ask only if you intend to follow up. Applicants frequently tell references to expect your call.

- **Residence.** "Do you rent? own? board?" Once a common question, it supposedly was a measure of stability. But it may evidence discrimination against minorities and others who tend to rent rather than own, and it's likely to be regarded as none of your business by many applicants.

- **Relationship of person to notify in an emergency.** Don't even ask the question at all until you hire an applicant.

- **Criminal records.** Generally, don't ask about *arrest* records on a job application. You may ask about *conviction* records in order to protect yourself from negligent hiring claims, as long as you place a statement nearby indicating that a conviction alone won't prevent hiring.

- **Type of discharge from military service.** Some states make it unlawful to discriminate on this basis.

- **Disability, health.** Don't ask medical questions. Defer medical or physical exams until after you make a conditional offer of employment.

- **Workers' compensation history.** The ADA (for employers with at least 15 employees) prohibits this type of questioning. Gather the information you need to comply with your obligations after an offer of employment has been made.

- **Citizenship.** Discrimination based on citizenship is unlawful under the Immigration Reform and Control Act of 1986.

- **Dates of school attendance.** Asking for dates attended might be viewed as a means of asking an applicant's age. Don't ask unless you can show a nondiscriminatory, legitimate business reason, such as to facilitate reference checks.

Using an Application To Limit Liability

The purpose of a job application is to gather the information you need to narrow down the pool of applicants and, ultimately, select your new employee. It can also be used to help protect you from liability by informing applicants about work rules and how the hiring process will work. An applicant's signature, acknowledging these statements, can help you to avoid or win claims later on. Always keep the original applications that are signed by applicants in a job file.

Release of information form. Include an information release statement on the application that gives you permission to check references. Here's sample language for a release.

Example

"I hereby authorize any person, educational institution, or company I have listed as a reference on my employment application to disclose in good faith any information they may have regarding my qualifications and fitness for employment. I will hold ABC Company, Inc., any former employers, educational institutions, and any other persons giving references free of liability for the exchange of this information and any other reasonable and necessary information incident to the employment process."

Employment-at-will statement. Employment-at-will means that an employer is free to terminate the employee at any time, with or without cause. The employee is also free to leave at any time. Employment-at-will statements included on an application form are designed to ensure that you don't create or imply that you will create an employment contract, should you hire the applicant. *Establishing an employment-at-will relationship is extremely important.* If an employee can point to a document you created and claim that it creates a contractual relationship, it can be expensive to sever the employment relationship.

Example

"I understand that, if hired, my employment would be "at-will" and could be terminated at any time by either party, with or without cause and with or without notice."

False information statement. You may want to terminate employees if you discover that they lied on a resume or job application. A statement to that effect in the job application gives prospective employees notice that submission of false statements will not be tolerated and gives you a clear way out if they are found out.

Work authorization statement. Although you can't discriminate on the basis of citizenship, proof of identity and work authorization are required of all employees by the Immigration Reform and Control Act. To bolster documentation of your compliance efforts, and to make sure that applicants understand what is required of them, include a statement that notifies applicants that they'll have to furnish proof of identity and legal work authorization prior to hire.

Confidentiality statement. A statement that all information will be kept strictly confidential should be included to allay applicants' fears that the information they provide might be disclosed.

Work rules. Some businesses use the application to inform applicants about work rules. The application provides an opportunity to have the applicant agree to abide by all work rules, if hired. If you have a drug and alcohol testing policy, now is the time to let applicants know.

Accepting Resumes

If you don't plan to hire or replace many people in your business, you may not want to create or use a job application. You may instead rely on resumes and cover letters when you have a job opening. Asking for resumes is also the way to go if you're hiring for a position where it would be normal for applicants to have resumes. And there are no questions regarding fairness, which can be an issue with a job application that you create.

The downside of resumes is that each resume is different and gives different information. The flexible format and individual license that applicants take can make it hard to figure out exactly what they did in past jobs because they can place things in the most positive light and exclude things that might damage their employment prospects.

On the other hand, resumes are usually accompanied by a cover letter in which the applicant tells about his or her experience and background. You can get a good idea about the applicant's communication and writing abilities from a cover letter. Well-written letters and resumes can give you a much clearer sense of the applicant's qualifications than a standardized application could. For these reasons, some employers use *both* a resume and an application.

Work Experience

Resumes usually consist of several main parts, which you'll need to evaluate. The first part will set forth work experience, and the second will provide information regarding education and references.

Work Smart

In resumes, form is important, but not as important as substance. A resume should give you the information you need to decide if you want to *interview* someone, not hire. Don't make a hiring decision based on a piece of paper. However, if the position you're filling places a premium on writing skills and accuracy, it might not be unreasonable to reject applicants whose resumes contain typographical or spelling errors.

In looking at the work experience portion of the resume, warning signs include large gaps in employment, many jobs in a short time span, and vague descriptions of work (the applicant could be trying to make the job sound like more than it was). On the other hand, the presence of lots of action words and specific information is a positive sign, in that it can indicate that someone is goal-oriented.

Education and References

The description of a person's education should be straightforward. It should indicate what schools the applicant attended, what degree or certificate, if any, was earned, and, if appropriate, the field of study or specialization. Some candidates may indicate that they're currently pursuing their education at night or on a part-time basis. Many applicants will also provide information regarding membership in professional associations in this portion of the resume.

Many people will simply state "references provided on request." Ask for this information *only* if you plan to check references. Applicants often tell references to expect a call from you. Don't put the applicant in an awkward position by not calling.

Requesting Other Application Materials

You may want to ask for other materials depending on the job. For example, if the job involves artistic talent, you may want to ask applicants for copies of work from their portfolios. If the job involves writing, you'll want to ask for writing samples.

Work Smart

Let applicants know if you don't plan to return writing samples, photos, or other application materials. You don't want to be responsible for throwing away the original copy of an artist's or writer's work. Offering to return submissions, or failing to say that you won't, can lead to big shipping costs. If you think you may get a lot of responses to an ad that requires such submissions, consider stating that you won't return submissions.

INTERVIEWING JOB APPLICANTS

Once you've reviewed the information provided by those who've applied for the job, it's time to start scheduling some appointments to interview the most promising candidates.

Assessing applicants' qualifications by talking to them is a highly subjective method of choosing employees. Used in conjunction with other screening methods, such as applications and background checking, it can be an extremely useful selection tool. After all, one of the most important qualifications a person must have for any job is the right personality to work well with others, and you can't determine that from a resume or application.

Work Smart

Although it might be tempting to schedule a large number of interviews in a short time to minimize your time away from the rest of your business, don't do it. You might find it difficult to stay on schedule, and it's awkward and unprofessional to have a group of applicants waiting around your business. More important, you don't want to minimize the effort you'll expend on each interview. You'll be meeting someone new, trying to follow an agenda of information gathering, and attempting to evaluate how well each applicant would fit your needs. Three interviews in a day can easily overwhelm you.

Planning for an Interview

Preparing beforehand is the key to a successful interview. Here are some steps to take:

- Limit the number of people you select for an interview. The more you pick, the more time it will take. For most jobs, try to interview three to six candidates. If you're filling more than one similar position, the pool can be somewhat larger.

- Compare each applicant's background and skills with what the job requires.

- Decide how you want to conduct the interview, and formulate the questions that you'll ask. Prepare a written outline of questions, which you can also use for taking notes. Practice asking questions until it becomes natural. A nervous interviewer means a bad interview.

- Think about the responses you'll give to questions that the applicant asks about you and your business.

- Decide where to conduct the interviews.

- Review the applicant's resume or application so you don't need to constantly refer to it during the interview.

- Allot plenty of time for the meeting. It can take anywhere from 15 minutes to two hours or more.

- Unplug the phone or do whatever you must to prevent interruptions.

Choosing Where To Interview

If you have an office, it's probably best to conduct interviews there so that the applicant can see the working environment. Don't sit behind your desk with the applicant sitting across from you. Try to create a less formal, conversational setting.

Over the phone. If you're screening a lot of applicants, or if an applicant is from out of town, phone interviews can be a reasonable alternative. The drawback to phone interviews is obvious: you can't see the person's facial expressions or body language. On the plus side, brief phone "pre-interviews" can help reduce the number of applicants you call in for a face-to-face meeting. If you do phone interviews, call applicants, rather than having them call you.

Work Smart

If you work in your home or are uncomfortable interviewing at your place of business, pick a neutral, public location, such as a coffee shop or library (many have conference rooms you can use). You don't want unsuccessful unhappy applicants knowing where you live. *Don't* try to conduct an interview over a meal, however. The social setting conflicts with the business nature of the meeting.

Choosing an Interview Format

Whatever form the interview takes, the interaction between you and the applicant helps to determine whether you're suited to one another. We suggest that you have a list of essential questions that you'll ask every applicant. You can choose when to seek further information based on how the interview progresses. Then, leave time for questions that arise during the course of the conversation. Candidates should have a chance to elaborate, where appropriate.

Some businesses use a standardized list of questions for a particular position in order to develop a format that doesn't discriminate. Others follow a less structured or "tell me about yourself" format. Deciding what you're comfortable with is a personal choice that will, unfortunately, involve a bit of trial and error.

You also need to decide who else will be involved in the interview process. It's not uncommon to have potential coworkers meet with candidates, at least briefly. That way, you can use their input to help select someone who's compatible with your existing workforce.

Conducting the Interview

There are distinct parts to an interview, and each of them is important. To make sure that you cover all the bases in your interview, use this outline as a guide:

- **Establish rapport.** Greet the applicant with a pleasant smile, firm handshake, and a casual statement or two. Outline the interview objectives and structure. For example, say "In the time we have, I would like to..." People are always more comfortable when there is a known agenda for a meeting.

- **Gather information.** Verify specific information from the resume or application. Use open-ended questions (how, what, when, etc.), and always follow up a yes or no answer with an open-ended question.

- **Give information about your business and even "sell" the position.** Do this *after* applicants answer your questions. If you tell people exactly what you're looking for first, they can adapt their answers to fit what they perceive to be your needs.

- **Close the interview.** Thank the candidate for his or her participation and interest. Indicate what the next step will be and the time frame within which it will occur.

- **Evaluate your notes and compare candidates.** As soon as the interview is over, complete an evaluation form or firm up your notes, noting specific information wherever possible.

Warning

Don't make any notes about an applicant that could be considered discriminatory, even if you're just noting physical characteristics to help you keep track of who's who.

Also, be specific about what you record in your notes. For example, a white male applicant for a receptionist job comes to the interview in a coat and tie. A black female shows up in torn jeans and a T-shirt. It's legally defensible not to hire the black female because of her clothing choice. But the documented reason for rejecting her should be that "the applicant appeared for the interview in torn jeans and a T-shirt." Don't ambiguously state that she was rejected because she "didn't have the proper appearance."

Providing the Information an Applicant Needs

As the interviewer, your responsibilities are broader than just information gathering. You also need to convey information regarding the job and the business to applicants so that they have the information they need to make an informed choice about working for you. This information generally includes the nature of the job and the skills you believe are required to perform that job; pay and benefits, although some interviewers don't discuss pay until a job offer is made; working hours and conditions; and general information about your business.

Most applicants will have some questions for you. Prepare for questions that the applicant might ask regarding your operations, your personal philosophy as an employer, and even your business's financial situation. Know what information you're willing to share and what you choose not to reveal. Don't get caught off-guard or flustered, and definitely don't lie or conceal important facts.

Example

An employer in Denver was held liable for getting an applicant to move from New Orleans and take a job even though the employer knew that the project the employee was being recruited for was in serious financial trouble.

Questions To Ask

Only ask for information that's needed to weigh an applicant's competence or qualifications. A certain amount of spontaneous conversation is helpful in determining whether you get along with one applicant better than another, but don't risk offending an applicant or damaging your reputation with inappropriate questions.

Throughout the interview, don't debate with or become adversarial toward an applicant. Your goal is to get an accurate picture of the person's employment history and suitability as an employee of your business. Listen carefully and evaluate the information you obtain. Follow-up questions may be needed to obtain additional information. If you don't understand something, ask about it.

Ask specific, performance-based, questions, one at a time, and let the applicant answer uninterrupted. Resist filling in every lull in the conversation; wait to see if the applicant will do so. Don't give applicants verbal or physical clues as to how you regard their answers; remain neutral. Do take notes, however, so you don't have to trust your memory regarding each candidate's qualifications.

Once you've gotten the information you need from an applicant, switch to the role of information provider and tell the applicant more about the job and your business. Then, close the interview graciously. If you've found a promising candidate, explore any doubts or reservations the applicant might have. Let the applicant know what happens next, whether another interview will be needed, and when you'll be making a decision.

If you've already decided not to offer an applicant a job, you can let him or her know at this point. Do so cordially and uncritically; you needn't be specific about why you've rejected the candidate. If you think that you would consider the applicant for another position in the future, say so. If pressed for a reason why an applicant won't be offered a job, you can say that you don't discuss the reasons for your hiring decisions. Or you may explain that, for example, you've already interviewed other, more qualified, applicants. Don't create an awkward situation by telling someone that he or she is unqualified or lacks experience. Be honest, but don't be confrontational.

Questions Not To Ask

If you have 15 or more employees, you're subject to federal laws prohibiting discrimination in hiring. Some states also have laws that mimic federal discrimination laws and apply them to employers with as few as one employee. The same types of questions that you can't include in a job application (see page 61) are also impermissible during an interview. In formulating your questions, ask yourself if the information is really needed to judge an applicant's competence or qualifications. Also ask whether the answer to this question, if used in making a selection, inequitably screens out minorities or members of one sex.

Many interviews involve at least some casual discussion regarding interests, history, and personal background. While these topics are being discussed, it's easy to forget that what you're saying could have legal repercussions later on. When chatting informally, limit your discussions to the weather, sports, or some other neutral topic. Questions are likely to be found discriminatory if they address topics such as marital or family status, origin, age, or religious affiliation.

Warning

If an applicant volunteers information about one of these areas, we recommend that you ignore it. Don't respond to it and don't follow up on it. *Don't* include it in your notes. It could be used to prove you discriminated if the notation concerns the applicant's status as a member of a protected group.

BACKGROUND CHECKING

After you've collected information about applicants and conducted several interviews, you're ready to check the background of your most promising candidate. Unfortunately, many people misrepresent their background and credentials, so it's important to do at least a little checking to verify an applicant's claims. Employers who don't do any checking often regret that decision. A check might have revealed information that would have shown the applicant to be unqualified or undesirable for other reasons.

Checklist for Reference Checking

❑ Tell each applicant that no employment offer will be made until satisfactory reference checks are made.

❑ Call or write to each reference given. If you aren't going to check references, don't ask for them.

❑ If you get no response to a written request to an employer, call. The call may reap more information than a letter would, although you should be aware that many employers are reluctant to disclose much about a former employee because they're afraid of being sued.

❑ If you request references in writing, include a release signed by the applicant allowing disclosure of the information.

❑ Document all information that you receive. Also document unsuccessful efforts to gather information, to protect yourself from negligent hiring claims.

❑ If a former employer won't tell you anything, record the fact that he or she refused to give any information.

❑ If you can't get the requested information from references, ask the job applicant for more information or to clear the way for you with the references he or she gave.

❑ Don't make a job offer until you've completed your reference checking.

Checking Employment References

Former employers are in the best position to tell you about an applicant's work history. Verify that the information you get agrees with what the applicant gave you. Former employers can give you valuable information regarding employment dates, job titles, pay rates, duties, and work habits, including conscientiousness, sense of responsibility, and ability to work with others.

Warning

Don't contact an applicant's *current* employer without getting permission. If you do and the employer retaliates, you can be sued by the applicant for causing the loss of the job.

Some employers won't discuss former employees because they fear being sued. If this occurs, ask the candidate if there is a coworker or supervisor you can contact. Often, they too are instructed not to discuss why the employee left or whether the employee would be rehired. However, a number of states *require* former employers to provide a job reference letter or some information about people who worked for them (see page 290). No matter what, document whatever information you do get and note who gave it to you. Also note the information they would not give you.

Contacting a Former Employer

Calling is the preferred way to check references because people will sometimes tell you things that they wouldn't put in writing. Whatever you ask, though, be sure it's job-related. You don't want to be accused of invading anyone's privacy or of discriminating against them. Here are some tips for successful over-the-phone reference checks:

- Call once to schedule the reference check and call back when you say you will. This gives the employer time to remember specific facts about the worker or look up that worker's file.

- Allot plenty of time in case a reference is willing to talk at length.

- Be sure it's quiet. You don't want to be distracted, and the check should be private.

- Take good notes during the conversation.

In some cases, employers won't give out any information unless they get a written request that includes the former employee's signed release of information form. Always keep a copy of the letters you send. Use certified mail to establish that someone received your letter. Include your phone number in case a former employer wants to respond verbally. And, to increase your chances of getting a response, enclose a self-addressed, stamped envelope.

Checking Personal References

Most employers don't check personal references, even when they ask for them. There is the perception that personal references are friends of the applicant, and that they will not convey any negative information, in the event that it exists. If you do ask for and check personal references, follow the same procedures you followed when contacting former employers. Since the applicant requested these people to provide references, you shouldn't encounter any resistance to their providing information.

Warning

Consider it a red flag if the applicant has lived in the area for a considerable period of time but can't list any local references.

Checking Public Records

Depending on the type of position that you're filling, there's a variety of other sources that might provide relevant information. Don't feel that you have to check everything that a prospective employee tells you. Only check those items that are significant to your assessment of the applicant's ability to perform the job.

Education Records

Education is one of the favorite places for applicants to misrepresent themselves because many employers don't check educational references. It's important to do it, though, to make sure that the applicant has the qualifications and background you want. Most colleges or universities will verify an applicant's degree or attendance, and many will do it over the phone. Some schools will send you a transcript if you follow the school's guidelines for obtaining records.

Work Smart

You can also pre-screen an applicant's education by asking for copies of diplomas or certified copies of transcripts.

Credit Reports

If an applicant is going to handle large sums of money or exercise financial discretion at your business, you may want to run a credit check. However, there are a lot of federal restrictions on credit reports, so doing them can be more trouble than it's worth.

Federal law. Hiring is a permissible reason to do a credit check under the Fair Credit Reporting Act of 1971, but you must keep the results confidential and *exclude* the results from the person's personnel file. You can't deny employment to a person solely because he or she sought protection under the Bankruptcy Act, was insolvent before seeking such protection, or has not paid a debt that is dischargeable under the Act.

Disclosures you must make. You must provide applicants with clear written notice that a consumer credit check is being conducted no later than three days after the report is requested. Inform them that the report might include information on their character, reputation, personal characteristics, or mode of living. Include a statement informing applicants of their right to request disclosure of the nature and scope of the investigation. If applicants request it, make a complete and accurate disclosure of the *nature and scope* of the information sought no later than five days after the applicant's request, or five days after the report was requested, whichever is later.

Work Smart

In most states, you don't have to share the *contents* of a credit report with an applicant.

You can either send this disclosure information to the applicant, or you can incorporate it into your employment application, which is generally easier. Make sure that the statement is clear and placed where it will be read. Be prepared to answer questions about your inquiries should an applicant ask. Here's a sample notice that's adaptable for use alone or as part of an employment application.

Example

"This is to inform you that, as part of our procedure for processing your employment application, it's understood that an investigation of your credit history may be made, whereby information is obtained through personal contact with individuals with whom you're acquainted. Inquiries will involve checking records that can include information as to your character, general reputation, personal characteristics, and mode of living. You have the right to make a written request within a reasonable period of time to receive additional, detailed information about the nature and scope of this investigation."

If you deny employment because of something on the credit report (and remember, it must be something other than bankruptcy), you must:

- inform the job applicant that employment was denied because of the credit report investigation, even if the credit report wasn't the only reason

- furnish the individual with the name and address of the consumer reporting agency that made the report

- show that there is an underlying history of financial irresponsibility shown by the report

- provide evidence that your position requires financial honesty

- show a business necessity for the credit check in order to prevent discrimination claims, if applicable

These disclosures alone may keep you from performing credit checks. Currently only two states, California and Minnesota, regulate the use of credit checks for job applicants.

State Laws for Credit Checks

CALIFORNIA Employers that request a consumer credit report for employment purposes must give the individual being investigated written notice and an option to request a copy of the report. If the employer denies the individual a job based wholly or in part on the credit report, the employer must identify the name of the credit reporting agency that prepared the report.

MINNESOTA Employers may use consumer credit reports for making employment decisions only if written disclosure is made to applicants or employees before the report is ordered. Applicants or employees must be notified in writing of the right to request more information on the nature of the report and, when investigative consumer reports are involved, indicate that the report may include character and reputation information obtained through personal interviews. Upon request, applicants and employees must be given a copy of the report within 24 hours of when the employer receives it. If adverse employment action is taken based on a report, the employer must advise the employee or applicant. The employer must notify the employee or applicant of the right to receive a copy of the report, the right to dispute and correct errors, and the name and address of the consumer reporting agency.

Driving Records

If a job requires any driving in an employee's own vehicle or in a company vehicle, check the applicant's driving record. Check with the state department of motor vehicles to get information about an applicant's driving record and to verify the applicant's identity. Generally, states keep records of all traffic violations (for a limited time, such as three or five years), driving-related offenses, and identifying information contained on the license. Some states charge for checking records. You may have to use a DMV form for the request. Call before you send a request to find out what's required.

Warning

Be aware that many people who drive for a living arrange to have driver's licenses in multiple states. This questionable practice lets them conceal traffic offenses by having them charged against more than one license.

Criminal Records

You'll need to protect your business from liability by doing criminal checks on applicants who:

- will be bonded because of access to money or valuables

- carry a weapon

- drive a company vehicle

- have access to drugs or explosives

- have access to master keys

- have a great deal of contact with the public, patients, or children

- be filling a position that requires a criminal record check under state law

Checking criminal records is a sensitive issue, and such checks are subject to a number of legal restrictions under federal law, and under the law of many states as well.

Warning

In general, checking *conviction* records is usually permitted. Checking *arrest* records is not permitted, except in special circumstances.

If you do check criminal records and the result is an adverse impact on minority applicants, you might be charged with violating applicants' civil rights.

Case Studies — Using Arrest Records

These case studies are legally applicable only if you're subject to federal antidiscrimination laws (have 15 or more employees). Even if you aren't, they are still good guides for evaluating and using arrest records. And, your state may have rules even more restrictive than federal law.

Case Study 1. Wilma applies to Bus Inc. for a position as a bus driver. In response to a pre-employment inquiry, Wilma states that she was arrested two years earlier for driving while intoxicated. Bus Inc. rejects Wilma, despite her acquittal at trial. Bus Inc. doesn't accept her denial of the conduct alleged and concludes that Wilma was acquitted only because the alcohol test performed at the time of her arrest wasn't administered in accordance with proper police procedures and was therefore inadmissible at trial. Witnesses at trial testified that after being stopped for reckless driving, Wilma staggered from the car and had alcohol on her breath.

Bus Inc.'s refusal to hire Wilma is justified because the conduct underlying the arrest, driving while intoxicated, is clearly related to the safe performance of the duties of a bus driver, and occurred fairly recently. Also, there was no indication of subsequent rehabilitation.

Case Study 2. Lola applies to Bus Inc. for a position as a bus driver. In response to an inquiry whether she had ever been arrested, Lola states that she was arrested five years earlier for fraud in unemployment benefits. Lola admits that she committed the crime alleged. She explains that she received unemployment benefits shortly after her husband died and her expenses increased. During this period, she worked part-time for minimum wage because her unemployment check didn't cover her rent. She didn't report the income to the state for fear that her payments would be reduced and that she wouldn't be able to feed her three young children. After her arrest, she agreed to, and did, repay the state.

Bus Inc. rejected Lola. In this case, Lola's rejection violates federal antidiscrimination laws. The commission of fraud in the unemployment system doesn't constitute a business justification for the rejection of an applicant for the position of bus driver. The type of crime that Lola committed is totally unrelated to her ability to safely, efficiently, and courteously drive a bus. Furthermore, the arrest was not recent.

State laws. Some state laws *prohibit* employers from considering certain criminal records in making employment decisions. Other state laws *require* certain employers to perform criminal checks. Some states have both. Some of these states permit record checks when employers are considering applicants for jobs that involve providing health care or being in contact with minors or senior citizens. States that have no laws regarding your ability to check criminal records are omitted from the listing.

State Laws on Criminal Record Checks

The following states currently have laws on the books that *restrict*, to some extent, the right of an employer to check criminal records of job applicants or employees:

California, Colorado, District of Columbia, Florida, Illinois, Maryland, Massachusetts, Michigan, Ohio, Oregon, Pennsylvania, Rhode Island, Vermont, Virginia, and Washington.

On the other hand, the following states *require* that criminal checks be performed for applicants for certain types of jobs with private employers:

Indiana (home health care and day care workers), Kentucky (workers who provide direct services to senior citizens, and workers for state-funded social service agencies or nursing facilities who will have personal or group interaction with seniors), Rhode Island (workers at state licensed or registered facilities who will have routine contact with patients or residents), South Dakota (applicants for child welfare licenses must undergo criminal records investigations), and Utah (no one with a felony conviction may provide child care, child placement services, foster care, or institutional care in state facilities or programs).

Conviction records. We recommend that you check conviction records only if you need to do so to protect your business from negligent hiring claims. Whether you're justified in requesting a criminal record check can be determined from the type of position being filled and the information that you had obtained from the applicant, former employers, personal references, and educational references before you started a criminal record search. You may also want to consider the cost of the search to be done.

The easiest way to check conviction records is to have a private detective agency do it for you. You can also do it by communicating directly with the state's central repository of records; state and local criminal agencies or department of justice; any county in which the applicant may have been living; the state's department of motor vehicles for records of driving-related convictions and violations; and the Federal Bureau of Investigation.

Arrest records. Routine checking of arrest records isn't permitted. An arrest record alone isn't proof that an applicant committed a crime. If you're permitted to check arrest records, you can deny employment based on that record only if there is a relationship between the conduct resulting in the arrest and the position applied for and it's likely that the applicant actually committed that conduct. Even if those conditions are satisfied, you need to offer the applicant a chance to explain, consider the surrounding circumstances, and make follow-up inquiries to evaluate the applicant's credibility.

Generally, applicants don't even have to disclose any information concerning arrest or criminal charges that did not result in conviction. Thirteen states have laws that grant applicants and employees certain protections against criminal disclosure based on privacy concerns.

Documenting the Reference Check

After you've taken the time and effort to check references for candidates you think are good prospects, you still have paperwork to do. In case of a lawsuit, or even just to protect yourself in case an employee you hire later proves unsatisfactory, you should document every step of your reference check. This documentation will help you demonstrate that you acted reasonably in hiring the applicant based on the information that you had.

It's a good idea to create a list of all references checked for each applicant. Include information regarding how you contacted each reference and either the letters you received or any notes you made during telephone conversations. Retain copies of any documents you receive, such as driving records, credit check results, etc. If you can't contact a reference, or the reference didn't provide the information you need, keep a record of the efforts that you made to contact the reference and get the required information.

Keep the records as long as the employee works for you as part of the hiring papers and keep these records in the employee's personnel file. Treat an ex-employee's reference records and reports as part of that ex-employee's personnel file. A common rule of thumb is to keep an ex-employee's personnel file for seven years. Also keep the records of your reference checks on unsuccessful applicants. They are employment records "having to do with hiring" that the EEOC requires employers to keep for at least one year after the date of the employment decision (if you have 15 or more employees).

Warning

Don't keep credit reports, criminal records, or medical records in a personnel file. Keep these separately in a secure place.

Avoiding Negligent Hiring

You can be legally liable for negligent hiring if you fail to check references, criminal records, or general background and, as a result, hire someone who harms another employee, a customer or some other business contact. Someone can sue, and possibly recover damages from you, for your failure to take reasonable steps to discover an employee's unfitness for a position, or your subsequent failure to take corrective action, such as training, reassignment, or discharge.

If you're served with a negligent hiring lawsuit, immediately call your lawyer. If you don't have a lawyer, find one right away. Once you have a lawyer, he or she can tell you more about your chances for winning or losing the lawsuit. Basically, however, you're at serious risk if your employee was at least partly at fault for the incident.

Failure to fire. A closely related concept is negligent *retention* of an employee. In this situation, someone will attempt to hold you liable for the conduct of an employee that you should have terminated. If you become aware that an employee is unfit, but you let the employee continue to work, you're opening yourself up to charges of negligent retention of an employee. Your best defense is to take immediate corrective or remedial action upon discovering that a particular employee presents a problem.

Reasonable investigation duty. You have a duty to make a reasonable investigation of an applicant's fitness *before* hiring. The extent of the duty may vary with the circumstances. You can be liable for damages if you don't do a background check or you hire an employee you should have known (through proper checking) was incompetent or unfit.

Example

A furniture store owner was liable for negligent hiring where a delivery person assaulted a customer while delivering furniture to her home. A routine background check would have revealed that he had a history of violent behavior. The customer could recover damages from the owner in this instance because it was reasonably foreseeable that a person with a violent past might attack a customer.

TESTING

There are many types of tests you *can* ask applicants to take, including proficiency and skill testing, physical ability tests, drug use, honesty, etc. *Don't even consider testing* unless you truly believe that the time, expense, and potential liability will be offset by the information that you get. In some cases, such as lie detector tests, the cost of testing includes long-term recordkeeping obligations to comply with federal law. Remember that you already have several sources of information: a resume or application, the results of a personal interview, and references to check. If a test merely adds a bit of incremental information, skip it.

On the other hand, we strongly recommend that you test each applicant's ability to do the specific job you're hiring for. So, for example, if you're hiring someone to handle word processing using a particular software application, ask applicants to type a document using your setup. If you're hiring someone to make flower arrangements, have applicants actually create a sample arrangement. There's no substitute for a hands-on demonstration to help you determine which applicant can really do the job.

If you have 15 or more employees. You're subject to specific federal antidiscrimination laws. Testing opens up plenty of opportunities to get accused of discrimination and creates recordkeeping duties. Before testing, check with your attorney.

Warning

Any person who applies for a job and isn't hired is in a position to claim that you somehow discriminated in the testing process. An unhappy applicant can charge that you picked an unfair test, administered the test unfairly, interpreted the results incorrectly, or anything else a clever attorney can think up.

Some businesses *must* test applicants. Drug testing is a condition of employment for many people engaged in the transportation industry. Other jobs may require skills or abilities that not everyone possesses. If you need the information a test will provide to pick the best candidate, then test each applicant you're still considering after the interviewing process has ended.

Choosing a test that's fair. If you're going to test, whether it's asking candidates to demonstrate their typing skills or federally required drug testing, you need to choose the right test. Or you can hire someone else, perhaps a human resources consulting firm, to do it for you. A good test is one that measures the criteria, behavior, or skills needed for particular job, and whose results are an accurate predictor of employee performance. Consult your attorney before you proceed with any type of testing; it's a subject that has generated a lot of litigation.

Administering tests. You have to administer any test to all applicant in a fair and even-handed manner. Give each applicant the test in as nearly identical a manner as possible. Set aside a quiet place where applicants can be tested in private. Give specific instructions and tell applicants the time limits. Encourage them to ask questions if there's something they don't understand. Explain the purpose of the test, indicate that the test is just one part of the hiring process, and confirm that scores will be kept strictly confidential.

Warning

Applicants with disabilities may require that a reasonable accommodation be made in order for them to take the test.

Schedule tests for a period that will not conflict with an applicant's religious beliefs.

Keeping scores confidential is a professional responsibility that must be taken seriously. Individuals taking the tests should always be permitted to see their own scores and have them fairly explained. However, don't share other applicants' scores. Results should be made available only on a limited basis and only after instruction has been given on the meaning of the scores. But you should retain the scores (or completed tests, if appropriate) so that you can demonstrate the fairness of your process if it's ever challenged.

Types of Tests

Achievement tests. These tests help identify applicants who already possess the skill, talent, or knowledge needed to perform a job. They are usually the most reliable and valid at predicting job performance, and they're the type of test that you probably ought to give. Many achievement tests are actually performances. An applicant is given a letter to type or a forklift to drive. Typing, knowledge of a word processing program, and other clerical tests are widely used employment tests because they are demonstrably job-related.

Warning

Do *not* give an applicant actual work to do. For example, don't ask a candidate for a welding position to work on something intended for a customer, or an applicant for a bookkeeping position to reconcile your bank statement.

Physical ability and agility. These tests assess an applicant's endurance, strength, or overall physical fitness needed to perform actual or simulated job-related tasks. Physical ability and agility tests aren't considered medical tests and can be performed before a job offer is made.

Any test that measures an applicant's physiological or biological responses to performance would constitute a medical examination according to the EEOC's interpretation of the ADA and cannot be given until after a conditional job offer is made. Therefore, employers with 15 or more employees must be mindful of what constitutes a test of health and what constitutes a test of ability to perform a task. The distinction isn't always easy to determine.

Example

A messenger service that tests applicants' ability to walk one mile in 20 minutes could perform the examination, if desired, before a conditional offer was made to an applicant.

However, if a messenger service tests applicants' ability to walk one mile in 20 minutes and then takes the applicants' blood pressure and heart rate, the test is a medical procedure and shouldn't be done, if at all, before a conditional job offer was made.

If you choose to administer physical ability tests, they must be given to all applicants regardless of disability. If the tests screen out or tend to screen out persons with disabilities, and you're subject to the laws prohibiting discrimination against disabled individuals, you would have to demonstrate that the test is job-related, it's consistent with business necessity, and a disabled person cannot perform the task, even with reasonable accommodation.

Polygraph tests. Lie detector tests are among the most controversial, and regulated, forms of testing. These tests should be reserved for instances when they are absolutely needed, such as for jobs where employees have access to *large* amounts of money or will carry guns. Employers engaged in providing security services, working on national defense or security contracts, or dealing with pharmaceuticals are likely to require such testing. Most small businesses just won't need to conduct lie detector tests.

Under the Employee Polygraph Protection Act of 1988, and the law in many states, most private employers are *prohibited* from requiring, requesting, or suggesting that job applicants or employees take polygraph tests as a condition of employment. Further, employers *may not retaliate* (e.g., fire, demote, etc.) against applicants or employees based on the results of a polygraph test or because they refuse to submit to testing.

Drug tests. Some businesses have decided that the benefits to be derived from drug testing outweigh the costs and potential liabilities that may result. Drug testing can help you avoid hiring alcohol or drug abusers, and it can help protect you from negligent hiring claims arising from an employee's conduct. And, it may be required if your employees will be operating vehicles.

If you have 15 or more employees and therefore are covered by the Americans with Disabilities Act, you should test only those people who have been given a conditional job offer. Why? Because as part of the test, the applicant is asked about prescription drugs or other conditions that could account for a false positive reading. If you asked for this information *before* a preliminary job offer was made, it might appear that you were trying to screen out medical disabilities. You can be selective about drug testing so long as you don't discriminate against protected groups. But you must comply with your state's laws, if any.

Remember, federal laws on testing are unaffected by state rules. Many state drug and alcohol testing laws require that job applicants be notified in advance that they will be tested. Generally, the fact that your company conducts drug and alcohol testing should be spelled out in the job application. In addition, written notice of the need for testing must be given before the job applicant may be tested.

State Laws on Employee Drug and Alcohol Testing

More than one-half of the states have laws regulating the use of drug and alcohol testing. Some states seem to encourage testing by tying an employer's right to test with maintenance of an employee assistance program, or by providing preferential treatment regarding workers' compensation premiums. Other states seem more interested in protecting the privacy rights of individual employees. Thus, many of the states with rules regarding testing limit the circumstances under which testing can be performed, while other states insist on procedural safeguards that preserve the dignity and privacy rights of the employees or applicants who might be subjected to testing. If you reside in one of the following 34 states, consult an attorney before embarking on a program of drug or alcohol testing:

Alabama, Alaska, Arizona, Arkansas, California, Connecticut, Delaware, Florida, Georgia, Hawaii, Illinois, Iowa, Kansas, Louisiana, Maine, Maryland, Minnesota, Mississippi, Montana, Nebraska, Nevada, New Jersey, North Carolina, North Dakota, Ohio, Oklahoma, Oregon, Rhode Island, South Carolina, South Dakota, Tennessee, Utah, Vermont, and Washington.

Medical Exams

A medical exam is any test that seeks information concerning the existence, nature, or severity of an individual's physical or mental impairment, or information regarding an individual's physical or psychological health. The purpose of asking job applicants to take a medical examination is to screen out those candidates who would not be able to properly perform their jobs for medical reasons.

Unless you're *certain* that medical testing will provide information needed to make an employment decision, don't get involved with medical testing. You'll probably have to pay for the exams yourself, and even routine medical exams aren't cheap. And information relating to a medical condition that wouldn't prevent a person from doing the job just isn't relevant to your business. Asking for such information merely provides grounds for invasion of privacy suits and disability-based discrimination actions.

If you have 15 or more employees, you're subject to the ADA. Should you decide to test, proceed carefully. The ADA and its requirements are specific and complex. Check with your legal advisor before requiring medical tests as part of the hiring process. Medical testing is generally prohibited prior to a making a conditional offer of employment.

Chapter 5

Extending an Offer of Employment

You've finally found one or more applicants whose abilities match the requirements of the job and whose references check out. All of the candidates seem like people you could work comfortably with, and they have all expressed an interest in taking the job. The next step is to bring the new employee on board. This will involve making an offer, and, perhaps, doing a little negotiating. Don't be surprised or offended if your offer is met with a counter-offer. In today's job market, people increasingly want to bargain in an effort to ensure that they are fairly compensated.

Example

Employees who are changing jobs after many years with the same company may want to negotiate for more vacation time than you might customarily provide to a new employee. They have become accustomed to the amount of time off their long service has earned them, and may place a significant premium on retaining that particular benefit.

Once you've reached an agreement, you'll have to start preparing to familiarize your new employee with how you do business. You'll also have to start keeping employment records. The end of the hiring process also marks the start of a transition period in which your new employee will have to be brought up to speed on exactly how your business works, and where he or she fits in this scheme.

HOW DO YOU MAKE THE HIRE?

After you've interviewed your top candidates for a job and checked their backgrounds, you must decide which one you want to hire. Use the notes that you've taken in interviews to help you.

Work Smart

If you're considering more than one applicant for a job, document why you selected the candidate you did, and why you rejected the others. Give solid, defensible reasons for your choice, such as experience or education, for example. Avoid subjective matters, such as appearance. If someone you chose not to hire files suit charging employment discrimination, a record of the selection criteria can show you acted fairly.

Now you're ready to make a job offer to your top candidate. A job offer may be made orally, either in person or over the phone, or in writing. We recommend that you do it over the phone so your chosen applicant doesn't get snapped up by some other employer while your written offer is still in the mail.

Work Smart

Give your choice a reasonable amount of time to decide. Career decisions are significant and almost everyone will want time to consider or to discuss the situation with a spouse. But don't wait so long that your chances of hiring another candidate are reduced. A weekend or a few days is usually a reasonable amount of time.

No matter what the form of the job offer is, the principle is the same. *Don't make promises, or statements that can be construed as promises, that you can't or don't intend to keep.* Those statements can sometimes lead to litigation if you later decide to terminate the employee.

When a job offer is extended, it should include the following information about the job:

- the position offered

- location

- salary (although sometimes salary must be negotiated before the applicant will accept) and benefits

- starting date

- any papers or information that should be brought on the first day of work

---

- a date by which the applicant must respond to your job offer, so you can move on to the next candidate if your first choice doesn't accept.

NEGOTIATE A STARTING SALARY

If you offer an applicant a job, and it turns out that this person wants the job but also wants more money than you're offering, you've got some hard decisions to make. The first thing to do when this situation arises is find out exactly how much the candidate wants. Always ask this. It may turn out that your offer wasn't too far from what the candidate wanted, and you may decide that the extra little bit isn't a problem.

But what if your offer is way off? The process is a little trickier if the candidate wants a lot more money than you want to pay. There are different approaches to take, depending on what you want to do.

If you can't pay. If the candidate's request is simply out of the question, but you want to try to hire this person anyway, make a counteroffer. There may be some ways to entice the candidate to work for you without paying the big bucks. If not, explain that you have to keep to your budget and call the next prospect on your list.

If you're uncertain. If the possibility exists for paying the candidate more, but you're on the fence about it, these questions can help you decide if the person is worth the extra money:

- **Special skills.** Is the candidate highly skilled (more so than other applicants) at performing tasks critical to your business?

- **Employment status.** Employed people are less willing than the unemployed to take a job for less than they want. If you really want this person, you may have to pay. Assess your bargaining position on this basis.

- **Future growth.** If you see the position growing from its present duties into something that will require additional skill and responsibility, you may be getting a deal by agreeing to pay more. Once the applicant takes on the additional responsibilities, you'll be getting your money's worth.

- **Alternative candidates.** If there were some "close seconds" in your applicant pool, you have more room to bargain. One of those applicants may take the job for the money you're offering.

- **Employee longevity.** While there's no sure way to predict, if you get the sense that an applicant will be a long-term asset, paying a little more up front may be the best thing to do.

- **Urgency.** How long can you let the position remain unfilled?

- **Impact on existing employees.** When a new employee is brought in for the same pay as an experienced employee performing similar work, the senior employee will likely feel that his or her years of service and additional experience aren't being recognized. Employees frequently talk about pay among themselves, and it's illegal for you to forbid them from discussing how much they make.

Once you've answered some of these questions, you should be in a better position to decide what to do. Remember, whenever you negotiate *anything*, the person who's willing to walk away from the deal is in the stronger position.

Making a Counteroffer

If you decide an applicant is worth more, consider the following:

- Offer additional benefits in lieu of extra pay. Additional vacation time may be an attractive alternative. Depending on what you offer, benefits may cost you less than a higher pay rate.

Warning

Federal nondiscrimination rules may prevent you from offering one employee more benefits than you offer to other employees in similar jobs.

- Consider keeping the wages you offered the same, but reducing the number of hours to be worked.

- Offer to give the candidate the extra money in increments, subject to performance appraisal.

- Agree to pay more, but add additional responsibilities to the job that may allow you to cut costs from somewhere else.

- Offer the candidate stock options in your company instead. (Obviously, this option is only available to corporations and there is an administrative burden in offering stock options.)

- Offer the candidate a commission, a gainsharing incentive, or a bonus in lieu of extra pay. If the candidate accepts, he or she will be even more motivated to do a good job.

Example

Offer the candidate 10 percent of the increase in net profits over a certain time period. If your business's net profits increase $2,500 over a six-month period, the employee's gain would be $250.

EMPLOYMENT CONTRACTS

In most cases, we *strongly* suggest that you *do not* enter into a written employment contract with an employee, unless there is a valid and compelling reason to do so. Employment contracts can interfere with the rights you have as an employer under the employment-at-will laws of most states. These laws permit you to terminate an employee, with or without cause, when you decide it's the right thing to do. They also permit employees to quit at any time.

You might want a contract to keep someone on board for a certain length of time. It can also serve as the vehicle for non-competition agreements, secrecy guarantees, or other collateral matters. You might even consider an employment contract because you feel that it's the only way to ensure a good relationship with a person who has needed skills.

Warning

If you think you need an employment contract to guarantee that an employee will perform according to your agreement, forget it. You're just buying aggravation. Find another way to obtain the necessary talent. Even a good contract can't make up for lack of trust.

Even if you need to gain written assurance of confidentiality from an employee or a guarantee that he or she won't compete with you, a written contract may not be necessary. You can legitimately enter into an agreement that requires confidentiality, but doesn't guarantee that the employment will last for any particular period of time. Similarly, an employee may sign a covenant not to compete with you without having an employment contract.

Warning

If there's a real possibility that an employee may leave and open a competing business, a noncompete agreement is probably appropriate. Be sure to limit the time period during which the employee may not compete, and to restrict the agreement to just your geographic market area. Courts are unwilling to enforce agreements that unreasonably restrict a person's right to make a living.

On the other hand, if you need to be certain that employees won't leave until a job is completed, you might want to enter into a employment contract that specifies the duration of the employment. If you do, have your attorney write the agreement so that there's nothing in the contract that will come back to haunt you later.

Avoiding Unintended Hiring Contracts

To avoid accidentally creating an employment contract, make the offer as narrowly and as carefully as possible. Any statement that alludes to job security can be interpreted by a court as a *promise* of job security, which might make it extremely difficult for you to fire an employee if you need to.

Example

Statements that designate employees as "permanent" rather than as "probationary" were found to constitute a contract for long-term employment. "You will have a long, rewarding, and satisfying career ahead of you" and "we will pay one-half your moving expenses now and the balance after one year" were statements construed as meaning that the employment relationship was intended to last at least one year.

When a prospective employee gives up something of value or quits another job in reliance upon an employer's promises, the courts tend to enforce the promises made in job offers more strictly. While these specific situations may not apply to you, you should be careful not to make any promises or statements that will lead the employee to give something up (like a house or another job) unless you're definitely going to hire him or her.

Example

When hired, a new employee was told he had to furnish his own car for the position. He had no car, so he borrowed the money and bought one. Thereafter, he was informed that someone else had been hired for the position. The company was liable for money damages because the man had relied on its statement, causing him to buy the car.

AFTER THE HIRE

After you've made the job offer and the candidate accepts it, you can begin to take steps to:

- complete the required paperwork

- set up personnel files

- orient the employee

- review your recruiting and hiring process

Completing Required Paperwork

One of the first things you should attend to after the candidate accepts your job offer and the hire is made is to get the employee to complete some important pieces of documentation that are required of all employees:

- Form W-4 (for payroll withholding and tax purposes)

- Immigration and Naturalization Service Form I-9

- any new hire reporting information required by state law

The Form W-4

The Form W-4 must be completed so that you know how much federal income tax to withhold from your new employee's wages. The importance of filing a Withholding Allowance Certificate, Form W-4, cannot be overstated, so make its completion a priority. Our discussion of payroll withholding will help you understand how the Form W-4 should be completed and how you should use it in doing payroll (see page 230).

The I-9 Form

Under the Immigration Reform and Control Act of 1986, all employers are required to verify the *identity* and the *eligibility to work* in the United States of all employees hired after November 6, 1986, using the Immigration and Naturalization Service Form I-9, "Employment Eligibility Verification Form." Once completed, the form isn't sent to the government, but you must keep it in your files in case an INS inspector ever wants to see it.

Provided the employee has the right documents, completing the form shouldn't take more than a minute or two. The form must be completed within three days of hire.

Required documents. The most common documents that an employee might present are:

- **A U.S. passport.** If an employee presents a passport, expired or not, supply the information under List A, and have the employee complete and sign his or her part. That's it, you're done.

- **A driver's license and a Social Security card.** The driver's license verifies the identity and the card verifies the right to work in the U.S. Just complete the information under List B, have the employee complete his or her part, and you're done.

Other documents you can accept. Some documents will fulfill both requirements of the I-9 form:

- Certificate of U. S. Citizenship, INS Form N-560 or N-561

- Certificate of Naturalization, INS Form N-550 or N-570

- an unexpired foreign passport that:

  — contains the following unexpired stamp: "Processed for I-551. Temporary Evidence of Lawful Admission for permanent residence. Valid until [DATE] Employment authorized," or

  — has Form I-94 attached and that form bears the same name as the passport and contains an employment authorization stamp with an unexpired endorsement and the proposed employment doesn't conflict with any restrictions identified on Form I-94.

- Resident Alien INS Form I-551

- an unexpired Temporary Resident Card, INS Form 688

- an unexpired Employment Authorization Card, INS Form I-688A

- an unexpired reentry permit, INS Form I-327

- an unexpired Refugee Travel document, INS Form I-571

- an unexpired INS employment authorization document that contains a photograph, INS Form I-688B

What if the employee doesn't have the necessary documents? If a new employee is unable to produce the required documents within three business days of hiring, the employee must present:

- a receipt for the application of replacement documents within the three business days

- the required document within 90 days of hire

It's illegal to hire an alien who indicates that he or she doesn't have work authorization at the time of hiring.

I-9 retention requirements. After you've completed the form, you must retain it for three years from the date of hire or one year after termination. You don't have to keep copies of the documents the new employee showed you, though we recommend that you do. If you do retain copies, they must be kept with the Form I-9s.

State employment agency certification. Referrals from state employment agencies may have certificates that fulfill the I-9 requirements. In that case, retain the certification instead of the I-9.

Creating and Maintaining Employment Records

All the information that you've accumulated about your new employee during the hiring process has a place. In fact, separate bits of information may have separate places. To create an efficient system of records and files, you need to know:

- if you need to maintain certain files

- what you have to keep and for how long

- who gets to see the information

For employers with fewer than 15 employees, it's not that complicated. You don't even have to have files, per se, but you *do* have to have information. A file may be the easiest way to keep that information under control.

Are Personnel Files Required?

There is no law that requires you to keep a personnel file on each employee. *Specific employee records* are what you must retain under federal laws. However, as a practical matter, personnel files are the easiest means of keeping track of employee information to comply with those requirements and to keep track of information for your own business purposes.

Bare-bones information. Most of the information you have to keep to comply with federal laws is basic and can be kept on a form (with the exception of payroll records) in a file or on a computer. For bare-bones compliance, include:

- full name and employee number (many use a Social Security number, some don't use one at all)

- home address, including zip code

- date of birth

- gender

- job title

- basic payroll records

Information collected about employees and retained in personnel files should *be strictly job-related.* You might consider keeping some of the records required by law in files separate from an employee's personnel file and limit the personnel file to information that applies only to the individual employee (such as resumes, performance evaluations, and work history).

Warning

Keep sensitive information (such as credit checks, drug test results, or medical records) separate from other personnel records. Store all personnel records in a secure location.

Personnel Information You Must Keep

The only records that you have to keep are those required by the government (we discuss federal law, but state law requirements may mean additional recordkeeping) and whatever information you need for your own business purposes. But the government requires that you keep an array of information under different laws.

Federal laws address the length of time that certain employee records must be kept, but not how long the entire personnel file must be kept. Some states require that personnel files be retained for a given period of time following an employee's termination. The retention periods range from 60 days to three years following termination.

We recommend that you retain such records and keep a personnel file for seven years after any employee terminates employment. Your business may be called upon to provide an employment reference for the employee in the future or may be drawn into a dispute over the reason for the termination. The following chart shows the federally required retention periods.

Information	Retention requirement
Employee name and any identifying number used in place of the name used on any work records	3 years
Social Security number	3 years from tax due date or payment of tax, whichever is later
Employee home address, including zip code	3 years from tax due date or payment of tax, whichever is later
Birth date of employees under 19	3 years
Birth date of all employees	3 years

Information	Retention requirement
Employee gender	3 years
Employee occupation	3 years
Service record to determine whether an employee has worked 1000 hours or has incurred a break in service	no time period specified by law
Form I-9	3 years after hire or for 1 year after termination, whichever is later
Complete job application	1 year
Resumes or other forms of employment inquiry	1 year
Other hiring material	1 year
Job orders submitted to an employment agency	1 year
Test papers for a position if the test paper discloses the result of the test	1 year
Results of any physical examination considered in connection with personnel action	1 year
Any advertisements relating to job openings	1 year
Records of job movement (promotions, demotions, transfers)	1 year
Material relating to layoffs	1 year
Material relating to termination	1 year from the date of termination
Selection for training or apprenticeship	1 year
Requests for physical job accommodation	1 year

Other records. Because of your obligations and potential liability under a variety of laws, both federal and state, there are other records that you should keep. You'll need attendance and payroll information to establish your compliance with wage and hour rules (see Chapter 12). Work history, including performance evaluations and disciplinary records, are important if you're ever charged with wrongful discharge or unfair conduct. Other records, such as benefit enrollments and beneficiary designations, should also be kept.

Who Can See Personnel Files?

The information you collect about employees is sensitive and few people should be allowed to see it, often not even the employee. Just as there is no federal law about keeping a personnel file, there is no federal law about who gets access to it. Many states, however, limit, guarantee, or otherwise regulate employee access to personnel files. Even if a state doesn't have any laws relating to employee access, employees can still choose to litigate their right to view the records.

Must you allow employees access? Despite the fact that you created and, therefore, own your personnel files, they contain information about employees that could affect their future. Employees often want to know what's in their files, whether the information is correct, and who has access to the information. We recommend that, whether or not your business is located in a jurisdiction requiring employee access, you allow each employee reasonable access to his or her own personnel file as part of a policy of treating employees with fundamental fairness.

State Laws on Employee Access to Personnel Files

Less than half the states have laws on employee access to personnel files. They are Alaska, California, Connecticut, Delaware, Florida, Illinois, Iowa, Maine, Massachusetts, Michigan, Minnesota, Nevada, New Hampshire, Oregon, Pennsylvania, Rhode Island, Washington, and Wisconsin.

If you live in one of these states, your obligation to allow access, and the conditions under which access must be permitted, are set by statute. Typically, employees must be given access to information that you use to determine the employees' qualifications for employment, promotion, and additional compensation, as well as information about disciplinary actions and terminations.

In the remaining states, the issue of employee access is open to dispute in court. In either case, handle requests for access in the way you think best serves the interests of your business. Consult with your attorney if you're unsure or uncomfortable about how to deal with a request for access to personnel files.

Who else can see the file? Other than an employee, the most likely source of "requests" to see information will be regulatory agencies charged with enforcing workplace regulations. For example, if you routinely hire minors, a state or federal inspector might demand to see records establishing that you're not in violation of child labor laws. Agencies charged with enforcing employment discrimination rules might also want to examine the make-up of your workforce.

TRAINING AND ORIENTATION

The first day of work is always a little scary for new employees. They're probably coming to a facility that they've only been to once or twice before. They're facing the challenge of a new job and working with people they don't know. You might feel some of the same anxiety, particularly if you're hiring your first employee.

As an employer, the first thing that you should do is take steps to make a new employee comfortable. The second thing you should do is provide a new employee with the information needed to either learn, or begin working on, the new job. During the hiring process, you discussed pay, working hours, vacations, and other issues in general terms. Orientation is the time to provide greater detail.

Example

If the price you charge your customers is based on the number of hours an employee spends on each job, orientation is the time to explain to the new employee how to keep track of and report his or her time.

In addition to the objective information you provide, also take the time to introduce a new employee to the rules of the road. Every business and every business owner is different. It's absolutely vital that you clearly convey your expectations to the new employee. It's awfully hard to hit a target if you don't know what it is.

Work Smart

If your business has close relationships with individual customers, suppliers, vendors, or service providers, introduce your new employee to these people early on in the orientation process. You'd be surprised how much "training" and support your new employee might get if cordial relations are developed early on. The people you deal with regularly know a lot more about how you run your business than you might think. And they're a great source of feedback regarding employee performance.

Don't trust other employees, if you have them, to provide full and accurate information regarding the job. You're the only one with the big-picture view of your business.

To some extent, the orientation began when you interviewed the employee and answered questions regarding your business. When the new employee starts, you want to reinforce the information provided during the hiring process. A good orientation will involve:

- a review of the job description, with additional details regarding specific duties, and a recap of your agreement on compensation and benefits

- a discussion of what your business does and what your business goals are, and how the employee's job fits into the overall picture

- basic work rules

- a tour of the workplace

Various parts of the orientation should happen at different times, so we've given you lists of what to do, before the employee starts, during the first day, and during the first week.

Before the Employee Arrives

You'll want to prepare a packet that contains all the information that the employee will need, including:

- necessary forms, like the W-4 and the I-9

- any written policies or rules, including safety information

- any benefits information, including materials that compare and explain specific coverage levels and benefits, and any enrollment and beneficiary designation forms

- information that explains the pay schedule, deductions from pay, availability of sick leave, and vacation time

- any marketing materials or product descriptions that can give your new employee insight into your business

On the Employee's First Day

When the employee arrives on the first day of work, some of the first things to do are:

- Show the employee where his or her work area will be, and where personal effects can be safely stored, if not in that area.

- Give the employee a tour of your workplace, pointing out the restrooms, break room, supply room or area, and first aid kit.

- Introduce the employee to any other employees or workers. Don't just pass the employee off to someone else and let them make brief introductions. It's easier for everyone if all your employees know who is responsible for each aspect of the business's operations.

- Explain what to do and who to contact in the event of an emergency, accident, natural disaster, etc.

Work Smart

If you have a lot of work to do yourself and you won't be able to spend a great deal of time with the employee, you might want to designate a trustworthy employee to be the new employee's "buddy" in case the employee has questions.

In the first few hours that the employee is at work, you should:

- Process any employment forms.

- Give the employee the information that you have gathered and explain what each piece of material is.

- Tell the employee that you're available for questions after the employee has reviewed the material.

- Arrange for lunch (if you like) with the employee and any other coworkers.

In the First Week

It's important to avoiding overwhelming an employee on the first day. There are things that don't need to happen on the first day, but that should happen soon thereafter, including:

- arranging for any training that is needed

- ensuring that you discuss the following:

  — job description

  — performance expectations

  — schedules

  — recording work time

  — equipment and materials

- finding out at the end of the week if any questions or problems have arisen and dealing with any concerns raised

Review Your Hiring Process

Hiring someone is hard work — especially the first time. You'll make mistakes. After you've made the hire and the employee has been oriented, it might be time to sit down and make some notes about what went right with your strategy and what went wrong. Some considerations in evaluating your success are:

- **Did you get too many applicants? Too few?** Maybe you need to think about tailoring your advertisement and recruiting to get the result you wanted.

- **Were the applicants over-qualified? Not qualified enough?** Try rewording your advertising to attract more appropriate candidates. Using a job description can help.

- **How cost-effective was your advertising?** A simple way to measure is to divide the cost (not only in dollars but in your time) by either the number of total applicants or the number of applicants that you considered seriously.

- **Were there questions you wanted to ask but didn't?** Provided the questions are job-related and not in violation of antidiscrimination laws you're subject to, make a note and ask them next time.

- **How did you do as an interviewer?** Maybe you can ask your new employee to critique you. Give him or her a chance to get to know you and feel comfortable around you first, or you won't get candid information.

- **Did your testing support or help you in your hiring decision?** If not, maybe you should reconsider the kinds of tests you're administering, if you can do so legally. If so, be sure the cost and time involved in testing are worth it. Would you have come to the same conclusion without testing?

Ensure that your selection procedures are in compliance with the law. Your hiring must be based on the *actual requirements of the job*. The ability of an applicant to perform a job is the major factor in supporting a hiring decision. Are you hiring without reference to a person's race, sex, religion, national origin, disability, or age? *Can you prove it?* Keep records showing why applicants were rejected for employment. Reasons should be objective, spell out the factual basis for not hiring, and be clearly written in order to avoid possible misinterpretation.

Part III

Life With Employees

People just aren't predictable. They have good days, bad days (hair and otherwise), and indifferent days. They may not share your most closely held beliefs about business, art, the world, or reality. Your employees aren't going to be any different in this respect than anyone else you know.

So, accept that life is going to be different now that you're sharing some of your business responsibilities with someone you may have met only a few times. It will be a while before things return to business as usual. And "business as usual" will unquestionably be different than it used to be. In the meantime, there are a few things you should do to increase the chances of a successful relationship.

Work Smart

Contact your insurance agent before your new employee reports for work. You need to make sure that your business owner's policy or commercial policy covers the increased risks that you run when you have an employee.

In many types of small businesses, the owner has a lot of contact with employees. You'll get a first-hand look at this person's way of dealing with situations that you used to handle. Be patient. This is your business, after all, and a new employee probably won't deal with situations exactly the same way you would.

Chapter 6: Dealing With Your Employees explores what it's like to actually run a business with one or more employees, including the additional legal risks you face because you have employees, how to coach your employees, providing feedback, and performance reviews.

Chapter 7: Work Rules and Policies discusses how to get your employees to perform well, act prudently, and represent your company well, and the disciplinary policies to back up your rules.

Chapter 8: Maintaining Employee Morale examines what steps you can take to ensure that your workers are happy and productive.

Chapter 9: Workplace Safety alerts you to the potential hazards that your workplace might present and provides guidance in creating a safety policy to minimize the risk of injury and accidents.

Chapter 6

Dealing With Your Employees

We realize that every employment relationship is different. You may have hired someone who'll sit at a desk in another room, answering phones and doing paperwork. Or, you may have hired someone who's going to work alongside you, or even instead of you. Regardless of the type of relationship, don't get lulled into an "out of sight, out of mind" complacency. Your employees are representing your business, and how they do it matters a lot.

PROBATIONARY PERIOD

This may seem like an odd topic to begin a discussion of what may well be a long-term relationship with an employee. However, for better or worse, you don't always hire the right person. There can be any number of reasons a new employee doesn't work out. The idea behind a probationary period is that an employer and a new employee may need some time to actually test the relationship in the fire.

Many laws regulating the employment relationship recognize this. For example, in some states, an employee terminated during an initial probationary period isn't entitled to collect unemployment compensation. Make sure you're familiar with the rules in your state, regarding how long an employee may be classified as probationary, and what protections that classification affords you.

RESPONDEAT SUPERIOR: LATIN IS FOR LAWYERS

As an employer, you'll be adding one little Latin phrase to your vocabulary. That phrase is *"respondeat superior."* It's an important one, and, if you're lucky, you'll never hear it again. It's used by attorneys to describe a legal doctrine that imposes liability on an employer for wrongful actions taken by an employee. The idea is that *you may be held liable for damages that result when an employee performing work on your behalf messes up* the job, or is otherwise responsible for an accident or problem. Respondeat superior liability can arise in a variety of settings.

Example

Anyone who drives a vehicle in the course of employment is subject to the risks of the road. A house painter can accidentally drop a can of paint, ruining an expensive plant underneath. A beautician can leave chemicals on a client's hair for just a little bit too long.

You can't avoid respondeat superior liability altogether. Imagine an employee whose delivery truck slides on the ice, bumping into the back of a car. In most states, the slippery conditions won't excuse the driver, and, therefore, you, from liability. It may have truly been an "accident," with fault assigned after the fact by the courts, but you (or your insurance company) may still have to pay for it.

Nevertheless, you can take steps to reduce the possibility of being required to pay for the consequences of an employee's mistake.

- The defense that works best is to establish that the employee violated a policy that prohibited the conduct that caused the problem. Obviously, you can't expect to rely on a policy that says, "Don't make mistakes," but if the facts are right, proving that an employee's actions violated your policies may get you off the hook. The obvious implication, however, is that you have policies in place and that you have effectively communicated them to your employees (see Chapter 7).

- You may also be able to avoid liability for damages caused by an employee if the employee committed an *intentional* wrong. Only actions that further your business purposes can result in respondeat superior liability. An intentional act of wrongdoing isn't likely to further your business purposes. Remember that the law imposes a duty of ordinary care on everyone, and a breach of that duty is negligent "wrongdoing." Only if your employee's intentional conduct is the overriding cause of the damages will you prevail with an intentional wrongdoing defense.

> **Warning**
>
> There are always gray areas. Consider a bouncer who intentionally decks a customer. You can bet some attorneys will argue over whether the bouncer was trying to further your business purposes (controlling a rowdy customer) or his own (mad at a mean drunk).

AVOIDING CLAIMS BASED ON YOUR NEGLIGENCE

If you've ever owned a car for a long time, you probably got used to some of its less desirable traits. Yes, the brakes pull to the right, but you know that, so you compensate and it's no problem. Well, it can be a problem if an employee who doesn't know that your delivery truck is long overdue for service has an accident because the brakes aren't up to par. Your failure to maintain a vehicle or equipment in safe operating condition exposes you to liability to whomever gets hurt as a result, whether it's your employee or a member of the public.

> **Warning**
>
> Make sure you handle all your responsibilities as an employer well, including the employee selection process itself. You don't want a jury rating how well you did in hiring your employees. If employees are going to drive company vehicles, make absolutely certain that you check drivers' records. If someone claims that he or she was injured because you hired the wrong person, you may need to prove that there was nothing wrong with your employee, or that you had no way of knowing that there was something wrong. (See page 79 for a discussion of negligent hiring.)

When you bring an employee on, make sure that you aren't exposing him or her to unreasonable risks. Take a close look at how you've been doing the jobs that the employee will now perform. Are there any maintenance or safety needs that you've let slide because you were the only driver or operator? Take care of them before they create a problem. Just because you got by, using a marginal piece of equipment, doesn't mean that an employee should. And you can pay a lot if a jury agrees you were in part responsible for damages resulting from your employee's actions.

Preventing Embezzlement and Theft

You don't like to think that you've made a mistake in hiring, but you have to face the fact that some employees will steal money or property from your business. You need to safeguard against that, even though it means that you're second-guessing your own judgment. We speak from painful (and expensive) experience when we warn you not to accept an employee at face value, at least not at first. Most people are honest, but you can't bet your business that your newest employee is among them.

Small businesses are particularly vulnerable to employee stealing because of the informality with which business is often conducted. Also, a small business usually has few employees, so you can't build in the kinds of checks and balances you'd like when setting up systems to handle cash, inventory, raw materials, or other valuables.

There's no simple way to prevent a determined employee from stealing from you. When you brought in your first employee, you gave up some control over your business. The opportunities are there, and some employees will give in to temptation.

Work Smart

The types of activities that you'll have to watch for vary tremendously, depending on the type of business and employee. Look for what employees might have access to that is of the most value, in any form. For example, a construction worker's time is the most valuable asset of your business that he has ready access to. Slipping off an unsupervised job site for a few hours may not seem like stealing, but it is.

In contrast, if you're hiring a bookkeeper, the risk of financial loss is much greater, and you need to consider what sort of internal controls you'll want to ensure that the money goes where it's supposed to go. Talk to your accountant or other financial advisor if you're unsure how to go about implementing internal controls. Be particularly cautious if you plan to let an employee do payroll, sign checks, or provide inventory control.

When you decided exactly what your employee would do for you, part of the process involved deciding how much trust you would place in the employee. Also consider what you can do to ensure that trust. Are your financial records password protected, or can anyone with access to the computer get in and manipulate your data? When you hire an employee, you have to take whatever steps are necessary to ensure the security of your business. This can be as simple as a daily cash register reconciliation or as complicated as an integrated software package that provides an audit trail of all financial, sales, and other activities that can affect your business.

DEALING WITH EMPLOYEE PERFORMANCE

In your ongoing relationships with employees, there will be times when an employee doesn't perform the way you had hoped or expected. When that occurs, you need to decide whether the situation requires support in the form of coaching and instruction, or discipline to correct inappropriate conduct. Then you have to follow up on that decision.

One way to reduce the stress of discussing performance with employees is to schedule a periodic performance review. That way, you have an opportunity to provide feedback without waiting for a problem to arise. It's also an important adjunct to periodic salary reviews, which are common in most businesses.

Problem Employees

After you've investigated a problem or complaint, if you find that action is necessary, you'll need to deal with the employee in question. Prior to disciplining an employee for violating work rules or engaging in other workplace misconduct, ask yourself the following questions.

- Was the employee aware of the rule and the possible or probable disciplinary consequences of breaking the rule?

- Is the rule reasonably related to the orderly, efficient, and safe operation of the business?

- Does the rule require conduct that might be reasonably expected of an employee?

- Has an effort been made to determine whether the employee actually engaged in conduct that violated the rule?

- Was the investigation of the conduct fair and objective? Did the investigation include an effort to get the employee's version of events?

- Did the investigation find substantial facts that show that the employee acted improperly?

- Has the rule in question been applied to all employees in a similar manner?

- Did the investigation reveal any facts that might justify or excuse the conduct?

If, after going through these questions, discipline still seems appropriate, you should then proceed with the process. Be sure that the steps you follow are the most appropriate for the problem, since different discipline methods should be employed depending on the problem. Generally, you can choose one of two courses of action in dealing with the employee. You can:

- Coach the employee, a preferable course of action for a

minor offense, a first-time, problem, or a performance problem.

- Discipline the employee, more appropriate for serious offenses, frequent offenders, and problems involving the willful disregard of a company policy or rule.

On the whole, coaching is more desirable because it focuses on changing the behavior and retaining the employee. However, there are times when you want to penalize or punish an employee, and discipline is necessary in those instances. It's important to understand the difference so that you can make an informed choice about your course of action.

Coaching and Feedback

Some employee performance problems aren't the result of improper conduct. It's one thing to have an employee who deliberately violates a safety rule and places another employee in jeopardy. It's quite another to have an employee who seems to be trying to measure up, but is falling a bit short. This is where you have to do some coaching. Effective coaching and providing constructive feedback can be difficult and challenging, but they can pay off:

- employees learn more about their jobs and perform better

- employees develop loyalty toward you and the business

- working conditions are improved

- productivity is enhanced

Obviously, some people are better suited to coaching than others. Accept the fact that coaching comes with the territory when you bring on your first employee. The most important thing is to communicate effectively. This includes listening and a fair measure of patience. Try to keep the discussion focused on goals, and on what you want the employee to achieve. Consider what business objectives will be better achieved if the employee's performance improves. The coaching process has certain perspectives and behaviors that can be duplicated in the workplace. They are:

- **Mutual respect.** Both you and your employees must accept the mutual dependence each has on the other in order for each of you to succeed. From that relationship, respect can grow based on the contributions of each party.

- **Supportive environment.** Where there is respect, it follows that the working environment will be supportive. The opposite is true where there is distrust or conflict.

- **Trust.** Where there is fear, there can be no trust. The workplace must encourage an atmosphere of trust, which includes candor and an acceptance of an initial level of failure.

As the coach, you must:

- set clear expectations

- set performance standards

- measure performance

- correct deviations from performance standards

- make it clear that you are on the same side as the employee

- provide guidance while preserving the employee's self-esteem

Steps in Coaching an Employee

A coaching session to improve poor performance might contain the following steps:

- Express the performance standards for the job and review past performance of the employee. Explain why it is important to the business for the employee to perform well.

- Describe the areas of performance that the employee must improve. As much as possible, describe desired performance in terms of results to be achieved. Explain the business consequences (e.g., lost sales) when the employee doesn't perform well. Describe what good performance looks like, providing concrete examples of good work, if possible.

- Ask for the person's view on why performance doesn't meet standards. Does the employee believe there is a problem?

- Discuss possible solutions. What does the person propose to do to solve the problem? Have the employee develop steps to solve the problem to create a sense of ownership in the solution. Suspend the session if the employee needs more time to develop a plan. If the employee can't develop a plan, develop one for the employee.

- Agree to a written action plan containing specific goals and timetables for meeting those goals.

- Have the employee orally commit to the action plan and provide the employee with a copy of the plan. Retain another copy as documentation of the meeting.

- Follow up on performance based on the goals stated in the action plan. Provide feedback on how the employee is doing. Offer suggestions to improve performance. Praise instances where performance has improved.

Coaching to improve poor performance is often the first step of the progressive discipline process. If the employee's performance doesn't improve, however, explain that you may be required to take more severe discipline steps.

What is required to give successful constructive feedback? Giving successful feedback requires that you:

- have explicit, clear expectations of what should occur

- know exactly what behavior and performance occurred and what must be done to resolve or improve the situation

- have honest, candid, and direct face-to-face communication

- know why the business requires a change in behavior

- know how you will monitor the work situation to ensure that the behavior change occurs

Checklist for Providing Constructive Feedback

❑ Do your homework — have personal knowledge of the reason to have the conversation. Allegations and rumors are not enough. Personally verify the facts.

❑ Be sure that you know the person well enough to predict the responses you'll receive.

❑ Have some notes with you. Practice what you're going to say and in what sequence.

❑ Know your own communication style, how you are perceived, and how you will react in the event of a challenge or emotional outburst.

❑ Pick the location and ensure privacy.

Pitfalls of Constructive Feedback

There are some things that can stand in the way of effective feedback. Some employment atmospheres are not open, and lack of candor inhibits true communication, especially about difficult issues. Remember, too, that criticism hurts. Avoid these pitfalls to make your constructive feedback most effective:

- **Procrastination makes the situation worse.** Behavior in the workplace doesn't often change and a problem usually gets worse. Waiting until a situation is desperate is unfair, wasteful, and counterproductive. It also makes it harder for you to keep your cool when the problem is finally addressed.

- **Conversation may seem artificial.** Initially it may seem artificial to follow a script. However, failure to act has more dangerous consequences than the perception that it is difficult to give constructive feedback. Try to be as conversational and natural as possible, but don't make it your primary focus — you're there to change behavior.

- **Timing the conversation is tricky.** Constant, regular communication is the ideal, and it is true that immediate feedback is most effective. But do not initiate any conversation if your own emotional state affects your objectivity or knowledge of the situation. Avoid feedback conversations if it is particularly busy, if privacy can't be guaranteed, if either party is tired or upset, or if it's too late for the conversation to have a meaningful impact.

- **Criticism may seem personal and mean-spirited.** Attacking the individual is beyond the scope of a business conversation. Besides that, it almost guarantees that the desired behavior change will not occur permanently and leaves you open to legitimate criticism. Never criticize the individual personally, but rather *focus on the actual behavior.*

- **Anger and defensive behavior are unpleasant, especially when directed at you.** When challenged, the best strategy is respectful and active listening. Let the other person vent. As difficult as it may be to have employees verbally attack you, the process of getting it off their chest may actually help them be less resistant to change and, by listening carefully, you may learn something that you need to know.

- **Failing to ask the right questions can be costly.** For the constructive feedback to be effective, it must be comprehensive. You must probe to get all of the facts and the perceptions. Have a list in front of you to ensure that you cover all of the issues.

- **Having hidden agendas is destructive.** Honest and open dialogue doesn't allow for either party to play games or use the situation to further another purpose.

- **Trying to do too much in one meeting isn't a good idea.** Focus on one issue at a time. Addressing many concerns may overwhelm the employee and may be too much to adequately address and resolve in one conversation.

- **Failing to plan and rehearse can be costly.** You can practice and learn to give feedback well. You must practice to improve your skill level until the complex process of putting together all of this material becomes second nature.

- **Failing to document the conversation and your actions is not a good idea.** Since there is always the possibility that the conversation may be misconstrued or may form the basis for disciplinary action at a point in the future, you must document that it occurred. Additionally, the documentation makes it easier to follow up in an organized manner.

Performance Reviews

It may seem a little strange to discuss performance reviews in a chapter that doesn't have anything to do with compensation. Nevertheless, many businesses are trying very hard to split performance reviews from salary reviews. Keeping the two topics separate can make it a lot easier to use each type of review to its fullest extent. A performance review provides an employee with a periodic evaluation of how well the work being performed measures up to your expectations. A salary review also reflects performance (at least in many businesses), but other factors (e.g., what others are paying, how well your business is doing, salary equity issues) figure in that don't relate to the employee's performance.

Consider a performance review to be a special type of constructive feedback. These periodic appraisals give you an opportunity to establish goals for each employee. Because you'll sit down with each employee at least once a year, these meetings, and other coaching or feedback sessions, will be less stressful for both you and the employee. Periodic reviews also provide an opportunity to get input from an employee's coworkers regarding their evaluation of the employee's performance. They also demonstrate that you've made a long-term commitment to your employees and that you don't consider them expendable.

EMPLOYEE COMPLAINTS

Eventually, it's likely that an employee is going to get upset enough about something at work to come see you and complain. If an employee complains about an employment-related situation, you should be prepared to handle it in a fair and consistent manner.

Informal Complaint Procedures

As a small business, you probably don't want to spend the time and resources or have the need to develop an involved procedure for dealing with employee complaints. Instead, you may want to have some general guidelines so that employees know what to do if they have a complaint. A set of basic procedures helps you make sure that you treat all complaints in a consistent manner.

Your informal complaint procedure can be just about anything you want to make it. Typically, small business owners can adopt an informal, open door policy, or a more formal process involving periodic employee meetings.

Open door policy. An open door policy is just what it sounds like. Basically, you make it clear to employees that if they have a problem or complaint, they are free to come to you with it. This is a good approach if you have a relatively small and reasonably happy workforce. It's not so good if you have many employees or employees who bring every situation to you for resolution. The time commitment may be just too great for you to manage.

Work Smart

If you adopt an open door policy, make it known that, while employees can come to you at any time, a detailed follow-up on their complaint or problem might not take place at that moment, depending on your schedule or business commitments. Explain that, in some cases, an appointment will have to be scheduled when the employee can come in and discuss the issue with you.

Periodic employee meetings. If your employees work as a team or if work requires periodic meetings anyway, you may want to allot some time during your meeting for complaints or problems that employees can share. This approach allows you to address an issue only once instead of individually. However, also allow employees the opportunity to speak with you individually, since some problems and complaints may be personal or involve other group members.

Communicating your policy. Be sure to communicate basic information to employees about what to do if they have a complaint. In a "policy" of this sort:

- explain that your business cares about its employees and wants to help solve any workplace problems that may arise

- encourage employees to come forward with problems and assure them they will be taken seriously, kept confidential, and handled fairly and consistently

- explain how employees should go about voicing a complaint (visit in person, submit a written complaint, schedule a time)

Case-by-Case Complaint Procedures

An alternative to having a traditional complaint procedure is to address complaints as they arise. This may be an effective approach for a business with only one or two employees.

If you find that, even though you have only a few employees, you are spending a lot of time dealing with complaint-oriented issues, you may want to consider a more formal complaint procedure to help you get control of how complaints are handled. It could end up saving you some time and help you ensure that complaints are handled fairly and consistently.

Save Time

Requiring employees to follow procedures may also curtail aimless complaining or griping that they may feel is justified because you don't have a specific policy governing complaints.

Handling Employee Complaints

Whatever the type of dispute or complaint resolution procedure — either an informal procedure or a case-by-case approach — it should:

- resolve disputes in a timely manner

- provide a binding resolution

- involve those who must live with the decision

- be externally defensible, in case the decision is subsequently challenged

- be perceived as being fair overall

If employees feel that they are being treated with respect and fairness, they are more likely to accept the resolution you suggest, even if it is not exactly what they wanted or expected.

Be sure to treat all complaints seriously:

- Allow the employee to talk without interruption.

- Ask questions until you have a clear understanding of the facts. Probe for specifics.

- Ask the employee what he or she would like to see in the way of a resolution.

- Remain calm and in control; do not lose your temper or become accusatory.

- Establish a record by taking notes. This will also assure the employee that you are taking the matter seriously. You may want to have the employee write down the complaint, as well.

- Repeat the complaint. This will ensure that you and the employee agree on the facts and the issues.

- Don't make a decision until you obtain all the facts. If you must talk to others, explain that to the employee. It's better to postpone a decision than to make one that you would regret or reverse later.

- Check to see if any of the business's other policies (if there are any) address the problem. Have there been other similar cases? How were they handled in the past?

- Consider the source and gather information about the complaining employee. The more you know about the employee, the easier it will be to handle the complaint.

- Advise the employee of the decision as soon as possible. Determine the most appropriate time and place to meet with the employee.

- If the employee's complaint is without merit, explain it to the employee in a pleasant, low-key manner.

- If the complaint is sound, thank the employee for calling it to your attention so that you can resolve it.

- Follow through with corrective action as soon as possible. Delay may result in other problems.

- Check back with the employee after taking action in order to determine if the issue has been completely resolved to his or her satisfaction.

CONDUCTING AN INVESTIGATION

Once you become aware of a problem with an employee or receive a complaint from another worker or a customer, you need to investigate the situation before you take any action. You need to be sure that you have all the facts and that you understand what went on, as much as possible.

A word about anonymous complaints. There is a natural tendency to ignore anonymous complaints. This may not be a good idea. Prior to going to an external third party, such as the EEOC or an attorney, some employees may complain anonymously. Put aside the fact that a complaint is unsigned or the complainer is unknown and decide if the complaint deserves a thorough investigation or if you should ignore it. If it seems likely that the complaint came from an employee, greater weight should be given to the complaint.

If you decide to investigate the complaint, do so as thoroughly as possible given the few details that you have. In the event that the investigation uncovers policy violations or errors, treat those the same as an employee complaint — rectify any errors that you can.

When you start looking into a problem or incident, begin by making sure that you are operating without bias against one or more people involved in the incident. Investigations are useful only if they are accurate and impartial.

Advanced Investigation Methods

Sometimes, normal investigative techniques, such as interviewing employees and other people, and checking documentary evidence, if any, won't provide the information you want. If this happens, you may consider some alternative information-gathering methods.

Warning

Before you get carried away, remember why you're conducting the investigation. If you're required to take some kind of employment action based on the outcome of your investigation, continue until you have all the information you need, or contact your lawyer on how to proceed with the investigation.

None of the methods you can use to move an investigation further are particularly pleasant. There are workplaces searches and surveillance of employees in the workplace, including monitoring phone calls and e-mail. (See the discussion of polygraph testing at page 83 for reasons why you probably shouldn't consider polygraph testing in most circumstances. If a situation has escalated to the point where you're considering asking employees to submit to polygraph testing, call your attorney and, perhaps, the police.)

The biggest danger with any of these techniques is that people expect, not unreasonably, to maintain their privacy. Employees who feel that their employer is spying on them, or listening in on private telephone conversations can respond with a lawsuit charging invasion of privacy or worse.

Chapter 7

Work Rules and Policies

The concept of a small business developing a set of formal work rules and policies may seem like overkill to many small business owners. This is particularly true of businesses with just one or a few employees. It's hard to understand the point of creating a written set of rules when it's just you and someone you've carefully screened and hired. However, something as simple as a page or two of clearly stated work rules can go far in protecting you from many potential liabilities, so it pays to consider having at least a few rules.

Keep whatever work rules you choose to have general, so that you retain flexibility in how you enforce them. Apply them in a fair and even-handed manner. Common topics to address include safety rules, absence policy, time reporting, meals and breaks, overtime, drug use, smoking, and confidentiality. Even if you decide against creating written policy statements, you have to provide employees with guidance regarding some or all of the issues that we'll address here.

Before we move on to specifics, a very important reminder. The mere fact that you're the boss is *not* a reason to create work rules. Each work rule should make sense from a practical standpoint and contribute to your business's operations. Unduly restrictive rules that don't serve a substantial business purpose won't help your business make more money or help you keep your employees happy.

Example

The owner of a small software development company whose employees don't interact with the public might not be too concerned about a programmer who doesn't show up until mid-morning, but who works late most nights and regularly puts in 65 to 80 hours a week.

In contrast, the owner of a coffee and donut shop serving early morning commuters relies on employees to be on time, all the time. A policy imposing severe penalties for tardiness might well be appropriate in the latter situation.

FORMAL WORK RULES AND POLICIES

We recommend that you adopt a few formal work rules so that your employees know what's expected of them and what happens if they disregard your rules or policies. You may be required to adopt certain work rules by state or federal law. And the existence of formal, written work rules and policies can help you establish a defense to legal actions relating to your employees.

Work Smart

Here's how work rules can save you money by establishing a defense for your actions:

- You can successfully defend against employee claims of discrimination or improper termination by showing that the action you took was appropriate under a written policy addressing the situation.

- If you're cited by OSHA for a safety violation, or an employee files a claim for workers' compensation, you can avoid liability if you can show that the citation or injury was a result of an employee's deliberate violation of a written safety policy.

- Unemployment compensation benefits will be denied (and your rates won't suffer) if you can establish that an employee was fired for violating a written policy or rule.

If you have enough employees, you might need to establish ground rules for how your business is run to ensure that your customers are presented with a consistent image. Finally, they enable you to take appropriate disciplinary action with less risk of legal repercussions (see page 133).

Legally Required Work Rules

State and federal laws regarding work rules differ in their scope and application, so you might not be required to have work rules with respect to some of these topics. We recommend that, even if you're not subject to these rules, you make sure your business has some mechanism to achieve the same goals. You might not have a written policy prohibiting sexual harassment, for example, but you had better be sure that you have some way of dealing with an employee who engages in what another employee believes is harassing conduct. See Chapter 9 for a discussion of safety rules that might be required.

Harassment of Other Employees

Harassment is verbal or physical conduct that denigrates or shows hostility or aversion toward an individual because of that person's (or that person's relatives', friends', or associates') race, skin color, religion, gender, national origin, age, or disability, and that:

- has the purpose or effect of creating an intimidating, hostile, or offensive work environment

- has the purpose or effect of unreasonably interfering with the individual's work performance

- otherwise adversely affects the individual's employment opportunities

If you have 15 or more employees, you're subject to federal antidiscrimination laws. You have a legal obligation to provide a work environment that is free from intimidation, insult, or ridicule based on race, color, religion, gender, or national origin. Even if you have fewer than 15 employees, you must also be concerned with preventing harassment because you can sometimes be sued in state courts, depending on your state's harassment laws. As an employer, you may be held liable not only for your own acts that affect employees in the workplace, but also for the acts of your employees, and even your customers, suppliers, and others who regularly do business with you.

Although harassing conduct must be *objectively* viewed as creating a hostile work environment to be unlawful, the subjective perception of complaining employees is still significant. After all, those subjective beliefs will play a large part in a decision to get an attorney and sue you if they feel strongly enough about it. If an employee doesn't perceive the work environment to be hostile as a result of someone's conduct, the conduct is not unlawful harassment.

Example

If five male employees and one female employee are telling "blonde jokes" at break, and none of the employees finds them offensive, hostile, or abusive, the conduct is not harassment. It might not be a bad idea, however, to caution the employees that others might construe the comments as harassment.

Sexual harassment. Sexual harassment occurs when sexual or gender-based activity or comment creates a hostile work environment that interferes with an employee's ability to do his or her job. Many states have enacted laws that specifically address the problem of sexual harassment in the workplace. These laws generally require you to create, clearly communicate, and fairly enforce a policy that effectively ensures a harassment-free environment. Such a policy generally contains:

- a definition of harassment (see page 119)

- a statement prohibiting harassment

- a complaint procedure to be followed by employees who feel that they've been harassed

- a statement outlining the disciplinary action that can or will be taken if an employee engages in harassing behavior

- a statement assuring employees that you won't retaliate against them for raising the issue of harassment

The following states have laws regarding sexual harassment that apply to private employers. Information is provided regarding coverage, policy, notice, and posting requirements. Remember that federal law, if it applies, is controlling, unless state law offers more protection *to the employees*, in which case the state law is controlling. If you live in a state and appear to be covered by the law, talk to your attorney regarding how to comply with the requirements. States with no laws on sexual harassment are omitted from the list.

State Laws on Sexual Harassment

State	Laws on Sexual Harassment
AL	Alabama courts permit employees to sue employers for sexual harassment based on an invasion of the employees' right to privacy. No employer policy, notice to employees, or posters are specified.
AK	Employers with 15 or more employees are subject. No employer policy is specified. Covered employers are required to post a notice prepared by the state Commission for Human Rights.
CA	Employers must act to ensure a workplace free from sexual harassment by distributing to each employee an information sheet on sexual harassment. An employer may either distribute a state-prepared brochure or develop an equivalent document. Employers must display a poster made available by the Department of Fair Employment and Housing.
CO	Harassment that results in discrimination in employment on the basis of sex is a violation of Colorado's Antidiscrimination Act. No employer policy, notice to employees, or posting is specified.
CT	Employers of three or more employees must post information concerning the illegality of sexual harassment in a prominent and accessible location in the workplace. Employers of 50 or more workers are covered by Connecticut's sexual harassment training law.

State	Laws on Sexual Harassment
HI	Sexual harassment is a violation of state law. Employers should affirmatively raise the subject, express strong disapproval, develop appropriate sanctions, inform employees of their right to raise and how to raise the issue of sexual harassment, and take any other steps necessary to prevent sexual harassment from occurring. No employer policy, notice to employees, or posting is specified.
ID	Information concerning sexual harassment is included in the educational brochure "Sexual Harassment on the Job," reprinted in 1984 by the Idaho Human Rights Commission. No employer policy, notice to employees, or posters are specified.
IL	It is a civil rights violation for any employer to engage in sexual harassment. No employer policy, notice to employees, or posters are specified.
ME	Employers must provide employees with an annual, individual written notice, delivered in a manner that ensures that all employees receive notice.
MA	Employers with six or more employees must adopt a policy and distribute it to employees annually. The state will furnish a policy on request.
MN	Minnesota courts have held that the state's statutory prohibition against sex discrimination in employment includes a prohibition against sexual harassment that impacts on the conditions of employment when the employer knows or should have known of the conduct alleged to constitute sexual harassment and fails to take timely and appropriate action. No employer policy, notice to employees, or posters are specified.
NJ	The New Jersey Division on Civil Rights has issued a statement discussing the illegality of sexual harassment, including coverage of employer liability. No employer policy, notice to employees, or posters are specified.
ND	Employers are responsible for their acts and the acts of their supervisory personnel if the employer knows or should know of the sexual harassment and fails to take timely and appropriate action. No employer policy, notice to employees, or posters are specified.
PA	Pennsylvania Human Relations Commission guidelines indicated that sexual harassment is a violation of the Pennsylvania Human Relations Act. No employer policy, notice to employees, or posters are specified.
PR	Sexual harassment is treated as illegal sexual discrimination and employers must have and express a policy to supervisors and employees.
VT	Every employer must adopt a policy against sexual harassment and individual written copies of the policy must be provided to each employee. New employees must receive a copy upon their being hired. Employers must post a poster providing, at a minimum, the policy elements specified above; a model poster is available from the Commissioner of Labor and Industry.
WA	Case law interprets the state's unfair labor practices law to include sexual harassment as an unfair labor practice. No employer policy, notice to workers, or posters are specified.
WV	The state supreme court has ruled that sexual harassment is a form of discrimination prohibited by the West Virginia Human Rights Act. No employer policy, notice to workers, or posters are specified.
WI	Sexual harassment is a violation of Wisconsin's fair employment practices act. No employer policy, notice to employees, or posters are specified.

Smoking Prohibitions

Workplace smoking is a controversial issue. Virtually every state has laws that affect smoking, and most small business owners will probably have some responsibilities regarding smoking at their business premises. There are two types of state laws that can affect you as a small business owner. First, some states directly regulate smoking in the workplace. These laws address the rights of employees to work in a safe environment, and the obligation of employers to take the steps necessary to ensure those rights. Second, many states regulate smoking in public places in general. Small business owners may have obligations to everyone who enters their business premises under these laws.

As a result, most employers prohibit smoking in the workplace or limit it to certain designated areas. Few employers allow unrestricted smoking in the workplace, and with good reason:

- Laws in some states require a written policy or certain practice to be followed.

- Most *employees* seem to be in favor of smoking restrictions.

- Smoking is a health hazard. Smoking endangers the smoker directly and the nonsmoker indirectly. Some employees are allergic to smoke and their needs must be accommodated, if the ADA or similar state laws apply to you.

- Nonsmoking employees are suing not only to restrict smoking, but also for disability, workers' compensation, and unemployment compensation.

- Employees who smoke account for higher insurance premiums, increased medical payments, and higher absenteeism rates.

There are no federal laws that require you to adopt a policy regarding smoking in the workplace. However, employers in some states are required to adopt and enforce written smoking policies. (See page 12 for a discussion of the state rules that prohibit you from considering an applicant's smoking preference in making employment decisions.) In general, a smoking policy will contain a general statement about where and when employees can smoke; the location of signs designating smoking and no smoking areas; information about quitting smoking programs, if you offer one; and, a statement indicating that you won't discriminate against smokers.

Warning

Whether or not you're required to have a formal, written policy on smoking, you *must* comply with any state laws that regulate when and where people can smoke in public places, businesses, and offices.

In effect, you may be required to have a "policy" on smoking even though there's no requirement that you write down the terms of that policy or communicate it to employees. Almost every state has taken steps to restrict smoking in places where the health risk is obvious or common courtesy dictates some restrictions. For example, few states permit smoking in hospitals, schools, day-care centers, elevators, or similar environments. Eating establishments are also frequently subject to special rules. If you're in an industry where it's likely that there are special, and more restrictive rules, be sure to follow up with local industry or commerce groups.

Most states that impose smoking restrictions place the responsibility on the person in charge of the workplace to post conspicuous notice of smoking and no smoking areas. Typically, business owners have some discretion about designating smoking areas or mandating a smoke-free workplace.

Drug and Alcohol Use

Some small businesses are subject to the federal Drug Free Workplace Act of 1988. Your business is covered by this law only if you have a contract with the federal government worth at least $25,000, or you receive a grant from the federal government. For the majority of small businesses, workplace rules or policies on alcohol or drug use are optional, not mandatory.

Warning

If you have at least 15 employees the ADA can complicate the question of employee use of drugs and alcohol. Substance abuse may be considered a medical condition or disability, in which case you'll have additional issues to consider in this area.

Employers subject to the Drug Free Workplace Act must publish a statement notifying employees that there is an absolute ban on controlled substances in the workplace, and informing them of the actions that will be taken for violations of your policy. If you're subject to the Act, you'll also have to establish an ongoing, drug-free awareness program, and take certain actions if employees violate a criminal drug statute.

If your business is involved in commercial transportation, it's likely that you'll be required by Department of Transportation regulations to have a workplace drug abuse program. This may well include a mandatory random drug testing program. (See the discussion at page 83 for rules on applicant and employee drug testing.) Consult your attorney if you think these rules might apply to you.

Also consult your attorney, if you're thinking about a written substance abuse policy. Because of the medical nature of substance abuse problems, it would entail more risk than it's worth to write your own substance abuse policy. Larger employers often tie their policies to employee assistance programs, which are designed to provide confidential help to employees with drug or alcohol problems.

Family and Medical Leave

Federal law requires employers with 50 or more employees to provide employees with family leave to deal with certain medical and family problems. Six states, California, District of Columbia, Maine, Minnesota, Oregon, and Vermont, have rules that are even broader in scope than the federal rules. If you're subject to these rules, you'll want to have a policy that explains how you administer this particular benefit (see page 202).

OTHER COMMON WORK RULES

You're under no obligation to adopt any work rules other than those outlined above, but we believe that you ought to have at least a few basic rules or policies. In general, work policies can be divided into two categories. The first group provides the details of how some aspect of the business is administered. A handout specifying paydays and paid holidays is an example of this first group. The other type of work rules defines conduct that is unacceptable and prescribe the penalties that can or will be imposed for such conduct. Rules relating to employees who get into fights are an example of this type of rule.

Take a long, hard look at your business before you decide that you need an extensive collection of work rules and policies. If you've done a good job hiring, your employees will exercise their own good judgment in dealing with the situations that arise in a business environment. Your rules can then be limited to addressing those situations where the right course of action might be difficult for an employee to determine without guidance.

Example

If your business involves manufacturing products for your customers, and you need to track the amount of time each employee spends working on each particular item, work rules can spell out how time is tracked and reported.

Absenteeism and Tardiness

An absenteeism and tardiness policy alerts employees to what you consider to be acceptable attendance practices. An absence policy should let employees know what is expected of them, clearly explain how your time off benefits are administered, and spell out the consequences for failure to comply. Consider the issues raised in the discussion of time-off benefits (see Chapter 11) in deciding what your absence policy will contain.

Two common types of time-off policies are traditional policies and so-called "no-fault" policies. Traditional policies distinguish between excused and unexcused absences, usually by listing situations where absences are excused. Unexcused absences result in disciplinary action, up to and including termination. A no-fault system permits an employee to take a specified amount of time off annually without providing a reason for absences.

Example

Traditional: Tom gives his employees vacation time based on how long they've been with the business. He also provides paid sick leave for up to 12 days a year. Some employees will take their vacation time and call in sick only when required. Others will treat the 12 days as additional time off to be taken, whether they're sick or not.

No-fault: Nancy allows employees with at least 5 years' service to take 30 days off each year. The amount is reduced for people who have worked for less than 5 years. Employees are free to schedule time off, or call in when necessary, without specifying why.

Dress Codes

A dress code may not be relevant to your business if your employees' work doesn't involve contact with the public. But if customers, vendors, or others visit your workplace, or your employees perform services outside you business establishment, a dress code can help maintain your business's image. Also, safety considerations might make certain clothing mandatory: open toe shoes have no place in a manufacturing facility, for example. You may also feel that there needs to be some minimum standards on what can be worn in order

---

to maintain a business-like atmosphere.

If you feel that a policy regulating how people dress is right for you, be specific. Your definition of "proper attire" might not mesh with your employees' ideas. Don't forget that you have the option to require employees to wear a uniform, which many businesses do in order to present a consistent and professional look. And a uniform can be something as simple as a tee shirt with your logo on it.

While there are no state or federal laws regulating your right to require your employees to dress in the manner you direct, you still have to consider whether your dress code discriminates against members of protected groups. For example, members of certain religions believe that they are required or prohibited from dressing in particular ways by the edicts of their faith. Rules relating to appearance, such as no-beard rules, and different dress codes for men and women, also have the potential to create problems for you. If you permit women to wear ponytails and earrings, but not men, you could be asking for trouble.

Violence in the Workplace

Workplace violence is, or should be, an issue that concerns every employer. An employee may attack a coworker, or be attacked by a customer. You're at risk too, since employers are all too often the victim of workplace violence. From your perspective as an employer, work rules can serve as a deterrent by making employees aware that there can be severe consequences attached to even minor incidents involving physical confrontation or contact.

In determining whether to have a formal policy on violence in the workplace, you need to realistically assess the chances of an incident occurring. The probability of workplace violence increases as the number of employees you have increases. Even if you do a good job in screening applicants and you avoid hiring people with a history of violent behavior, there's no guarantee that your employees will get along with one another. Stress and pressure resulting from the demands of the job are also likely causes of workplace violence.

If you decide that a formal policy is warranted by the particular circumstances of your business, explain in clear and simple terms exactly what types of conduct are prohibited, and what sanctions you'll impose on those who violate the policy. While the policy itself is unlikely to get you in trouble with any employment laws, your enforcement of the rules must be even-handed and fair.

Example

Two employees who are members of a minority group get into a fight on your business premises and you fire them both. Later, two other employees (who aren't minorities) get into a fight and you suspend them, without pay, for a week. One or both of the employees that you fired may now sue, charging that you discriminated against them by imposing a more severe punishment on them than on your non-minority employees. They'll have a good chance of winning, too, unless you can show that the circumstances surrounding the two incidents justified the differing treatment.

Regardless of whether you have a formal policy, it's important to keep your head when an incident occurs. Don't respond to a situation rashly. Your first priority should be to stop the fight or other violent incident. Then, investigate what happened, and why. Impose sanctions only after you're sure of the facts and you've documented them so you can explain your actions if they're ever challenged. To curtail violence among employees in your business, take the following steps:

- Review your recruiting and hiring procedures — institute criminal background checks and carefully check all references and former employers.

- Check external and internal security. Use external security to prohibit uncontrolled access by outsiders throughout the company.

- Identify those members of your staff (such as yourself) who may be likely targets, and establish procedures to control access to them.

- Take every known threat seriously. Follow up and investigate.

- Know the warning signs of a troubled employee (see the box that follows).

- Prohibit the possession of all weapons, either inside the workplace or in an employee's vehicle on company property.

- Make sure all employees know how to reach your local police, ambulance, and security company if you have one.

- If you need to fire an employee, do so with sensitivity, in a way that preserves the employee's dignity.

- Establish exit interview procedures that collect company keys, identification, etc., and alert you to any potential problems.

Warning Signs of a Violent Employee

In many cases, there are early warning signs of a potentially violent employee that are not communicated to the people who could take action or that are not taken seriously:

- depressed or paranoid behavior

- recent acquisition of a weapon

- talking about or posting a clipping of a violent incident in another workplace

---

Off-Duty Conduct, Including Moonlighting

There's not a lot you can do to control what your employees do when they're not at work. What you can do, however, is let them know in advance what types of off-duty conduct are objectionable to you, and what steps you'll take if an employee engages in activities that you deem inappropriate. Don't even try to regulate lawful activities unless: (1) there's a relationship between the off-duty conduct and the employee's job performance, (2) the conduct puts your business in an unfavorable light with the public, or (3) the conduct has the potential to harm your business.

Some state laws (see page 12) prohibit employers from discriminating against employees who engage in lawful off-duty conduct, such as smoking, participating in political demonstrations, or drinking alcoholic beverages.

Illegal activities. If an employee engages in illegal activities outside the workplace, you should follow up with the law enforcement authorities. Determine how long it will be until the matter is resolved through the legal system. Based on this estimate, you can choose a course of action ranging from doing nothing more, to suspending the employee without pay pending resolution, to terminating the employee. If you choose to terminate, be certain that the misconduct meets one of the three criteria listed above. An employee who's terminated for what you believe to be illegal off-duty conduct can sue for wrongful discharge, defamation (if the employee didn't do what is alleged), or invasion of privacy (if you discuss the alleged conduct with other people).

Moonlighting. Whether you have a policy restricting moonlighting should be based on how much of a problem a moonlighting employee will pose for your business. Typical problems include employees not working effectively because they're too tired, employees not available to work when required due to scheduling conflicts, employees diverting work time to perform activities relating to their other jobs, and the potential for conflicting interests between you and other employers.

If you decide that moonlighting is an issue that you need to address, focus on the ways that it interferes with your business and not on the employee's conduct. Don't forbid employees from having a second job: instead, couch your policy in terms of noninterference with the duties that you hired the employee to perform. You might indicate that the needs of your business limit your flexibility in adjusting work assignments to accommodate an employee's second job. And you might make it clear that you expect your employees to give their job with you first priority in arranging their affairs.

Understand that your employees are probably not working a second job just for the fun of it. It may demonstrate that they have goals they can't achieve on what you're paying them, or it might indicate that it's time to review the compensation levels you've selected. If working a second job doesn't negatively impact, or have substantial potential to negatively impact, your business, you probably shouldn't do anything about it.

Selling or Soliciting on Work Time

If you're like most people, you probably know someone who sells Girl Scout cookies or cosmetics or who solicits people to give blood. It's commonplace for employees to engage in these activities at work. Most small business owners don't have any problems with this. In many cases, it's for a good cause. And it's not particularly disruptive or time-consuming. Unfortunately, it can be a source of trouble if an employee goes beyond the bounds of what you feel is appropriate, particularly if the activity you object to relates to the unionization of your workplace. If you have no policy prohibiting *all* solicitations and *all* distributions in the workplace, objecting to a particular solicitation or distribution can be considered discriminatory.

Example

An employee brings in and distributes literature prepared by a union regarding the benefits of joining the union. You're not too thrilled about the prospect of having your business turned into a union shop, and you ask the employee to stop distributing the pamphlets. If you've permitted others to distribute literature, perhaps in an effort to get people to support a charity, it can be hard to justify your position to the National Labor Relations Board. (If you prohibit *all* solicitations at work except for the United Way, the NLRB won't assert that you're interfering with protected union organizing activities.)

When the issue isn't unionization, however, you're generally free to develop and enforce a policy that prohibits solicitation and distribution by employees during work time in work areas. And those in retail can generally prohibit employees from solicitation or distribution in selling areas. You *can't* prevent such activity off your premises or during breaks and lunch time.

Personal Use of Business Property

Most employers expect that employees will make occasional photocopies and use the telephone for calls relating to personal, rather than business, matters. But this can get out of hand all too easily.

If you're careful about not letting employees abuse the privilege, permitting a reasonable amount of personal use of your business property shouldn't be a problem. But if you're going to let employees use company vehicles, or expensive tools and equipment, definitely consider a written policy that spells out the conditions under which you allow that use. Pay particular attention to the issue of who bears the risk if business property is damaged or destroyed.

English-Only Rules

The EEOC presumes that English-only rules are discriminatory. Requiring employees to speak only English in the workplace may disadvantage workers on the basis of national origin and can create an atmosphere of inferiority, isolation, and intimidation. An English-only rule will be upheld only if the use of English is required by business necessity. This area of the law is unsettled, however, since some courts have rejected the EEOC's position.

Warning

Don't assume that this is an issue you can ignore if you don't have English-only rules. Recently, an English-speaking worker sued her employer because her coworkers were isolating her by consistently speaking a foreign language she didn't understand.

Confidential Information

Most small businesses probably don't need a written policy requiring employees to maintain the security of confidential information, trade secrets, or customer lists. But for some small businesses, protecting a proprietary process or customer list is absolutely necessary to maintaining a competitive edge. If that's the case for your business, a written policy is probably in order. Another option is to ask employees to sign a confidentiality agreement at the time that they're hired (see page 89).

If you want to formulate a written policy, identify exactly what it is you want to protect. Explain to employees that there is a need to protect that information and prohibit them from disseminating it to anyone. Explain what the penalty for revealing confidential information will be. It should probably be quite severe if loss of confidentiality poses a serious risk to your continued success. Be prepared to take legal action against someone who violates your policy. If the loss of secrecy destroys your business, it may be your only recourse.

Betting on the Winners

Gambling in the workplace is a difficult issue, particularly for the sports fan. Many offices and businesses have pools on the Super bowl, World Series, NBA championship, college basketball championships, etc. As an employer, however, you place yourself at risk if you permit, or participate in, this type of gambling. Let your employees know where you stand on gambling before gambling gets out of hand.

Criminal Activities, Theft, and Insubordination

You don't need to have a written policy in order to discipline or fire someone for insubordination or stealing from you. You'd think that you really shouldn't need a written policy to tell employees not to engage in criminal conduct or that you expect them to do as they're asked. These are things every person should know without being told. Unfortunately, people don't always do what's right, and you need to be prepared to deal with unpleasant situations that can arise.

In this context, a written policy can be more helpful in doing damage control than in preventing improper conduct. It's easier to justify your actions when they're taken in accordance with a pre-existing written policy. A written policy doesn't ensure that an employee won't steal money, or disobey or threaten a supervisor. But it makes it possible for you to respond to the conduct appropriately without fear of employee retaliation. A employee is unlikely to prevail in a suit charging discrimination or wrongful discharge after being terminated for conduct that violates a written policy.

Warning Signs of Theft

Detecting theft can be difficult, especially if the thief is good at what he or she does. Watch for unusual occurrences, such as cash drawer shortages, missing merchandise or supplies, unlocked exits, and employee vehicles inappropriately parked in loading areas.

Employee behavior can also provide clues to potential problems with theft. Look for unusual working hours or poor work performance, unjustified complaints about employment or defensiveness when reporting on work, an unexplained relationship with a supplier or customer, or a personal lifestyle that doesn't match salary.

COMMUNICATING WORK RULES TO EMPLOYEES

Even if your relationship with your employees is informal and the job offers little chance for misinterpretation, there are advantages to written policies. As we suggested at the outset of this chapter, a brief handout describing the basic ground rules is a good idea. But even if you don't create a written policy, be sure to orally communicate your expectations regarding employee conduct.

Work Smart

Whatever you do, don't turn a simple policy statement into an employment contract. Contact your attorney before distributing any written policy statement. There should be no language that even suggests that you have a contractual relationship with your employees.

Written Policies

A written policy ensures that all employees receive a consistent message regarding your expectations of how they'll conduct themselves. You'll also save time because you don't have to read a list of paid vacations, work hours, break rules, etc. to each new employee. Distribute written policies to new employees at the beginning of their first day. We suggest that you give a new employee time to review your written policies, then ask the employee to sign a statement acknowledging that he or she has read, understood, and will abide by your work rules. This can be useful if an employee who is terminated, penalized, or disciplined claims that he or she didn't know about the policy whose application resulted in the employment action being challenged.

Anytime you alter your work policies, or adopt a new one, you should provide notice to *all* employees. Some business owners find that they have to adopt specific policies in response to employee practices that don't violate existing policies, but are inconsistent with the owners' wishes. In other situations, employers have to adopt new policies to reflect the changing business climate in which they operate. You must communicate your policies to employees in terms they understand to obtain their compliance and the protection that written policies can afford you if employees don't follow the rules.

Employee Handbooks

An employee handbook is a manual that contains an employer's work rules and policies. It can also contain other information that is useful to the employee, such as the business's history, its goals, and its commitment to customer service. Handbooks can be helpful, but there's a real danger that a handbook will create an employment contract. If it does, it can be difficult to terminate employees and you might be liable to them if you change any of the rules, employee benefits, or working conditions described in the handbook. Most small businesses don't need a handbook because there are just a few written policies to distribute.

Warning

We generally don't recommend handbooks, but if you decide to create one anyway, be sure your lawyer reviews it before you give it to employees.

WHEN EMPLOYEES DON'T FOLLOW THE RULES

Disciplinary action is the appropriate response when employees fall short of your expectations by failing to conduct themselves in the manner you require. We're not talking about employees who are incompetent or in over their heads. Instead, we're dealing with employees who choose not to comply with the rules that you've set forth. A disciplinary policy can help you if you have to defend against a wrongful firing action filed by an angry ex-employee.

We strongly suggest that the first thing you do is call the employee aside and talk about the conduct informally. Sometimes people aren't quite aware of what you want. As we said, you're dealing with people, and they aren't predictable. But, except in the case of serious misconduct, talking with an employee is the best first response. (See Chapter 6 for a discussion of how to coach employees.)

If you've decided to discipline an employee, keep your temper and don't react hastily or angrily (easy to say, tough to do, sometimes). Before you react, verify that the employee misconduct in fact occurred, and that there aren't any unusual or extenuating circumstances that might explain apparent misconduct. Measure the gravity of the offense in terms of its potential consequences to your business and the safety of others. Then, respond in a manner appropriate to the seriousness of the conduct you find unacceptable.

Documenting Disciplinary Actions

After you've investigated the situation and dealt with the employee, document the entire process starting with the complaint or incident and ending with the final resolution or action taken. Document your reasons for taking any employment action, the fact-finding you did, and the actions that you took. This will help if your actions are ever challenged later, and can provide evidence that you acted in accordance with your own procedures. Here's a sample form that illustrates the type of information that you should record.

Discipline Documentation Form

Employee Information

Name of Employee: _____

Employee's Job Title: _____

Incident Information

Date/Time of Incident: _____

Location of Incident: _____

Description of Incident: _____

_____

_____

_____

Witnesses to Incident: _____

Was this incident in violation of a company policy?   Yes   No

If yes, specify which policy and how the incident violated it. _____

_____

_____

Action Taken

What action will be taken against the employee?_____

_____

_____

Has the impropriety of the employee's actions been explained to the employee? Yes   No

Did the employee offer any explanation for the conduct? If so, what was it? _____

_____

_____

Signature of person preparing report: _____Date_____

Summaries are good way to document disciplinary action where behavior is being tracked over an extended period of time. A summary is a written record of the events that led up to disciplinary action being taken, a description of the disciplinary action that was taken, and any future steps to be taken to ensure compliance or in the event of future infractions. Include specific details that illustrate the problem. Be sure that the employee's version of events is included in the record. If you can, get written statements from witnesses.

Get the employee's signature. Regardless what form the documentation takes, allow for employee comments and signature:

- If the employee makes comments about changing or rectifying the behavior, you have documentation that the employee understood and accepted the discipline.

- If the employee disagrees with the action, you have documentation that you participated in this process with the employee. Allow the employee to record his or her disagreement on the form, but also try to work with the employee to come to an understanding. Document that process as well.

- If the employee refuses to sign the document, you at least have proof that the employee refused to participate in the process should the employee later challenge your actions. Note on the document that the employee refused to sign.

Chapter 8

Maintaining Employee Morale

It's easy to see how an employee who sells a lot of your product helps your business's financial bottom line, whereas an employee who misses important deadlines hurts your company's profitability. But what about the employees who fall somewhere in between? They aren't performing *badly*, but they aren't excelling either. How do those folks fit in? They aren't costing you anything, right? Think again. If employees aren't satisfied with their jobs, it can cost you money through low productivity, high turnover, decreasing loyalty, and high absenteeism.

PRODUCTIVITY

What is productivity? A simple way to think of your business's productivity is in terms of:

- how much product you produce over a certain period of time

- how much product you sell over a certain period of time

- how quickly you perform a certain service

- how many customers you serve over a certain period of time

Did You Know?

It's been estimated that the cost to a business of "doing things wrong" (e.g., missing deadlines, shipping the wrong goods, etc.) is, on average, 10 percent.

There are a variety of factors, such as the quality of your equipment, the management of materials flow, and general economic considerations (e.g., inflation or recession), that can affect your business's profits. However, your business's profitability depends, in large part, on the quality of your employees' performance. You can evaluate the quality of your employees' work through performance evaluations and productivity measurements.

Measures of Productivity

Choose a convenient measure of productivity, based upon the type of operation your business is involved in and what you're producing. You'll also need to choose a time frame in which to measure it. Productivity will mean something different to each business. One standard measurement of productivity is output per worker-hour, or the ratio between the number of hours worked to total output. You can also measure your productivity per week or month, if each unit of production takes more than an hour to create. Output can be measured in terms of volume or quantity of items produced, or dollar value of items produced or services provided.

Example

A graphic designer's productivity may include aspects of how many jobs he or she completes in a month, as well as how quickly the jobs were produced. A company that builds and sells widgets, on the other hand, might measure productivity in terms of the number of units built and sold over a month's time.

Manufacturing businesses. If you manufacture goods, consider using output per worker-hour or number of worker-hours required to produce a single product.

Example

You have 5 employees who each work 160 hours per month to produce 100 widgets.

The unit cost of a widget is: 5 employees x 160 hours = 800 worker-hours

800 worker hours divided by 100 widgets per month equals 8 worker-hours per widget.

If you pay each of the workers $5.00 per hour, then the production cost of the unit is:

$5.00 x 800 worker-hours = $4,000 per month

$4,000 per month divided by 100 widgets per month equals $40 per widget.

Service industries. It can be a bit harder to measure productivity in a service industry due to the somewhat intangible nature of the product involved. Service industries can measure productivity by considering the number of tasks performed or the number of customers served in a given time period. Other measures might be whether the service delivered measured up to company or customer standards and whether performance deadlines were met.

Professional employees can keep personal time sheets to indicate the number of hours spent on a given task. Quantity of work is a possible measure, such as number of service calls made per day or number of contracts written. Clerical workers can be given specific amounts of work to determine the relative time it takes to complete a given task.

Sales performance. The most effective means of measuring performance by sales representatives is by taking into account and measuring each of these factors:

- The volume of sales in dollars per given unit of time: sales volume alone won't indicate how much profit or loss each sale represents, as a salesperson may make too many concessions or sell to poor credit risks in order to make the sale.

- The number of calls made upon existing accounts: the number of calls made by a sales rep alone doesn't indicate if those accounts with the most profit potential are being serviced.

- The number of new accounts opened.

- The dollar amount expended per sale: comparing sales over given periods of time, say monthly periods each year, will not account for changes in price, product, competition, or routes.

Other methods. Another method for measuring productivity involves determining the time an average worker needs to generate a given level of production. You can also observe the amount of time that a group of employees spends on certain activities (such as production, travel, or idle time spent waiting for materials or replacing broken equipment). The latter method can reveal if employees are spending too much time away from production on other aspects of the job that can be controlled by the business.

Work Smart

If you use multiple measures of productivity, be sure that the standards are comparable. A productivity measurement based on the dollar amount generated per activity should allow for inflation adjustments in order to compare productivity rates over time.

How To Improve Productivity

Once you've figured out how to measure your business's productivity, you need to determine whether your productivity is where it should be. This task can be tricky, especially if you're getting this information for the first time. Factors to take into consideration are:

- the cost per unit compared with price

- your competitors' productivity levels, cost per unit, and price

Some of this information may be available from your trade or industry association, or through networking with contacts in similar businesses. Once you've established a baseline measure, you can assess your productivity periodically and be able to spot trends and track your progress over time.

How to improve productivity? Identify potential problem areas. The quality of leadership in the business can have an effect on productivity, so make sure that you, as a leader, ensure that your business isn't suffering from:

- poor planning or scheduling of work

- unclear or untimely instructions to employees

- an inability to adjust staff size and duties during light or heavy work-load periods

- poor coordination of material flow

- the unavailability of needed tools

- excess travel time

Ultimately, the key to improving productivity lies with the employees themselves and the way that you work with those employees. Studies have shown that most workers think it's important to do their best at their jobs. Chances are that most of your employees feel that way. People want to do a good job, and you should provide them with every opportunity to do so. It becomes your challenge to tap into that desire to perform and make it work for your business.

TURNOVER

A tell-tale sign of low morale and dissatisfied employees is high turnover. Employees who are satisfied with their jobs generally don't give them up, so high turnover usually indicates a problem.

That's not to say that every employee who leaves your company is dissatisfied — after all, some will retire, leave town, quit because of family circumstances, desire to change professions, or even start a business of their own. But if you have high turnover and you're losing good employees, you may want to give some thought to the possibility that there is a morale problem.

Causes of High Turnover

The causes of turnover are related to the same factors that contribute to absenteeism and low morale. If workers aren't interested in their jobs, they will either stay away or leave. But being unhappy in a job isn't the only reason people leave one employer for another. If the skills that they possess are in demand, they may be lured away by higher pay, better benefits, or better job growth potential. While you can't control other companies, you can take steps to improve morale at your business and make those employees who are with you happy and productive. That's why it's important to know and recognize the difference between employees who leave because they are unhappy and those who leave for other reasons.

Following are some of the more common reasons for high turnover in businesses:

- **A bad match between the employee's skills and the job.** Employees who are placed in jobs that are too difficult for them or whose skills are underutilized may become discouraged and quit. Inadequate information about skill requirements that are needed to fill a job may result in the hiring of either underskilled or overqualified workers.

- **Substandard equipment, tools, or facilities.** If working conditions are substandard or the workplace lacks important facilities, such as proper lighting, furniture, clean restrooms, and other health and safety provisions, employees won't be willing to put up with the inconvenience for long.

- **Lack of opportunity for advancement or growth.** The job should be described precisely, without raising false hopes for growth and advancement in the position.

- **Feelings of not being appreciated.** Since employees generally want to do a good job, it follows that they also want to be appreciated and recognized for their work. Even the most seasoned employee needs to be told what he or she is doing right once in a while.

- **Inadequate or lackluster supervision and training.** Employees need guidance and direction. New employees may need extra help in learning an unfamiliar job. Similarly, the absence of a training program may cause workers to fall behind in their level of performance and feel that their abilities are lacking.

- **Unequal or substandard wage structures.** Inequity in pay structures and low pay are great causes of dissatisfaction and can drive some employees to quit.

Measuring Turnover

You can learn a lot about your workforce by keeping track of employee turnover. A little simple analysis can reveal problems with the bundle of duties you've created for each position within your business.

Follow these steps for tracking turnover:

- Keep a list or file of employees that leave. Include:

  — the length of time that the employee worked for you

  — the position that the employee held

  — the reason that the employee left (information from an exit interview can help here)

- Over time, try to spot trends in turnover.

  — Are there positions that you have trouble keeping filled?

  — Do employees tend to stay for the same length of time before they leave your employ?

  — Do employees seem to be leaving for similar reasons (like receiving more pay or a more responsible position)?

- If you suspect there is a problem with one or more positions, try to remedy or prevent the problem.

  — If possible, redesign a job by adding more attractive duties and reassigning some less desirable ones.

  — Examine the working conditions closely to ensure that employees aren't being asked to meet unreasonable demands or deadlines, or to work with the most difficult customers or employees.

- If you suspect that you're not paying enough, find out what other businesses are paying for similar positions.

- If you suspect that people are leaving because positions

elsewhere allow them more growth, emphasize in the hiring process that the position has limited growth potential so that they know what to expect.

Turnover Costs

Monetary and hidden costs associated with employee turnover are also of concern. When an employee leaves your business, it costs your company in:

- **Productivity.** When the employee leaves, productivity will usually take a downturn because other workers may have to add the former employee's duties to their own workload, at least temporarily.

- **Money.** In addition to the costs associated with lower productivity, you may have to pay employees overtime to get them to take up the slack left by the former employee until a replacement can be found. You may also have to face unemployment claims and pay for the cost of recruiting and hiring a replacement.

- **Time.** Not only may you be distracted from your regular duties to cover for a former employee, but you'll have to spend time and money advertising, interviewing, and hiring a replacement employee. And don't forget the time that you spent training and hiring the former employee.

Once you find and hire a new employee, you'll still experience flagging productivity while the employee learns his or her new job. In other words, it costs your business money every time an employee leaves because it takes even more resources to return to the same level of productivity or level of performance that you had before.

The flip side. Sometimes, though, if the worker in question was a problem performer, productivity may not suffer. In fact, you may be better off than if the dissatisfied employee had stayed on the job. On the whole, though, you're going to want to prevent turnover as much as possible because of the high costs associated with it.

Preventing Turnover

If a business wants to ensure that employees remain with the business, it has to identify and emphasize the positive aspects of the business that make employees want to stay.

Some internal factors that may influence your employees' desire to stay are benefits and compensation, pleasant working conditions, opportunity for growth/advancement, and job security. In addition to the internal factors that make employees want to leave or stay, there are also outside factors that can influence your turnover. You can't do much about these factors, which include family responsibilities, financial obligations, marketability of their skills, and jobs offered by other companies. What you can do is try to make the job as desirable as possible, to minimize the chance that external factors will lead your workers to leave.

To minimize turnover, give employees perks that are perceived by them as benefits that make or break a job. Trade on your strong points. Job perks like flexible hours or better-than-average benefits might keep employees in a job that they would otherwise leave. Attempt to make work fulfilling and rewarding for your employees.

Sometimes the jobs that you have may not be particularly exciting or offer a great potential for growth, but they are still important and must be done. So how can you handle this sticky situation? Some possible options are to hire temporary employees, or to use part-time workers who are simply looking for a low-effort paycheck.

EMPLOYEE LOYALTY

Some would say that the days of loyal employees and employers are gone. There used to be an almost family-like relationship in employment, where employees and employers looked out for one another. Now, employees are forced to look out for themselves as employers no longer promise a lifetime career.

People, especially younger people, don't remain in jobs as long as they used to. They change jobs to get new skills, more money, and more responsibility. This lack of permanency is one reason that the leased worker and temporary worker industries are booming.

Did You Know?

The Bureau of Labor Statistics reported that, from the years 1987 to 1991, the average length of time that employees had worked for their current employers was 4.5 years.

But this trend doesn't have to apply to your business. You can work to engender feelings of mutual interest and concern between your business and your employees. Before employees will feel loyal to you, they have to know they can trust you to be fair and to consider their interests as well as your own.

Gaining an Employee's Loyalty

There's no foolproof method for gaining someone's loyalty, but many of the same things that hold true in a personal relationship apply in an employment relationship, as well. The keys to a positive relationship are trust and respect. When employees feel respected, they will generally respect you and the business in return. Following are some hints for gaining an employee's respect and trust:

- Listen and respond to an employee's questions and concerns about the job.

- Treat your employees with courtesy and respect. Never lie. Don't abuse or swear at employees.

- Recognize and reward your employees for a job well done.

- Get your employees' input when making decisions that affect their work.

- Give employees greater responsibility or latitude in making decisions as they demonstrate their ability and honesty.

- Treat all your employees fairly and impartially.

- Be firm, but not tyrannical, when making decisions and disciplining employees. Don't belittle employees, in private or in front of others.

- Apologize or admit to employees when you are wrong.

- Give employees credit where it's due. Don't claim credit for an employees' work or ideas.

- Keep your employees informed about work-related matters. Don't treat your employees like children.

- Lead, don't manage, your employees. Your willingness to participate in getting the job done can demonstrate that you consider your employees as important members of your business's team.

- Don't build false hopes for raises or advancement.

- Don't be intimidated by aggressive employees.

- Consider your employees' personal needs.

- Don't discuss employees with other employees, except when you're getting input for a performance evaluation.

Once employees know that you'll treat them fairly, you're more likely to inspire a concern for the well-being of the business and the quality of their work.

Keeping It Professional

It's tough to develop a relationship of mutual trust and respect and avoid getting personally involved with your employees. There's no law that says you can't get personally involved in your employees' lives, apart from harassment laws, but it's not a good idea. Your employment relationship requires a certain amount of distance. When it becomes apparent that your relationship with an employee is becoming personal, take a step back and evaluate the situation. You don't want to create resentment among other employees, or lose credibility as a leader. And you certainly don't want to open yourself up to harassment charges. Keep your personal life out of your business, and vice versa.

Knowing What Makes Morale High

Employees are likely to feel good about themselves and your business when they're treated fairly, paid well, and recognized for the good work that they do. Unfortunately, many employers don't have a good grasp on what makes employees happy and productive. In a recent study, employees were asked to rank 10 items, in order of importance, that they wanted from their jobs. Their employers were then asked to guess how they thought their employees would rank the same 10 items. The results are set out below.

Employees' Rank	Item	Employer's Rank
1	Interesting work	5
2	Appreciation and recognition	8
3	Feeling "in on things"	10
4	Job security	2
5	Good wages	1
6	Promotion/growth	3
7	Good working conditions	4
8	Personal loyalty	6
9	Tactful discipline	7
10	Sympathetic help with problems	9

(Niebrugge, Vicki, *Declining Employee Morale: Defining the Causes and Finding the Cure*, NOVA Group, July 1992.)

What does it mean? It's good news for you, since employees of small businesses tend to wear a lot of hats and have more interesting jobs. It also means that factors such as feeling "in on things" and having their work appreciated mean a lot more to employees than you may think. If you're interested in keeping your employees happy and productive, take these soft issues seriously.

Some skeptics say that it's all about money and that if you pay people enough, they'll be productive and loyal. But pay usually becomes important only when the employee feels his or her pay is below standard for what similar workers earn elsewhere. If your pay is in line with industry averages, your employees' job satisfaction probably hinges more on the soft issues than on the fact that they may earn a few dollars more or less than their peers.

Interpreting the signs. The simplest way to find out how your employees are feeling is to ask them. Are they getting what they want out of the employment relationship or is there some problem with working conditions that you can correct? Annual or semi-annual performance reviews are a good time to discuss this. Recognize that workers may not always be honest with you, either because they fear that you may retaliate, or because they don't really know *why* they are unhappy. But in most cases, you'll learn enough to be able to make changes where necessary.

IMPROVING MORALE AND MOTIVATION

If you suspect that you may have a problem with morale, you need to determine which aspects of your workplace are creating the dissatisfaction with the job and then remedy them. Even if you don't have a morale problem, you may want to jump-start your workforce into higher levels of productivity.

Build employee involvement. Every employer's dream is to have employees who care as much about the success of the business as they would if the business were their own. You may never get employees to care *that* much, but you can foster a sense that what's good for the business is good for them.

- Look for the types of problems that lead to low morale and take the steps necessary to eliminate them.

- Get employees involved and establish a team mentality. As the leader, set goals and challenge employees to meet them.

- Give your employees the authority necessary to achieve the goals that you've made them responsible for achieving.

- Let employees have the latitude (within reason) to experiment and try to find new ways to help the business reach its goals.

- When your employees do well, reward them.

- Participate in community or recreational activities as a team (e.g., softball team, charity runs, etc.).

Building Employees' Self-Esteem

Many people believe that work performance is a reflection of how employees feel about themselves and their work. If an employee is proud of the job that he or she does, the work quality will reflect that. Employees who have bad self-images are more likely to exhibit those negative feelings in their work.

So how can you boost employees' self-esteem? There are any number of ways, depending on the employee and the means at your disposal. Some ways are as simple as recognition — a simple thank you or a reward for a job well done. This can be particularly gratifying for an employee with a behind-the-scenes job.

Other ways to help build employee self-esteem are:

- Pay for employees to attend public speaking or other professional development classes.

- Ask employees to teach you and other employees a skill or procedure that they do well (this has the added bonus of doubling as cross-training of the staff).

- Recognize successes, both personal and professional, such as an employee completing her graduate degree or an employee earning his black belt in martial arts.

Recognizing/Rewarding Employees

Many, perhaps most, employees are willing to work just a little bit harder to help a business overcome a problem or meet a tough deadline. But if the extra effort goes unnoticed, eventually employees will wonder why they should bother. A moment of your time spent thanking an employee and recognizing how that employee's efforts have helped cost nothing and go a long way toward increasing the employee's self-esteem and motivation.

When To Recognize and Reward

There are no hard and fast rules about when or what types of occasions merit special recognition. Some of the more common reasons for recognition and reward are length of service, retirement, or attendance awards. More recently, businesses have come to recognize employees for their productivity, customer service, or superior performance on a particular project. In a manufacturing business, awards for safe operations are also common. And many companies have periodic employee recognition programs, such as an employee-of-the-month award.

What Rewards Can You Give?

Awards need not have great monetary value, although employees certainly don't mind an occasional cash bonus. Typical rewards given in conjunction with employee recognition include certificates, plaques, trophies, or ribbons; and jewelry (pins, pendants), pens or desk accessories, watches, and clocks. Cash bonuses, vacations, and numerous types of entertainment are common ways to recognize employees' achievements.

Recognition on a shoestring budget. Even if your small business can't go all out due to budget constraints, recognition is one case where the thought does count. If you can't afford something expensive, consider a nice card and a gift certificate to a restaurant. Or consider taking the employee to lunch or just having an informal "thank you" party for the employee or group of employees you want to reward. A small cash award, accompanied by a simple certificate, can mean a lot.

Save Money

Many word processing programs have built in templates that can help you create an award certificate from your printer in a matter of minutes. For example, some word processing software contains templates for several different styles of award certificates. All you have to do is fill in the information.

Don't give awards out every day or they will lose their meaning. Be especially careful not to give them to everyone, but only to those people whose work really stands out. Giving out awards just to give them out is a *de*-motivator. Use them sparingly and when deserved.

If you have any kind of employee publication, you can use it to recognize employee achievement. You can also express your thanks for a job well done in private, if you feel that's appropriate. A simple thank you note, or an afternoon or day off can demonstrate to employees that the work they're doing is appreciated. Taking employees on a junket to a sporting event or some other cultural activity can do a lot to boost morale and build team spirit.

How To Reward and Recognize

How you present your reward and recognition is almost as important as what you recognize and, arguably, more important than what you give as a reward. If in giving the best reward you can afford for a special occasion you simply drop the award off on the employee's desk while mumbling a "thank you" on the way out the door, you've wasted your money and may even have done more harm than good.

Recognition that means anything is given with sincerity and thoughtfulness. It must be treated as special, because that's what it is. It should *not* be treated as some necessary evil. If it's worth doing, it's worth doing right. Recognizing an employee isn't an end in and of itself. It's a means to an end — making the employee feel valued and reinforcing desirable behavior.

Work Smart

The way in which praise is delivered may not always produce the hoped-for results. Some employees are shy and may feel self-conscious about a big show of appreciation. Be sure to take the employee's feelings into account in planning a celebration or other observation.

How to give recognition. Generally if something is worth recognizing, it is worth publicizing. Unless you have an employee who is extremely shy and introverted, a little celebration is a good way to bestow recognition, whether it takes the form of a plaque, a bonus, a certificate, or just some words of praise and a "thank you."

Some suggested ways to recognize employees include:

- Bring donuts and coffee, and make the presentation during the morning coffee break.

- Set aside some time at a regularly scheduled (weekly, monthly, yearly) meeting to recognize achievements.

- For more formal presentations, have a dinner.

- If the employee is shy and likely to feel uncomfortable, you may choose to send an e-mail message or a memo publicizing the achievements of the employee instead of having an in-person gathering.

Chapter 9

Workplace Safety

Workplace safety is important to every business, even those that have no employees. Any place of business should be free of hazards for your protection and the protection of your customers, vendors, and anyone else who spends time in your workplace. Yet, despite the best efforts of many employers, thousands of Americans are killed each year in on-the-job accidents, and many more incur work-related disabilities or contract occupational illnesses.

In addition to the incalculable cost of pain and grief, there are high monetary costs attached to workplace accidents. These costs can include the inability to meet your obligations to customers, wages paid to sick and disabled workers, wages paid to substitute employees, damaged equipment repair costs, insurance claims, workers' compensation, and administrative and recordkeeping costs.

Avoiding the problems associated with workplace injuries and accidents makes good business sense. It can also help you avoid being penalized further for failing to comply with state or federally mandated safety requirements. It's true that most small businesses are unlikely to even see a federal safety or health inspector, unless there's a workplace accident. Unfortunately, if an accident occurs or an employee files a complaint, you'll be the one spending time dealing with inspectors and paying the cost to make your business a safer place to work.

WORKPLACE SAFETY REGULATION (OSHA)

Your legal obligations to provide a safe work environment for your employees arise primarily from a federal law known as the Occupational Safety and Health Act (OSHA). *All businesses* have a duty to comply with some general safety and health rules. OSHA is administered by the Department of Labor.

State safety regulation. Although your safety obligations originate at the federal level, states have the right to develop their own federally approved state workplace safety plans. Standards under a state plan may differ from federal OSHA regulations, but must be at least as effective as the federal standards. If your business is in a state that has a state plan, you must comply with it. If your state doesn't have a state plan, you must comply with federal OSHA laws.

States With Workplace Safety Plans

Alaska, Arizona, California, Hawaii, Indiana, Iowa, Kentucky, Maryland, Michigan, Minnesota, Nevada, New Mexico, North Carolina, Oregon, Puerto Rico, South Carolina, Tennessee, Utah, Vermont, Virginia, Washington, and Wyoming have established and administer their own state plans for workplace safety. You can get more information about your state's rules by contacting your state department of labor.

Who and What OSHA Regulates

If you have control over the actions of your employees, and you have the right to fire them, OSHA makes you responsible for providing a safe workplace. Your obligation to ensure workplace safety may also extend to non-employee workers such as temps or independent contractors. If you have control over workplace hazards, you're going to be the one held responsible if something unfortunate occurs.

Small business exemptions. Businesses with no more than 10 employees that provide personal or business services, many types of retailers, and eating and drinking establishments are exempt from OSHA-mandated *injury and illness reporting*. Small businesses in specified low-hazard industries are exempt from programmed inspections. But *all businesses*, regardless of size or classification, must comply with OSHA's *accident reporting* rules.

OSHA's General Requirements

OSHA contains a "general duty clause" that requires *every employer* to provide *every employee* with a place of employment that is free from recognized hazards that cause or are likely to cause death or serious physical harm. This obligation is open-ended and, therefore, your potential liability under the Act is also open-ended. OSHA also addresses specific hazardous activities and conditions in four employment settings: general industry, construction, maritime, and agriculture. In these settings, OSHA's published standards address general issues such as personal protective equipment, means of egress, fire protection, and first aid. These standards also address highly specific activities, such as welding, electrical wiring, and concrete and masonry. Complying with these specific requirements, which address known hazards, is far easier than anticipating and correcting hazards that have yet to be officially identified.

Two Safety Issues for All Employers

All business should be concerned with OSHA standards in two areas:

PERSONAL PROTECTIVE EQUIPMENT — These standards, included separately in the standards for each industry segment (except agriculture) require you to provide employees, at no cost to them, with personal protective equipment designed to protect them against certain hazards. This can range from protective helmets in construction and cargo handling work to prevent head injuries, to eye protection, hearing protection, hard-toed shoes, special goggles (for welders, for example), and gauntlets for iron workers.

HAZARD COMMUNICATION — If you are a manufacturer and/or importer of hazardous materials, you must conduct a hazard evaluation of the products you manufacture or import. If the product is found to be hazardous under the terms of the standard, containers of the material must be appropriately labeled and the first shipment of the material to a new customer must be accomplished by a material safety data sheet (MSDS). Employers who receive hazardous materials must train their employees, using the MSDSs they receive, to recognize and avoid the hazards the materials present.

Compliance. You can be called on to engage in a wide variety of activities to ensure your business is safe and legal:

- **facilities:** installing physical safeguards or engineering controls (e.g., guardrails or fire extinguishers); monitoring for air contaminants; testing and inspecting equipment; using safety devices and equipment; determining when hazard warnings are required

- **employees:** meeting work practice requirements through employee training, company work rules, and supervision on the job; providing employees with personal protective equipment; deciding what training, protection, and medical examinations are necessary

- **recordkeeping**, as discussed below.

Enforcement. You can be found to be in violation of the general duty clause if it's shown that workers were exposed to a foreseeable hazard likely to cause death or serious harm, and you had knowledge of the hazard, or should have had knowledge because the hazard had been recognized by you, your industry, or common sense.

How To Comply With Workplace Safety Standards

To ensure that your workplace conforms to the general safety standards imposed by OSHA, take the following four steps.

Step 1: Get a copy of the OSHA standards and identify which of the standards apply to your workplace. Contact the nearest OSHA area office if you need a copy of the OSHA standards or if you have any problems determining whether a standard applies to your workplace. You can also check with a safety consultant. Unfortunately, there is no shortcut in locating which of the 144 general industry standards might apply.

Step 2: After you have a copy of the current standards, review the introduction, often called *scope and application*, for *every* standard that is potentially applicable to the workplace.

Work Smart

Almost every business needs to pay particular attention to the standards that govern general office worksites with respect to walking and working surfaces, means of egress (entrance and exit), occupational health and environmental control, fire protection, and materials handling and storage.

Step 3: Once you determine which standards apply to your workplace and become familiar with them, implement the requirements of all standards that apply to the particular workplace and the particular work task or operation.

Save Money

If a particular standard applies to your workplace, and you need more time to comply with the standard or you have different but equivalent safeguards from those required by the standard, you may apply to OSHA for a temporary or permanent variance.

Compliance may involve ensuring equipment design specifications, training employees, and establishing prohibited and required practices. Compliance may also involve generating records, certifying compliance, or documenting required practices for that standard. These recordkeeping requirements are in addition to the general recordkeeping applicable to all employers.

Step 4: Make sure that any occupational hazard not covered by an industry-specific standard isn't covered by a general industry standard or by the general duty clause.

If you need financial help in complying with federal or state standards, loans are available (either directly or in cooperation with banks or other lending institution) to assist any small business in "effecting additions to or alteration in the equipment, facilities, or methods of operation of such business."

Hazardous Material Requirements

Hazardous materials are given special treatment by OSHA regulations because of their great potential to cause serious harm. If your business involves the use or storage of hazardous materials, you're required to take appropriate safety precautions. You're also subject to rules that require recordkeeping and communicating to employees and the public about potential hazards. Your obligations include creating a written program for communicating with employees and the community, ensuring appropriate labeling of containers, and posting material safety data sheets in the workplace.

Almost any chemical qualifies as a hazardous material. Common sense exceptions are provided for food, tobacco, drugs, cosmetics, and consumer products. But anything else, even as simple as photographic solution, qualifies as a hazardous material. We strongly suggest that you contact OSHA directly, or a safety consultant (which your local OSHA office can help you find), if your business involves hazardous materials.

State law. When states regulate this process, generally the focus is on increasing access of local safety officials and health care providers to the material that the company must maintain on hazardous chemicals in the workplace.

OSHA Recordkeeping

OSHA requires every employer, unless exempt, to comply with certain recordkeeping requirements. These include:

- **accident reporting:** The exemption from injury and illness reporting requirements for businesses with 10 or fewer employees doesn't apply if an accident results in one or more fatalities or hospitalization of three or more employees. In that situation, you must report the accident by telephone or in person at the nearest OSHA office within eight hours.

- **illness or injury reporting:** Every employer with at least 10 employees that isn't exempt must maintain certain records of job-related accidents and injuries. OSHA has developed Form 200, the injury and illness log, for this purpose.

- **posting requirements:** Regardless of the size of your business, if you have employees you must display posters that inform employees of their job safety rights. Spanish and English copies of these posters (OSHA 2200 and 2203) are available by contacting the nearest OSHA office.

OSHA Inspections and Penalties

OSHA enforces occupational safety and health regulations by inspecting workplaces, issuing citations, and imposing monetary penalties for violations of safety and health standards. What can trigger an inspection of your business? The government's priorities for scheduling OSHA inspections are as follows:

1. **investigation of imminent dangers:** conditions or practices that could reasonably be expected to cause death or serious physical harm to employees immediately or before enforcement action could be taken (these investigations are conducted within 24 hours).

2. **fatality and catastrophe investigations:** a work-related incident that results in the death of an employee or the in-patient hospitalization of three or more employees.

3. **investigations of complaints**, such as complaints made by employees, and referrals.

4. **programmed inspections** (regularly scheduled) in "high hazard" industries.

We strongly suggest that you call your attorney if an OSHA or state safety inspector appears, without warning, to inspect your workplace for hazardous conditions or other violations.

Citations. If a workplace inspection reveals violations of safety and health regulations or of your general duty to provide a safe and healthful workplace, OSHA will issue you a citation. The citation will charge you with a particular violation, set a time for abatement or correction of the condition, notify you of proposed penalties, and inform you of the procedure for contesting the charges before the Review Commission, should you choose to do so.

Citations are issued only to employers, *regardless of whether the violation may have been caused or committed by an employee.*

When an employer receives a citation, it has the choice of correcting the violations and paying the penalties, negotiating with OSHA to have the citation or penalties amended or withdrawn, or contesting the citation before the Review Commission. Before making the decision, the employer may request an informal conference with the OSHA Area Director. OSHA policy is to attempt to settle most cases, reserving litigation for the most significant cases. Only in the most egregious cases will OSHA interfere with the operation of your business by shutting it down.

If you can't correct the condition, you can apply for a variance.

Variance. You may apply for a temporary variance from a safety standard when compliance cannot be achieved by the standard's effective date because of unavailability of professional or technical personnel, materials, or equipment, or because necessary construction cannot be completed within the prescribed time.

A permanent variance may be granted if you can show that you can provide equivalent protection for your employees through alternative means.

Work Smart

You should apply for a variance as soon as you know that there's a hazard in your workplace that will take some time to fix, *before* OSHA gets involved, since the agency may decline to consider a variance application when a hearing is pending on a citation.

Penalties. The minimum penalty for a serious willful violation of OSHA is $25,000; the maximum penalty is $70,000. The minimum penalty for a nonserious willful violation is $5,000. However, in April 1995, OSHA announced its intention to drop the minimum penalty requirements for small employers with 50 or fewer workers, and replace it with a sliding scale that sets a minimum penalty of $5,000 for employers with no more than 10 employees. If a penalty is assessed against you, the penalty amounts may be reduced if the violation doesn't present a risk of death or serious physical harm, you act in good faith in addressing the problem, you have no history of safety violations, and payment would cause financial difficulty.

Defenses. You may defend against a citation by showing that:

- You lacked knowledge of the violation.

- No employees were exposed to a hazard.

- The violation was caused by an unanticipated employee violation of your work rule.

- Compliance with the standard would have created a greater hazard to employees.

- Compliance with the standard was impossible or not feasible.

Defenses to a general duty violation. In order to establish that it was the employee's misconduct and not you who is responsible for a citation under the general duty clause, you must show that the employee violated a well-enforced work rule, and that the conduct could not be predicted or prevented.

Warning

Employers have been penalized even when employees deliberately violated safety rules, because the employer did not consistently enforce discipline for safety violations or provided inadequate training.

Employers are responsible for the acts of supervisors even though they have no knowledge or may not approve after the fact of a supervisor's actions. Thus a supervisor who fails to prohibit unsafe practices is condoning the unsafe practice and the company is responsible.

Employees' Rights Under OSHA

You can't discharge or discriminate against employees who exercise their OSHA rights by filing complaints or instituting proceedings under or related to the Act. Moreover, you have to provide employees with required information regarding workplace safety, particularly if OSHA has found any problems with your workplace. Fortunately, the posters that OSHA requires you to display to inform your employees of their job safety rights provide a clear summary of your obligations in this regard. The posters are available from your nearest OSHA office. Don't forget, the number one reason that OSHA inspects businesses is employee complaints.

DEVELOP A WORKPLACE SAFETY PROGRAM

Once you know what OSHA requires, you can develop and implement a safety program for your workplace. Consider your company's immediate needs and provide for ongoing, long-lasting worker protection. After your plan is designed, it's important to follow through and enforce it in the workplace. You then have a program to anticipate, identify, and eliminate conditions or practices that could result in injuries and illnesses.

If you have difficulty in deciding where to begin, a phone call to your state consultation program (or the services of a private consultant) will get you the assistance you need. A consultant will survey your workplace for existing or potential hazards. Then, if you request it, he or she will determine what you need to make your safety and health program effective. The consultant will work with you to develop a plan for making improvements and establishing procedures to make sure that your program stays effective.

Impact of the ADA. Since the passage of the Americans with Disabilities Act, there are several unresolved issues within the broad scope of safety planning, workers' compensation, COBRA, and group health insurance that over time will be resolved by government regulation and the courts. In the meantime, you should continue to be governed by the policies, plans, and procedures you have established. In the event that you feel you have a conflict between the various laws (for example, your safety program appears to prohibit you from making certain accommodations for a disabled worker), seek advice from an experienced attorney or consultant.

Here are the steps to follow in order to develop a safety program:

Identify Workplace Hazards

You need to concern yourself with the types of accidents and health hazard exposures that could happen in *your* workplace. Because each workplace is unique, your program will differ from that of your neighbor or competitor. It's your responsibility to know what you have in your workplace that could hurt your workers. Worksite analysis is a group of processes that helps you make sure that you know what you need to keep your workers safe.

Gather specific facts about your situation. Before you make any changes in your safety and health operations, gather information about the current conditions at your workplace. This information can help you identify any workplace problems and see what's involved in solving them. We strongly suggest that you obtain expert assistance from a safety consultant in this process.

A professional consultant can help you assess both safety and health hazards so you get a complete picture of what risk your business poses to workers. Try to get information from vendors and industry trade groups to keep current on newly created or recognized hazards. Also examine the processes and equipment employed by each employee to find any hidden hazards. You should also plan on routine self-inspections to make sure procedures are being followed and that no new hazards have developed as your business grows.

You can rely on employees to let you know when they think there is a potential problem, provided you make it easy for them to do so. In the unfortunate event that someone gets sick or hurt, do a thorough investigation to prevent recurrences. Don't just look at each experience in isolation. Look for patterns over time that might reveal a less than safe practice.

Once you've identified hazards and potential hazards, you're ready to put in place the systems that prevent or control those hazards. Your state or private consultant can help you do this. Whenever possible, eliminate hazards. When you can't eliminate hazards, set up a system to control them and limit the risk.

- Set up safe work procedures, based on the analysis of the hazards in your employees' jobs, and make sure that employees understand the job procedures and follow them.

- Be ready, if necessary, to use disciplinary rules to enforce employee adherence to safe work procedures.

- Where necessary to protect your employees, provide, at your own cost, personal protective equipment (PPE) according to published standards and be sure that your employees know why they need it, how to use it, and how to maintain it.

- Provide for regular equipment maintenance to prevent breakdowns that can create hazards.

- Plan for emergencies, including fire and natural disasters, and drill everyone frequently so that if the real thing happens, everyone will know what to do, even under stressful conditions.

- Ensure the ready availability of medical personnel for advice and consultation on matters of employee health. This doesn't mean that you must provide health care. But if health problems develop in your workplace, you're expected to get medical help to treat them and their causes.

  — Have an emergency medical procedure for handling injuries, transporting ill or injured workers, and notifying medical facilities with a minimum of confusion. Posting emergency numbers is a good idea.

  — Survey the medical facilities near your place of business and make arrangements for them to handle routine and emergency cases. Cooperative agreements could possibly be made with nearby plants that have medical personnel or facilities on-site.

  — If your business is remote from medical facilities, you're required to ensure that a person or persons be adequately trained and available to render first aid. Adequate first aid supplies must be readily available for emergency use. Arrangements for this training can be made through your local Red Cross chapter, your insurance carriers, your local safety council, and others.

Work With Employees To Reduce the Risk

Involving employees and managers (if you have them) in the process of developing workplace safety policies from the beginning has several benefits. First, you obtain the insight of everyone in the workplace regarding hazardous, or potentially hazardous, conditions or processes. Second, it's likely that employees will take safety rules more seriously if they participate in developing them. Third, gathering your employees together as a group to discuss how the safety rules will work gives you an opportunity to get everyone to share your personal concern in maintaining a safe workplace. Fourth, you can prepare for inevitable employee turnover if there are several people in the workforce who are familiar with the safety rules and can provide safety training to new hires.

A good way to get everyone involved early on is to have a general workplace clean-up. If your business permits, set aside some time when everyone can participate in the effort together. This can help identify and eliminate minor safety problems, such as blocked halls and doorways, rag piles, etc. Once your safety program is in place, challenge employees to find better and safer ways to get the work done, and reward those whose improvements you can implement.

Develop and Document Your Program

A written safety policy is the best way to convey necessary information to employees. At the same time, it documents your efforts to provide a safe and healthy workplace. A safety policy should contain:

- a strongly worded affirmative statement that acknowledges and supports the company's responsibility

- a system for any employee to report violations of safety rules confidentially

- documentation that establishes that the policy was given to all employees, posted prominently, and included in policy manuals

- a statement that supervisors are held to act as agents for the company

- a statement that any deviation from known policy by supervisors will not be tolerated

- a process to address how questions are to be answered and emergencies handled

- the penalties for employees who don't follow safety rules

Having a policy doesn't mean that you've done enough to ensure safety. Make sure the policy is understood and followed. To protect yourself, you'll also want to document that you have shared your policy and enforced it, in the event of an accident. Follow these guidelines to make sure that your policy is implemented and applied:

- All employees should sign a document stating that they have read, understood, and will follow the company policy.

- Retain the signed document in the employee's personnel file.

- Require that new employees sign prior to actual work.

- Provide clear notice when policies change or are updated, and secure new signatures.

- Provide appropriate safety training for all employees.

- Be consistent in the application of disciplinary action when employees don't follow safe procedures and practices.

- Perform independent follow-up inspections to ensure that work areas and employees are conforming to safety rules.

In a written safety program, accountability is the key. Some states allow for a reduction in a workers' compensation award when an employee fails to follow a safety rule or fails to use safety equipment.

Documentation. An important part of the on-going administration of your safety program and efforts is documentation. Document your activities in *all* elements of your workplace program. Essential records, including those legally required for workers' compensation, insurance audits, and government inspections, *must* be maintained as long as the actual need exists.

Keeping records of your activities, such as policy statements, training sessions for management, and employee safety and health meetings held, information distributed to employees, and medical arrangements made, is also a smart idea. Maintaining essential records also will aid:

- the demonstration of sound business management, for showing "good faith" in reducing any proposed penalties from OSHA inspections, for insurance audits, etc.

- the efficient review of current safety and health activities for better control of operations and for planning improvements

EMERGING SAFETY ISSUES

New technology and materials are constantly altering the workplace, and medical science is revealing more about the connection between work and health. As a result, new safety issues are constantly arising. In some cases, OSHA is taking action, or is considering taking action, to address some new workplace hazards. Two safety issues that are presenting unique workplace challenges are hazards associated with office automation and the risks associated with AIDS. Because the law in these areas is in the process of being developed, we recommend you watch the news for new developments.

Office Safety Hazards

Today's modern office is full of potential hazards that both you and your employees need to be aware of and for which you need to take appropriate precautions. For example, cloth and vinyl chairs, carpeting and drapery, and the large quantity of paper found in many offices can create a fire hazard. Misplaced wastebaskets, poorly lighted halls, a muddy floor, frayed carpet, a file drawer left open, telephone and electrical cords on the floor, and office machines being used by those who don't know how to use them are other examples of office safety hazards.

Another potential source of employee injury is a poorly designed workspace. Many recently recognized work-caused health problems result from the cumulative effects of physical actions that are repeated over a long period of time. Carpal tunnel syndrome, which can affect those who use computers all day, is an example of this type of repetitive stress injury. Thus, it has become increasingly important to ensure that the design of the workspace is well-suited to the range of movements and activities that employees will perform. Interestingly, an employer can be found to have violated the general duty imposed by OSHA to provide a safe workplace based on allegations of ergonomic violations.

AIDS in the Workplace

AIDS has become a workplace safety issue because some employers and employees fear that this fatal disease can be transmitted in the workplace. Medical literature generally suggests that the possibility of AIDS being transmitted in an ordinary business environment is exceedingly remote. Obviously, this isn't true for some types of businesses, such as medical practices. However, in addition to the medical issue, employees who have AIDS fear that they will lose their job, benefits, friends, and more. Since AIDS has become a workplace issue, other medical conditions, such as Hepatitis B virus, have also raised workplace concerns.

As an employer, you should worry about the health and peace of mind of *all* employees. You can't segregate or penalize individuals with AIDS, or you risk running afoul of civil rights laws. You can't treat their medical expenses differently if you provide health benefits for your employees. If you have at least 15 employees, the ADA may require you to make some reasonable accommodation for an employee with AIDS to permit him or her to remain employed.

If an employee has AIDS. If you find out that an employee has AIDS, you have responsibilities to that employee and to your other employees as well. This will require you to weigh the individual's right to privacy against your other employees' right to have complete information regarding potential hazards in the workplace. Either one can sue you if they don't like how you handle the situation. We strongly suggest that you contact an attorney if you're faced with this difficult situation.

Work Smart

Keep protective clothing, such as rubber gloves, in your first aid kit. This will help prevent direct contact between the potentially infected blood of an injured employee and an employee assisting an injured employee.

Part IV

Compensation and Benefits

One of the most important aspects of a job, from an employee's perspective, is the compensation and benefit package that will be received. When you hired your new employee, you competed against every other employer in the area. Part of getting the best employee was how your compensation and benefits package measured up. You now know that good pay and benefits are the price of admission if you want quality help.

Once you get that help, however, you'll find that there are many responsibilities that go along with having an employee. There are a large number of state and federal laws that regulate many aspects of paying your employees. There are rules saying how much you have to pay, how often you must pay, what information you must keep, and for how long, and a number of other topics. When you provide even the most basic benefits, such as paid holidays, sick leave, or vacation pay, paying your employees gets more complicated.

If you've been in business for a while, and you operate in corporate form, you've already had to face many of these issues as a paid employee of your business. If you operate as a sole proprietor, completing Schedule C has probably given you some insight into your added responsibilities.

Chapter 10: Paying Your Employees details the steps you'll have to follow to pay your employees, from establishing a payroll system to tracking hours worked and ensuring compliance with minimum wage and other legal requirements.

Chapter 11: Employee Benefits examines the types of benefits that you're required to offer your employees as well as those that you may choose to offer.

Chapter 12: Your Payroll Tax Obligations addresses the taxes you'll have to pay yourself, the amounts that you'll withhold from your employees' wages, and how to remit these taxes to the government.

Chapter 10

Paying Your Employees

At the time you decided to hire someone, you took steps to determine how much you'd have to pay to get a person with the skills needed for the job (see pages 3). You then had to negotiate the amount of compensation and benefits the employee would receive. Now that you're an employer, you have to deal with compensation issues on an ongoing basis.

While the mechanics of paying an employee don't seem that difficult, there's a lot you have to do to make sure that the amounts you pay your employees each payday are correct and in compliance with federal and state wage and hour laws.

CREATING A PAYROLL SYSTEM

Many small business owners handle their own payroll, with or without the assistance of payroll software. But you also have the option of using an outside payroll service to take care of these administrative tasks for you. An outside service will lift most of the burden from your shoulders, for a price.

Whether you handle payroll yourself or farm it out, you'll need to get a federal Employer Identification Number (EIN). The EIN is an employer's account number for the collection and reporting of taxes withheld and wages paid to the employees. Complete and submit IRS form SS-4 to get your EIN. If your state doesn't use the federal EIN for state tax reporting, you'll also have to get a state (and perhaps local) ID number. You'll also have to establish a payroll process, which involves setting pay levels, making periodic payments to your employees, withholding and remitting taxes, and keeping records of everything that you do.

HOW MUCH WILL YOU PAY?

Starting pay. When you first decided to hire someone, you estimated what it would cost you. You had to make sure that you could afford to hire an employee and that the pay would be in line with the market for your area, your industry, and your jobs. The actual amount was probably negotiated at the time of hire.

Review your compensation structure. To ensure that your starting salaries remain competitive, stay on top of the employment market in your area. What's reasonable in 1997 might not be so reasonable in 1999. Keeping up with the employment market also enables you to do a better job of keeping your long-term employees by providing information regarding pay for jobs at other than the entry level. See the discussion at page 47 regarding methods for obtaining and updating competitive pay information.

Giving raises. Most employees expect their pay to increase over time. Many employers have policies that call for salary reviews on a periodic (usually annual) basis. In 1996, the average business gave employees a 4 percent raise. We strongly suggest that you establish both periodic performance (see page 112) and compensation reviews. As part of this process, you'll be called on to determine how much more to pay an employee than he or she is currently earning.

The logical starting point is the same as it was when you decided to hire an employee in the first place. Determine how much more you can pay employees this year than last. Then, based upon your appraisal of each employee's performance, decide how to divide up the amount among your employees. Some businesses choose to give everyone the same percentage or dollar amount raise. This makes it easy to predict the impact on your budget. But it doesn't recognize that some employees may be doing a better job than others.

Example

If one employee earns the minimum wage and another earns 10 or 20 times more, is it really equitable to give each a 4 percent raise? Similarly, consider the impact on employee morale if a newly hired employee is paid nearly the same amount as a long-term employee.

If you want to use compensation to reward employees for doing a good job, then you'll adopt a policy that ties the amount of a raise to an employee's performance. The key element to making that connection is the decision to provide periodic performance appraisals that give employees direct feedback on how well they're performing. It's easier to decide how large a raise to give if you can track an employee's progress against clearly established goals. Increases will be based on merit, not just on the fact that an employee has stayed on for another year. Many employers believe that this is a good way to recognize each employee's unique contribution to the business.

THE FLSA AND EMPLOYEE CLASSIFICATION

In Chapter 1, we noted the federal laws that can affect your relationship with your employees. Foremost among those laws in a compensation setting is the FLSA. Most employers are subject to the wage and hour rules of the FLSA. Moreover, under both state and federal law, workers are classified as either "exempt" or "nonexempt," and your responsibilities vary tremendously depending on how each employee is classified.

Exempt employees *aren't* entitled to the benefits and protections of the FLSA. *Nonexempt* employees *are protected* by the FLSA.

Employee Classification

Only employees who are paid salaries, as opposed to hourly wages, may be exempt. However, you can have nonexempt employees who are paid a salary. People who are paid by the hour are automatically classified as nonexempt employees.

Exempt employees include executives who spend at least half their time exercising managerial functions; administrative staff; and professionals, such as attorneys, doctors, artists, or teachers. Other employees who aren't protected by the FLSA include learners, apprentices, and full-time students employed in agriculture or retailing; workers with disabilities; and employees who deliver newspapers to consumers. Even if you and your employees aren't subject to the FLSA (which is unlikely), always keep the exempt/nonexempt distinction in mind.

Minimum Wage Requirements

The FLSA requires, among other things, that all nonexempt employees be paid a minimum wage of $4.75 per hour. On September 1, 1997, the rate will go up to $5.15 per hour. This rate must be paid to all nonexempt employees for each hour worked up to 40 hours in a calendar workweek. Any time beyond 40 hours must be paid at time-and-a half overtime, currently $7.125 an hour, and $7.73 per hour as of September 1, 1997.

Though the minimum wage is expressed as an hourly rate, it applies to workers paid on any basis as long as the minimum requirement of $4.75 per hour is satisfied. For example, a salaried nonexempt employee working 40 hours a week must be paid at least $190.00.

Federal law allows you to count board, lodging, and other facilities as part of wages for purposes of meeting the minimum wage requirements. A common example is meals provided by a restaurant to its employees. To take advantage of the rule, however, you have to meet several criteria, and it's unclear if you can *require* employees to accept these facilities as part of their pay.

Who Must Be Paid Minimum Wage?

The general rule is that nonexempt employees must be paid the minimum wage. Employees engaged in certain occupations, however, don't have to be paid the federal minimum wage. Many of these occupations have limited relevance to a small business because they involve activities that aren't likely to be conducted by a small business. Workers who might be engaged by small businesses who don't need to be paid the federal minimum wage include outside sales staff; workers with disabilities; learners, apprentices, and messengers, and students employed in retailing or farming; certain employees in Puerto Rico, Virgin Islands, and American Samoa; employees of amusement or recreational establishments having seasonal peaks; and tipped employees, in conjunction with the tip credit.

If you're considering paying someone a subminimum wage, there are rules to follow and permission from the federal government to obtain. You may find it to be more trouble than it's worth. To obtain forms, contact your local office of the Employment Standards Administration's Wage and Hour Division.

Counting Tips Toward Minimum Wage

Special rules apply for tips received by employees. Federal law allows you, within limits, to presume that your tipped employees are receiving a certain level of tips each pay period. Thus, you can claim a credit against the minimum wage for tips. The rules are as follows:

- The tip credit is 50 percent of the former minimum wage of $4.25, or $2.13 per hour. Although the minimum wage was raised to $4.75, the tip credit was not increased.

- The credit cannot exceed the value of tips received; thus, the employee must actually be receiving $2.13 in tips per hour before you can get the whole credit.

- The employee must be notified that you're taking the credit.

- All tips received by the employee must be kept by the employee — the employer may not keep any tips received.

- Only "tipped employees" qualify for the credit, (defined as employees who regularly and customarily receive over $30 a month in tips).

State laws. Some states also address tip credits. If your state's minimum wage, minus the state tip credit, is higher than the federal minimum wage, minus the federal tip credit, you must pay the worker the higher amount. The following list summarizes each state's law regarding tip credits. States with no law are excluded from the list.

State Laws on Tip Credits

State	Amount allowed as a tip credit is:
AL	Tips may not be counted towards the state minimum wage.
AR	$2.13 per hour (50% of state min. wage), increasing to $2.38 per hour on July 1, 1997 and $2.58 per hour on Oct. 1, 1997.
CA	Tips may not be counted towards the state minimum wage.
CO	$1.90 per hour (40% of state min. wage) increasing to $2.06 on Sept. 1, 1997.
CN	$1.10 per hour (23% of state min. wage) in the hotel and restaurant industry (rising to $1.19 on Sept. 1, 1997), and $0.35 per hour in other industries.
DE	Minimum wage is $2.23 per hour for tipped employees.
DC	$3.16 per hour (55% of state min. wage) increasing to $3.38 on Sept. 1, 1997.
HI	$0.20 per hour, provided the employee receives at least $0.70 per hour in tips.
ID	$1.06 per hour (25% of state min. wage).
IL	$1.90 per hour (40% of state min. wage) increasing to $2.06 on Sept. 1, 1997.
IN	$0.80 per hour (40% of state min. wage); $1.34 for employers with at least 3 employees.
IA	$1.90 per hour (40% of state min. wage) increasing to $2.06 on Sept. 1, 1997.
KS	$1.06 per hour (40% of state min. wage).
KY	$2.13 per hour (50% of state min. wage).
ME	$2.38 per hour (50% of state min. wage) increasing to $2.58 on Sept. 1, 1997.
MD	$2.38 per hour (50% of state min. wage) increasing to $2.58 on Sept. 1, 1997.
MA	$2.38 per hour (50% of state min. wage) increasing to $2.58 on Sept. 1, 1997.
MI	The minimum wage may be fully offset by tips.
MN	Tips may not be counted toward the state minimum wage.
MO	$2.38 per hour (50% of state min. wage) increasing to $2.58 on Sept. 1, 1997.
MT	Tips may not be counted toward the state minimum wage.
NE	Minimum wage is $2.13 per hour for tipped employees.

State	Amount allowed as a tip credit is:
NV	Tips may not be counted toward the state minimum wage.
NH	$2.38 per hour (50% of state min. wage) increasing to $2.58 on Sept. 1, 1997.
NJ	The minimum wage may be fully offset by tips.
NM	Minimum wage is $2.125 per hour for tipped employees.
NY	$1.35 per hour.
NC	$2.13 per hour.
ND	$1.40 per hour (33% of state min. wage).
OH	$2.38 per hour (50% of state min. wage) increasing to $2.58 on Sept. 1, 1997.
OK	$2.38 per hour (50% of state min. wage) increasing to $2.58 on Sept. 1, 1997.
PA	$2.14 per hour (45% of state min. wage) increasing to $2.32 on Sept. 1, 1997.
RI	Minimum wage for tipped employees is $2.30 per hour.
SD	$2.13 per hour (50% of state min. wage), increasing to $2.58 per hour on Sept. 1, 1997.
TX	$1.68 per hour (50% of state min. wage).
UT	Minimum wage for tipped employees is $2.61 per hour (55% of state min. wage) increasing to $2.83 on Sept. 1, 1997.
VT	$2.25 per hour (45% of state min. wage) increasing to $2.32 on Jan. 1, 1998.
VA	The minimum wage may be fully offset by tips.
WV	$0.85 per hour (20% of state min. wage).
WI	Minimum wage for tipped employees is $2.19 per hour for nonprobationary adults, $2.07 for probationary adults, and $1.86 for minors.
WY	Minimum wage for tipped employees is $1.10 per hour.

State Minimum Wage Laws

Sometimes individual states set minimum wages either above or below the federal minimum wage. In some cases, a state's minimum wage will vary by the type of worker.

If you're subject to both state and federal laws, you must pay *the higher amount.*

If you're not subject to federal minimum wage law, it doesn't mean that you're also exempt from state minimum wage requirements. If you're subject to state requirements but not federal ones, you must pay the minimum wage set out by your state. The following list presents each state's minimum wage rules. States that have no minimum wage law are excluded.

State Minimum Wage Laws

State	Minimum wage is:
AL	$5.25 per hour, increasing to $5.65 on Sept. 1, 1997.
AR	$4.25 per hour, increasing to $4.75 on July 1, 1997 and $5.15 on Oct. 1, 1997.
CA	$4.75 per hour, increasing to $5.15 on Sept. 1, 1997.
CO	$4.75 per hour, increasing to $5.15 on Sept. 1, 1997.
CN	$4.77 per hour, increasing to $5.18 on Sept. 1, 1997.
DE	$5.00 per hour, increasing to $5.15 on Sept. 1, 1997.
DC	$5.75 per hour, increasing to $6.15 on Sept. 1, 1997 .
GA	$3.25 per hour.
HI	$5.25 per hour.
ID	$4.25 per hour.
IL	$4.75 per hour, increasing to $5.15 on Sept. 1, 1997.
IN	$2.00 per hour. Employers with at least 2 employees must pay at least $3.35.
IA	$4.75 per hour, increasing to $5.15 on Sept. 1, 1997.
KS	$2.65 per hour.
KY	$4.25 per hour.
ME	$4.75 per hour, increasing to $5.15 on Sept. 1, 1997.
MD	$4.75 per hour, increasing to $5.15 on Sept. 1, 1997.
MA	$4.75 per hour, increasing to $5.25 on Sept. 1, 1997.
MI	$3.35 per hour.
MN	$4.25 per hour for firms with annual receipts of $362,500; $4.00 for firms with annual receipts below $362,500.
MO	$4.75 per hour, increasing to $5.15 on Sept. 1, 1997.
MT	$4.75 per hour, increasing to $5.15 on Sept. 1, 1997; $4.00 for businesses with annual gross sales of $110,000 or less.
NE	$4.25 per hour.
NV	$4.75 per hour.
NH	$4.75 per hour, increasing to $5.15 on Sept. 1, 1997.
NJ	$5.05 per hour.
NM	$4.25 per hour.
NY	$4.25 per hour. Other wage rates are in effect in specific industries.
NC	$4.25 per hour.
ND	$4.25 per hour.
OH	Current federal minimum wage for employers with $500,000 or more in gross annual sales; $3.35 for employers at least $150,000 but less than $500,000; $2.80 for employers with less than $150,000 in gross annual sales.
OK	$4.75 per hour, increasing to $5.15 on Sept. 1, 1997.
OR	$5.50 per hour, increasing to $6 on Jan. 1, 1998; increasing to $6.50 on Jan. 1, 1999.

State	Minimum wage is:
PA	$4.75 per hour, increasing to $5.15 on Sept. 1, 1997.
PR	Minimum wage rates vary for workers in different categories of agricultural work.
RI	$4.75 per hour, increasing to $5.15 on Sept. 1, 1997.
SD	$4.75 per hour, increasing to $5.15 on Sept. 1, 1997.
TX	$3.35 per hour.
UT	$4.75 per hour, increasing to $5.15 on Sept. 1, 1997.
VT	$5.00 per hour, increasing to $5.15 on Jan. 1, 1998.
VA	$4.75 per hour, increasing to $5.15 on Sept. 1, 1997.
WA	$4.90 per hour for employees 18 and over.
WV	$4.25 per hour.
WI	$4.75 per hour; $3.80 for probationary adults; $3.45 for minors.
WY	$1.60 per hour.

Federal Overtime Requirements

In addition to the minimum wage requirements of federal wage and hour laws, employers must pay nonexempt employees one and one-half times their regular rate for any hours worked in excess of 40 hours in a workweek. The overtime pay requirements apply to nonexempt employees regardless of whether they're paid by the hour, on salary, or on a piecework basis.

There are some occupations that don't have to receive overtime pay under the FLSA (but may be covered by other provisions such as minimum wage, child labor, or equal pay). Most of these occupations aren't relevant in a small business context. Thus, in most cases, you can assume that you'll be paying your nonexempt employees overtime. However, a partial exemption is granted under certain circumstances to one group of employees commonly found in small businesses: commission employees of retail or service establishments.

What is a workweek? Understanding the workweek concept is vital to meeting your overtime pay requirements. A workweek can be any *fixed and recurring* period of 168 hours (seven days at 24 hours each). While it's not uncommon for a workweek to begin on Monday morning and to end on Friday night, it doesn't have to. A workweek is seven, consecutive, 24-hour periods that can begin at any time on any day. Therefore your employees' workweek, for pay purposes, may start at noon on Wednesday and end at 11:59 am on the following Wednesday.

State Overtime Pay Laws

As is the case with minimum wage, many states have laws pertaining to overtime. Many state minimum wage laws don't cover exempt employees, commission salespersons, family members, people subject the FLSA, and persons otherwise exempt from state minimum wage requirements.

If your state's law is less demanding than federal law. If the federal law is more demanding than your state's law, and you're subject to the federal law, you must meet the federal minimum, even though your state requires less to be in compliance.

If your state's law is more demanding than federal law. If your state's law is more inclusive or more generous regarding overtime pay than federal law, you must follow that law, even though you will exceed the minimum compliance requirements of the federal law. The following list identifies those states whose requirements are *tougher* than federal law. In the states that aren't listed, you have to comply with the federal rule, either because your state doesn't have an overtime pay law, or its law is the same as, or less stringent than, the federal rule.

State Laws on Overtime Pay

State	Overtime must be paid at:
AK	1.5 times regular pay for hours over 8 daily or 40 weekly. Doesn't apply to employees working for employers with less than 4 employees.
CA	1.5 times regular pay for hours over 40 weekly in any workday up to 12 hours, and for the first 8 hours on the seventh day of work; 2 times regular pay for hours over 12 daily and hours over 8 on the seventh day. Employees may work 7 days with no overtime required if total hours don't exceed 30 weekly and 6 daily. Certain alternative schedules involving more than 8 hours daily , but no more than 40 hours weekly, are permitted.
CO	1.5 times regular pay for hours over 40 weekly or 12 daily.
KY	1.5 times regular pay for hours over 40 weekly, and 1.5 times regular pay for all hours worked on the seventh day for workers who work 7 days. Doesn't apply to employees in retail sales, purchasing and distribution, or restaurants.
MA	1.5 times regular pay for hours over 40 weekly (includes tipped employees). Doesn't apply to, seasonal employees, and employees of restaurants, garages, or amusement parks. Employees who work 7 days must be paid 1.5 times regular pay for all hours worked on the seventh day.
NV	1.5 times regular pay for hours over 40 weekly or 8 daily (unless there's an agreement for 4 10-hour-day weeks). Doesn't apply to businesses with gross revenues of than $250,000 a year, employees paid at least 1.5 times the state minimum wage, outside buyers, and taxi and limousine drivers.

State	Overtime must be paid at:
PR	2 times regular pay for hours over 40 weekly or 8 daily (1.5 times for employers subject to the FLSA).
RI	1.5 times regular pay for hours over 40 weekly or for work in a retail business on a Sunday or holiday. Doesn't apply to salaried employees making at least $200 weekly.

HOW OFTEN MUST YOU PAY EMPLOYEES?

Federal law doesn't regulate how frequently you must pay your employees. Most states, however, require employers to pay wages on regular paydays designated *in advance*. Many states also regulate how much of a holdover you can take. For example, if you pay employees every Friday for the work they performed through the preceding Friday, you're holding over pay for one week. You might consider local or industry practices when selecting a payroll period.

Overtime. Federal law generally requires overtime compensation earned in a particular workweek to be paid on the regular payday for the period in which that workweek ends. If you can't determine the correct amount of overtime pay until after the regular pay period ends, you're required to pay the employee as soon after the regular pay period as is practicable.

State laws. The following list summarizes the general requirements each state imposes with respect to how often you must pay employees. Many states impose different rules for particular business types, such as mining, agriculture, logging, utilities, etc.; for designated (frequently exempt) employees, such as executives, managers, supervisors, professionals, outside and commissioned salespeople, etc.; or for overtime pay. If you're engaged in an industry subject to special rules, it's likely that industry practices reflect statutory requirements. States with no payroll frequency requirements are omitted from the list.

State Laws on Frequency of Wage Payments

State	Wages must be paid:
AL	at least monthly or semimonthly (at the employee's choice).
AZ	at least semimonthly with payments not more than 16 days apart; 5-day holdover permitted.
AR	at least semimonthly; corporations grossing $500,000 or more must pay managers grossing at least $25,000 per year at least monthly.
CA	at least semimonthly. Exempt employees must be paid at least once a month.
CO	at least once a month no later than 10 days after the end of the pay period.

State	Wages must be paid:
CT	at least weekly unless application for less frequent periods is granted; 8-day holdover permitted.
DE	at least monthly, within seven days from the close of the pay period.
DC	at least twice a month (nonexempt employees); 10-day holdover permitted. Payment once a month, by custom or contract, may lawfully be continued.
GA	at least semimonthly; no holdover permitted.
HI	at least twice a month, within 10 days after the end of each pay period.
ID	at least once a calendar month, within 10 days of the end of the pay period.
IL	at least semimonthly, not later than 13 days after the end of the pay period. For weekly pay periods, not later than 7 days after the end of the period. Wages paid on a daily basis must, insofar as possible, be paid the same day and, in any event, not later than 24 hours after the day they were earned.
IN	at least semimonthly or biweekly; within 10 days after the end of the pay period.
IA	at least monthly, semimonthly, or biweekly within 12 working days of the pay period's end.
KS	at least monthly, within 15 days of the end of the pay period.
KY	at least semimonthly (doesn't apply to exempt employees); 18-day holdover permitted.
LA	at least once every 2 weeks or twice during a calendar month with paydays 2 weeks apart whenever possible; 10-day holdover permitted. Applies to employers engaged in manufacturing who employ 10 or more persons, excluding clerical force or salespersons.
ME	at least weekly (most employers); 8-day holdover permitted.
MD	at least once every 2 weeks or twice a month (doesn't apply to executive, administrative or professional employees).
MA	at least biweekly; 6-day holdover permitted for 5- or 6-day workweeks, or 7 days for 7-day weeks.
MI	at least semimonthly, with wages payable on or before the first day of the month for wages earned in the first half of the preceding calendar month, and on or before the 15th day of the month for wages earned during the last half of the preceding month.
MN	at least once every 30 days. Laborers must be paid at least at 15-day intervals. Migrant workers must be paid at least every 2 weeks.
MS	at least every 2 weeks, twice during the calendar month, or the second and fourth Saturday of each month; 10-day holdover permitted. Applies to nonexempt employees of manufacturers with at least 50 employees.
MO	at least semimonthly (corporate employees) or monthly (exempt and commissioned employees); 16-day holdover permitted; manufacturers must pay at least every 15 days, 5-day holdover permitted. Employers who fail to pay within the required period must pay double the amount of wages due.
MT	at least every 10 business days, except for professional, supervisory, or technical employees who by custom are paid at least monthly; 5 day holdover permitted.
NE	on regular pay days designated by the employer.
NV	at least semimonthly, with wages for the first 15 days of the month paid by 8 a.m. on the last day of the month and wages for the last half of the month paid by 8 a.m. of the 15th day of the following month.
NH	at least weekly, for employees who work by the day or week; 8 day holdover permitted.

State	Wages must be paid:
NJ	at least twice each month (monthly for executives and supervisors); 10 day holdover permitted.
NM	at least semimonthly with wages earned the first 15 days of the month paid by the 25th of the month and wages earned the last half of the month paid by the 10th of the next month.
NY	at least weekly (manual workers); 7 day holdover permitted; at least once each calendar month (salespersons); semimonthly (in any other case).
NC	daily, weekly, biweekly, semimonthly, or monthly.
ND	at least once each calendar month.
OH	at least semimonthly, wages for the first half of the month must be paid by the first day of the next month, and wages for the last half of the month must be paid by the 15th of the month. Employees absent on payday are entitled to payment thereafter on demand.
OK	at least semimonthly. 11 day holdover permitted. Employers are allowed 3 days after a payday in which to make payment as required.
OR	on regular paydays that can't extend beyond 35 days from the time the employee entered employment or from the date of the last regular payday.
PA	at least semimonthly (except salaried workers) within 15 days from the end of the pay period, or by custom in the trade.
RI	weekly, except for employees whose compensation is fixed at a yearly, monthly, or semimonthly rate. 9 day holdover permitted.
SC	Employers with fewer than 5 employees at all times during the preceding 12 months are exempt from wage payment laws. Employers of 500 or more in Barnwell County and employers of 50 or more in Chesterfield County must pay wages biweekly with no holdover permitted. Other textile industries must pay on a regular payday with no holdover.
SD	at least once a calendar month, or on agreed upon, pre-designated, paydays.
TN	All employers must establish regular paydays. If 5 or more persons are employed, their wages must be paid at least semimonthly, with 20 days holdover. Businesses that allocate tips to employees must pay the amounts allocated at the close of the business day on which the tip or charge is collected or on the following payday.
TX	at least once a month (employees exempt from the overtime pay provisions of the FLSA); semimonthly (all other employees).
UT	at least semimonthly; 10 day holdover permitted. Employees on yearly salary must be paid at least monthly; 7 day holdover permitted.
VT	weekly, with 6 day holdover permitted, but employees may be paid biweekly or semimonthly if a statement of intent is filed.
VA	at least once a month (salaried employees); at least twice a month (hourly employees).
WA	at least once a month; 7 day holdback permitted.
WV	at least biweekly.
WI	at least monthly, within 31 days of the end of the pay period.
WY	at least semimonthly, but other intervals are permitted; 16 day holdover permitted.

Establishing a Pay Period

A major consideration in selecting a pay period is the availability of tax withholding tables. The IRS has published tables that make it easy to withhold the proper amount of taxes for designated payroll periods. We strongly suggest that you adopt one of these periods. Regular payroll periods are daily, weekly, bi-weekly, semi-monthly, monthly, quarterly, semi-annually, and annually. A miscellaneous payroll period is any payroll period other than a regular one (for example, a payroll period of 10 days). Sundays and holidays are included in computing the number of days in a payroll period. The timing of your payments to the government of taxes you've collected is determined by the payroll period that you select.

Part-time and temporary employees. Compute withholding for part-time workers who regularly work less than five days per week on a miscellaneous (daily) basis, even if you pay the worker weekly or on some other regular basis. However, an employee who works five or six days a week and is ordinarily paid at regular weekly intervals is considered to have a weekly payroll period. An exception to this rule is available if the worker has only one employer.

HOW MANY HOURS DID AN EMPLOYEE WORK?

You need to know how many hours each employee works each pay period to ensure that you pay each the proper amount. You also need this information to ensure that you're complying with both minimum wage and overtime rules.

Time You Have To Pay For

Generally, you have to pay nonexempt employees for the time they spend performing work for you while: (1) on duty, (2) on your premises, or (3) at the workplace. However, there are a lot of rules to remember about what counts as hours worked and what doesn't. Here's a few special rules that you should know about:

- **Employee absences.** Hours worked excludes time that an employee is away from work due to illness, or under your time off or holiday policies. This is true even if you're required, or choose, to pay employees for the absences.

- **Meals and breaks.** Generally, you have to include as working time, and to pay employees for, breaks or rest periods that last no longer than 20 minutes. Meal periods (generally, at least 30 minutes) are also excluded in computing work time. However, a meal period counts as work time if it's less than 30 minutes long, the employee isn't completely relieved of duties, or the employee can't leave the work post.

- **Working at home.** If an employee works at home without your knowledge, you don't have to pay for that work. If, however, you have reason to believe the employee is working at home, you have to pay the employee for that work.

- **On-call time.** Depending upon the circumstances, you may have to pay an employee for time on call. It comes down to how much control you have over the employee. If a nonexempt employee has to sit by the phone and be available for a phone call and come in to work immediately, you have to pay that employee. But an employee who is free to do whatever he or she wants to do, even though required to carry a beeper, isn't on call and doesn't have to be paid.

- **Orientation or training.** You must pay for any time spent on activities that you require, such as training or completing forms. This is true even if you send an employee to a class before or after the work day or on a non-work day.

- **Travel time.** You must pay employees for time spent traveling during normal working hours. You don't have to pay for time spent commuting and time spent traveling from home to a train station or airport. If overnight travel is required, only a portion of that time requires compensation.

- **Unauthorized overtime.** You have to pay an employee who works overtime you didn't authorize and you have to include that time as working time, if you knew or had reason to know that the employee was performing the work. If you know an employee is working overtime that you didn't authorize, you have an affirmative duty to stop the employee from performing the work to avoid having to pay.

- **Incidental work.** In addition to the principal duties that you hire an employee to perform, employees frequently perform, and must be paid for, some incidental activities. In general, you must pay an employee for time spent on activities that further your interests, but not for time spent on activities that are merely incidental to the employment relationship.

Example

An employee who stays late to set up equipment for the following day must be paid for his time. Similarly, an employee who is on call and must respond if summoned must be paid.

State Laws on Meals and Break Time

Federal law doesn't require that breaks be given at all, but some states regulate both meal and rest periods, either generally, or for specific industries. The following list sets forth the meal and rest break requirements established by the various states. Note that many states have very specific rules regarding when during a shift a meal break must be given. Also, some states permit meal and break rules to be determined under collective bargaining agreements. States that have no laws that generally apply to small businesses regarding rest and meal periods are omitted from the list.

State Laws on Meal and Rest Breaks

State	Meal and Rest Break Requirements
AR	Truck drivers must have at least eight hours' rest following 12 consecutive hours of driving. Rest periods of 20 minutes or less, when granted, are counted as hours worked.
CA	Wage orders regulating meal and rest periods exist for 15 industries and occupations: manufacturing; personal services; canning, freezing and preserving; professional, technical, clerical, mechanical and similar occupations; public housekeeping; laundry, linen supply, dry cleaning and dyeing; mercantile; industries handling products after harvest; transportation; amusement and recreation; broadcasting; motion pictures; industries preparing agricultural products for market on the farm; agricultural occupations; and household occupations.
CO	Employees who work at least 5 hours must be given a 30-minute meal period. Applies to laundry and dry cleaning, retail trade, public housekeeping, beauty service, medical professionals, janitorial service, and food and beverage service. Meal periods can be excluded from time worked unless the employee is required, by the nature of the work, to eat on duty. Meal periods are optional when a work period of less than 6 hours will complete the day's work. Employees must be given a paid 10-minute rest break for every 4 hours worked.
CT	Employees engaged in the trucking and railroad industries who work for seven and one-half or more consecutive hours must be given at least 30 consecutive minutes for a meal.
DE	An unpaid meal period of at least 30 minutes must be provided for employees who work seven and one-half or more consecutive hours in a day.
IL	Employees who work seven and one-half continuous hours must have at least 20 minutes for a meal period.
KY	Employees must be provided with a paid rest period of at least 10 minutes during each four hours worked, in addition to the regularly scheduled lunch period. Employers must grant employees a reasonable period for lunch.
ME	Employees may not work longer than 6 consecutive hours without taking at least 30 consecutive minutes of rest time that may be used as a mealtime. Doesn't apply to small businesses with less than 3 employees or in jobs that allow employees frequent breaks during the workday.
MA	No person may be required to work for more than 6 hours during a calendar day without at least a 30-minute meal break.
MN	An employer must permit an employee who works for 8 or more consecutive hours sufficient time to eat a meal, although the employer is not required to pay the employee during the meal break. An employer must allow each employee an adequate break from work during each 4 consecutive hours of work to utilize the nearest convenient restroom.

State	Meal and Rest Break Requirements
NE	Employees who work at assembling plants, work shops or mechanical establishments must have not less than 30 consecutive minutes for a meal. It's unlawful to require the employees to remain in the workplace during that period.
NV	An employer may not employ an employee for a continuous period of 8 hours without permitting the employee to have a meal period of at least 30 continuous minutes. Every employer must authorize and permit employees to take paid rest periods based on the total hours worked daily at the rate of 10 minutes for each 4 hours or major fraction thereof. Rest periods need not be authorized if total daily work time is less than 3.5 hours. One-employee establishments are exempt.
NH	An employer may not require an employee to work more than 5 consecutive hours without permitting a 30-minute eating period, except if it is possible for the employee to eat while working and the employer allows this arrangement.
NY	Persons employed in or in connection with a factory must be allowed at least 1 hour for a midday meal. Additional meal periods must be provided for people who work split shifts. Persons employed in or in connection with a mercantile or other establishment or occupation coming under the provisions of the labor law must be allowed 30 minutes for a meal. Additional rules apply to workers who work split shifts.
ND	Wage orders for agricultural, mercantile, manufacturing, professional, technical, clerical, and similar occupations provide for a 30-minute uninterrupted time period for meals, if desired, on each shift of work exceeding 5 hours when there are 2 or more employees on duty. Employees not allowed to leave the premises during the break period must be compensated at the regular rate of pay or provided with in-kind compensation, such as a meal whose value is equal to or greater than the minimum wage.
OR	Employers must provide a meal period of not less than 30 minutes. A period in which to eat while continuing to perform duties or remain on call, but which is not deducted from hours worked, is permitted only where the nature of the work prevents the employee from being relieved of all duty. Employers also must provide a paid break of not less than 10 minutes for each 4 hours or major part thereof worked in one work period, in addition to the usual meal period.
PR	Employees must be given a 1-hour meal break. Employers who permit an employee to work during the time fixed for taking food will be obliged to pay double time.
RI	No person may be employed for more than 6 consecutive hours in a factory, workshop, mechanical or mercantile establishment without at least a 20-minute meal period.
TN	Each employee scheduled to work 6 consecutive hours must have a 30-minute, unpaid rest break or meal period. If the nature of the workplace is such that employees may take breaks during the workday, the scheduled rest/meal period need not be provided.
TX	Employees who work at least 30 hours a week may not be required to work 7 consecutive days in a retail establishment without a 24-hour day of rest. The time off must be in addition to the regular periods of rest allowed during each workday.
WA	Employees must be allowed a meal period of at least 30 minutes. Meal periods must be paid working time when the employee is required by the employer to remain on duty on the premises or at a prescribed worksite in the interest of the employer. Employees working 3 or more hours longer than a normal workday must be allowed at least one 30-minute meal period prior to or during the overtime period. Employees must be allowed a paid rest period of not less than 10 minutes for each 4 hours of working time. No employee may be required to work more than 3 hours without a rest period.

State	Meal and Rest Break Requirements
WV	All employers must provide meal breaks of at least 20 minutes for employees who work 6 or more hours in a workday. Meal breaks must be provided for all employees who aren't afforded necessary breaks and/or are not permitted to eat a meal while working.
WI	Every employer operating a factory or mercantile establishment must allow each employee at least 24 consecutive hours off in each 7 consecutive days.

Keeping Track of an Employee's Hours

You need to have a reliable system for keeping track of your employees' hours to pay them properly and to ensure compliance with wage and hour laws. An easy place to find a time sheet appropriate to your type of business is at an office supply store. If you use computers, you can have employees track time in any number of spreadsheet, word processing, or database applications. While you may rely on your employees to keep their time, it's up to you to make sure that what they record is correct. Many businesses use time clocks, which are difficult to tamper with.

Generally, you're required to determine precisely the time for which you must pay your employees, including fractional parts of an hour. There is, however, an exception to the rule. You can use a rounding convention (for example, to the nearest tenth of an hour), if, over a period of time, the rounding results in employees getting paid for all the time they actually work.

Giving "Comp" Time

Giving comp time refers to the practice of giving compensatory time off to nonexempt employees who work extra hours instead of paying them time and a half. Under federal law, the practice is illegal. Of course, there's nothing wrong with giving comp time to an employee who doesn't work 40 hours in a week, even with the extra time.

Example

Bob Rollin stays late three days in a row to help you finish an important project. To thank him for his efforts, you give him the next week off. Bob normally works 25 hours a week but the extra time meant that he worked 35 hours for the week. You haven't violated federal law because he's not entitled to overtime until he works 40 hours in a workweek.

Deducting Pay for Tardy Employees

Depending on how you choose to pay your employees, you may deduct pay from *nonexempt* employees who are late or fail to punch the time clock (if you have one). However, if you choose to do so, be sure that the deductions don't result in an employee being paid less than the government mandated minimum wage or not being paid for overtime.

By definition, exempt workers are paid a salary, which means that they get the same amount of pay regardless of how many hours they work in a week. Deducting pay from an *exempt* employee for absences of less than one day is illegal. You can, however, choose to *not* pay exempt employees who are absent for a whole day. (You might make up for the loss from a sick or vacation leave plan, if you offer those kinds of benefits.)

Calculating Employees' Regular Rates

Paying your nonexempt employees requires you to calculate what's known as their "regular rate" of pay. When employees are paid by the hour, the regular rate of pay is the hourly wage. Unfortunately, the computation of the regular rate of pay becomes extremely complicated and time-consuming if you pay your nonexempt employees on some other basis.

Work Smart

We strongly recommend that you pay all your nonexempt employees on an hourly wage basis. You'll spend many extra hours doing payroll work if you don't. If you pay your nonexempt employees a salary, you still must calculate a regular rate for them to determine how much to pay them for overtime. Since the hours a salaried employee works can fluctuate from week to week, you have to calculate the regular rate for such employees each week, regardless of how often you pay them.

The regular rate is computed before any kind of payroll deduction is made. Regular rates aren't based on take-home pay. Regardless of how you pay employees, the rate must not fall below the current minimum wage rate.

MAKING DEDUCTIONS FROM PAY

What seems simple on the surface, deducting money from an employee's paycheck, can be extremely complicated. Several federal laws apply and, potentially, many state laws may apply as well. Deductions can be broken into three types:

- deductions required by law — examples are income and Social Security taxes (see Chapter 12), and wage garnishments

- deductions for the employer's convenience — examples are

those made to cover overpayments, wage advances, docking (for things such as spillage, breakage, or cash register shortages), or deducting for tardiness

- deductions that are done as a favor for employees — examples are benefit premiums, charitable contributions, and uniforms

Wage Garnishment Orders

A garnishment is a court order letting you know that a legal claim has been made against an employee's wages. The order generally will have arisen from a legal proceeding filed by someone to whom your employee owes money.

The most common reason for garnishment is that the worker owes child support payments to a divorced spouse; in many states everyone who is paying child support will automatically have their paycheck garnished. But other creditors may obtain garnishments against your employee as well; if your employee is unable to pay the amount, the court will order that the amount be deducted over time from the employee's wages. In effect, you, as the employer, will be responsible for collecting the money from the employee's pay and getting it to the court for payment of the debt.

How does a garnishment happen? In many cases, your involvement in a garnishment case will begin not with receipt of a garnishment order but with receipt of what is usually called a notice of garnishment. Here's how the situation usually unfolds: a creditor wants to collect a debt from your employee. The creditor finds out that the employee may be working for you and sends you a notice of garnishment telling you of the debt and asking you to confirm that the employee works for you.

If you get a garnishment order. Contact an attorney right away. Writs of garnishment are serious business. In some states, you have a limited amount of time to respond (sometimes just a few days) and if you don't honor the writ and begin withholding, you can be held responsible for the entire debt of the employee.

Generally, you can deduct garnishments from wages without violating the minimum wage rules because federal law treats money paid to a third party for the employee's benefit as the equivalent of payment to the employee. However, the amount that can be garnished is limited to 25 percent of the employee's disposable earnings (after legally required deductions like payroll taxes, workers' compensation, or unemployment compensation premiums), or the amount by which disposable earnings exceed 30 times the current minimum hourly wage set by the FLSA (currently, that amount is $142.50). And you can't terminate employees because their wages were garnished.

If the garnishment is issued under a state law, and that state law provides even more protection than the federal law, you would have to honor those additional protections. State laws on garnishment are detailed and complex. When you talk to your attorney, be sure to ask how much can be garnished, how to deal with multiple garnishments, and what fees you can charge the employee to recover the cost of compliance.

Docking an Employee's Pay

When we talk about docking pay, we mean reducing an employee's pay to recoup expenses due to breakage, spillage, cash register shortage, and the like. Technically, reducing an employee's pay for hours not worked is not "docking." Federal law doesn't prevent you from docking your employee's pay, but it does require that any such deductions not reduce pay below the statutory minimum. So if you're docking for things like spillage or shortages, you might have to carry over some of the amount to the next pay period, to avoid breaking the minimum wage law.

If you dock an *exempt* employee for any reason, other than for a major safety violation, that employee loses their exempt status for that *pay period*, not just that week. If this occurs, then you'll have to pay any overtime that may be due for the period.

Miscellaneous Deductions

Overpayments. Generally, if you paid an employee too much because of a legitimate bookkeeping error, you can deduct the mistaken overpayment from wages, even if the deduction reduces the pay below the statutory minimum wage for a particular pay period. However, if the deduction would cause a hardship, you're required to spread the repayments out over time. It's in your interest to work with the employee on this to avoid leaving an employee with insufficient money to pay bills.

Uniforms. You can't reduce an employee's wage for the pay period below the minimum hourly rate by deducting the cost of purchasing, renting, or maintaining a required uniform. Spread those costs over a sufficient number of pay periods to avoid this problem.

Benefit premiums. If you offer benefits and employees must share in the cost, you should deduct the amounts of premiums for those benefit plans to ensure that premiums are paid. It's in your best interest because, as an employer providing benefits, you're responsible for the payments. Be sure you have the employee's signature before making any deductions. If the deductions for pension or health plans cut into statutory minimum wage and overtime pay requirements, you can deduct them only if the employee voluntarily agrees and you don't get any profit or benefit from the transaction.

GOVERNMENT MANDATES RELATING TO PAY

One of the most important parts of paying your workers is making sure you're in compliance with the many federal and state laws that regulate the paying of employees. We've already looked at a number of these rules, including laws on frequency of payroll, minimum wage and overtime requirements, and wage credits for tips. In addition to these, which directly impact your payroll system, there are other laws that affect your relationship with employees.

Federal Child Labor Requirements

The federal FLSA *restricts*, but doesn't prohibit, businesses from employing children. Virtually all businesses are subject to these federal child labor rules. However, there are a few situations in which businesses are exempted from the child labor restrictions. These include *parents who employ their own children*, farm employment outside of school hours, and theatrical employment. If one of these doesn't apply, then the federal child labor rules specify what types of work children can do, when they can do it, and how old they have to be to do it.

Employees under 18. The FLSA doesn't limit the hours that employees under 18 may work when the next day is a school day. It does, however, specifically prohibit minors under the age of 18 from working in occupations deemed to be hazardous. Hazardous occupations that might be found in the small business context include driving motor vehicles, operating power equipment and construction machinery, installing roofs, and excavating. The prohibitions aren't absolute; an employee under 18 may engage in some hazardous occupations if special safety procedures are followed.

Employees 14 to 16. The FLSA provides additional restrictions on work by minors between 14 and 16 years of age. People in this age group are prohibited from engaging in most industrial and manufacturing activities, acting as public messengers, and working in some types of retail establishments. You can employ people between the ages of 14 and 16 for office and clerical work; sales or cashiering; window trimming; order processing and merchandise tagging; bagging; errands and delivery work by foot, bicycle or public transportation; cleanup work (but not with a power mower); kitchen work; pumping gas or washing cars; and newspaper delivery.

Minors between 14 and 16 may only work outside of school hours, may not work more than three hours a day and 18 hours a week during school, or eight hours a day and 40 hours a week when school is out; and must work between 7 a.m. and 7 p.m. except during the summer (June 1 through Labor Day) when the evening limit is 9 p.m. The limitations don't apply to students working in an approved work-training program where written documentation of the student's work time is authorized by the principal of the student's school.

State Child Labor Laws

All states have some laws restricting the employment of children or minors. Generally, there are restrictions in the type of occupation and on the hours of employment. In addition, many states require minors to obtain age certificates or work permits as a prerequisite to employment.

All states list hazardous occupations in which minors below a specific age cannot be employed. Many times, there are separate lists for minors under 18, minors under 16, and minors under 14. A substantial number of states prohibit most employment for all minors under age 14. Usual exceptions include newspaper delivery, family businesses, and agricultural work.

Almost all states restrict the hours of employment for minors under the age of 16. Several also have hours restrictions for 16- and 17-year-olds. Employment may be restricted to a specified number of hours a day or week and to daytime or early evening hours. In addition, permissible hours of work usually are less for school-aged minors while school is in session than during vacation periods.

State child labor law is detailed and complex. If you decide to hire a minor, check with your state labor agency about what you should do to comply with the state's child labor law. A primary area of concern is obtaining age or employment certificates. Many states require employers to get such certificates, usually from the superintendent of schools, but sometimes from the state department of labor, before employing minors of school age. State certificates are accepted as proof of age in almost every state.

States Requiring Employment Certificates for Minors

All but six states require age or employment certificates when businesses employ minors. The states that don't require such certificates are Arizona, Idaho, Kentucky, Mississippi, South Carolina, and South Dakota.

Equal Pay Requirements

If you're subject to the FLSA, you're also subject to the Equal Pay Act. The Equal Pay Act (part of the federal wage and hour laws) requires you to provide equal pay for equal work. The Act is very limited in its scope. It applies only to pay differences between men and women. In a nutshell, it says that you can't pay a person of one gender less than an employee of the opposite gender who is doing the same or substantially the same work. Pay inequities based on membership in protected groups other than gender groups are covered by federal antidiscrimination rules. Equal pay requirements apply to executives, administrative and professional employees, and salespeople who are exempt from other FLSA provisions.

If no two people in your office do the same job, you probably won't need to address this issue at all, but if you have people of different genders who do the same or substantially the same job, you should look for differences in the pay they receive. The difference doesn't have to be large. If you find them, make sure that you can prove that those differences are based on something other than gender, such as seniority, education, shift differentials, additional responsibilities, or experience.

You also have to look for more subtle types of equal pay violations. For example, are there situations where males predominantly occupy a certain kind of job that pays more than other jobs? While this situation may say something about your recruiting and hiring practices, it may also lead to problems with Equal Pay Act claims.

Example

You employ three salespeople and five customer service representatives. Salespeople get paid an average of $20,000 annually, and customer service representatives get paid an average of $15,000 annually. All of your salespeople are males, while four out of five of your customer services representatives are female.

While this situation in and of itself doesn't put you in violation of the Equal Pay Act, it should raise a red flag. If men are in most or all of your highest paying jobs while women are in most or all of your lower paying positions, you'll want to look into this problem and make sure that the differences in pay and in gender/job distribution are motivated by factors other than gender.

If you're sued and found in violation of the Equal Pay Act, you may have to pay any wages owed to the suing parties plus other penalties.

If you see a situation where there is clearly a problem with females being paid less than males for the same work, or vice versa, you need to fix the problem by making the wages more equitable. *It is illegal to reduce the pay of one gender to match the lower pay of the other.* You have to raise the pay of the employees being paid less. Fix the problem as soon as possible. Don't wait until the employee's next raise to bridge the salary gap. If the problems are more subtle, as in the example above, your hiring and promotion procedures may be the problem. Be sure to give females the same opportunities to get the higher paying jobs as males.

Posting Requirements

If you're subject to the FLSA, you'll also have to display a poster created by the federal government in your workplace, publicizing the federal minimum wage and overtime pay standards. You should place the poster in a place where employees will see it as they come and go from work. Any person who willfully violates any of the provisions of the FLSA, including failure to post, is subject to a fine of not more than $10,000 or to imprisonment for not more than six months, or both.

Work Smart

If your worksite is fairly large, you might also consider hanging these posters in a break room or on bulletin boards where employment-related information is posted.

The poster can be obtained from your local Wage and Hour Division office. To locate the Wage and Hour Division closest to you, check your phone directory (in the federal government listings). Under Employment Standards Administration, you should find a listing for the Wage and Hour Office.

State wage and hour laws. Individual states may also have posting requirements that you'll have to comply with. In general, you have to post the state minimum wage and overtime laws, or summaries of these laws. In many cases, the state will, on request, furnish you with the posters that you need. The posting must be conspicuous or in a place accessible to employees.

States With Wage and Hour Law Posting Requirements

Posting of minimum wage and overtime laws or orders is required of employers in Alaska, Arkansas, California, Colorado, Connecticut, Delaware, District of Columbia, Georgia, Hawaii, Idaho, Illinois, Indiana, Kentucky, Maine, Maryland, Massachusetts, Michigan, Minnesota, Missouri, Nebraska, Nevada, New Hampshire, New Jersey, New Mexico, New York, North Carolina, North Dakota, Ohio, Oklahoma, Oregon, Pennsylvania, Rhode Island, Vermont, and Wisconsin.

Recordkeeping Requirements

If you have employees who are covered by the federal minimum wage, equal pay, and overtime provisions, you must maintain and preserve records. What's more, even if your employees are exempt from the federal law, you'll have to keep records to prove that fact.

Your payroll records must be kept for three years from the date of the last entry you made on them. Supplementary records (including basic employment and earnings records; wage rate tables; order, shipping, and billing records; and records of additions to or deductions from wages paid) must be kept for two years, but it's easier to just keep everything for three years (or longer, if your state requires it).

What Records You Need To Keep

The information that you'll need to keep will vary depending on each employee's status. And you'll keep some information just to prove that each employee's status was correctly determined.

All employees. There's some information that you'll need for all employees. This information includes:

- name in full, as used for Social Security recordkeeping purposes, and, on the same record, the employee's identifying symbol or number if used in place of name on any time, work, or payroll records

- home address, including zip code

- date of birth, if the employee is under 19 years of age, for child labor purposes

- gender (for purposes of the equal pay provisions)

- occupation in which employed

- time of day and day of week on which the employee's workweek begins (if all employees have a workweek beginning at the same time on the same day, a single notation of the time of the day and the beginning of the workweek for all employees will suffice)

In addition, federal law requires you to keep specific additional information for each of the various classes of employees.

Nonexempt employees. Federal wage and hour laws require that your records show additional information for nonexempt employees. For each employee, you need to retain the information that you use to compute the amount of pay. Basically, if you keep and organize all of the records you create in order to do payroll, you should have what you need. If an employee has earned overtime pay, you need to retain the information necessary to show how much overtime was worked, and how the overtime pay was computed.

Exempt employees. If have employees who are classified as exempt under the federal FLSA, you're required to retain the information you used to determine that each employee is appropriately classified. If your employees qualify as exempt because they're classified as executive, administrative, or professional employees, you must keep records of the total wages paid each pay period days covered, and the date of payment.

Because these employees aren't paid by the hour, you don't, and should not, keep track of the number of hours they put in. Doing so could make it seem to a wage-hour auditor that you're indeed basing pay on the number of hours worked, which would mean that the employee was not exempt and that you might end up being liable for overtime for that employee.

Homeworkers. A homeworker is any person who produces goods for an employer from a home, apartment, or room in a residential establishment. Where the homeworker gets the materials—either from the employer or elsewhere—doesn't change the homeworker's status. Once again, the information that you'll need to keep is the same information that you use to determine how much to pay each worker. If you work through agents or distributors, you'll need to keep records identifying them as well. Organize the information so that you can establish that you've complied with all applicable wage and hour laws.

Tipped employees. If you have any employees who customarily receive tips from customers, patrons, or other third parties, you have additional recordkeeping to do. In addition to the records you keep for nonexempt employees, your pay records must identify the employees who are tipped and account for the tips reported by each employee. If tips are treated as wages for purposes of meeting minimum pay requirements, you'll need records showing that.

Federal Rules on Retaining Your Records

The federal government has certain requirements related to how and where you keep your records. According to those requirements, you must:

- Keep your records at your place of business or at an established central recordkeeping location.

- Keep your records safe, accessible, and open to inspection and transcription at any time by auditors from the Wage and Hour Division. If your records are kept at a central location apart from your place of business, make the records available at the place of inspection within 72 hours after notice from the Wage and Hour Division.

- Make any extensions, recomputations, or transcriptions of your records and submit them to the Wage and Hour Division, if the auditor makes such a request in writing.

- Request permission from the Wage and Hour Division if you want to convert your old records to microfiche or microfilm.

Recordkeeping form or media. The law doesn't specify what form your records should take. Whatever method you use is sufficient if the records establish the information or data required by law. You may choose to keep the records on paper, on computer, or on microfiche or microfilm.

Warning

If you keep records on microfiche or microfilm, you must have the equipment available to read them, should Wage and Hour Division auditors drop in. If you keep your records on your computer, make sure you have a backup on a disk.

State Laws on Recordkeeping

In addition to federal recordkeeping requirements, some states with wage and hour laws have their own requirements for keeping and storing records related to their wage and hour requirements. You must comply with both state and federal rules. For practical purposes, it's best to keep all your records for the longest time period specified by the laws that apply to you. If your state's requirements are less demanding, you must still keep all necessary records for three years to comply with federal law.

State requirements for wage and hour recordkeeping are summarized in the list below. The records required to be kept generally include the information you're required to prepare in order to pay your employees. For example, most states want each employee's name and identification information, occupation, payroll period, pay rate, hours worked, amounts withheld or deducted, and payment date.

State Laws on Payroll Record Retention

Period	State
3 years	ID, NY, OR, ME, MO, UT
4 years	AZ, CA, CT, DE, DC, GA, IN, MA, NE, NV, NJ, NM, OK, PA, RI, SD, TX, VT, VA, WA, WY
5 years	AL, AK, AR, CO, FL, HI, IL, IA, KS, LA, MD, MT, NC, ND, OH, PR, SC, WV
6 years	KY, MI, NH
7 years	TN
8 years	MN
not specified	MS

GETTING THE MONEY TO EMPLOYEES

Most small business owners with one or a few employees will generally pay employees in person by cash or check. However, some employers have found that electronic fund transfers can be a convenient way to pay employees. If you have enough employees to make it worthwhile, check with your banker regarding this option.

Distributing Pay to Employees

- Deliver pay to each employee personally and discreetly.

- Encourage employees not to leave checks or money in an unsecured area.

- Don't leave one employee's pay with another employee (unless it's a supervisor) to be delivered.

- Don't allow relatives of the employee to pick up an employee's pay if the employee is out unless you have express permission from the employee (preferably in writing).

- If you have a regularly scheduled pay period, try to distribute the pay at the same time of day on payday, so employees know when to expect their pay.

- In the interest of confidentiality, put checks or cash in individual envelopes.

- If you have to mail an employee's check because the employee is out on sick leave or vacation, use certified, insured mail.

- Never demean employees or require them to perform tasks or make statements to get their checks, even if you're just joking with them.

Other Information To Provide With Pay

If your employees are paid by check or participate in a direct deposit program, you should provide them with a statement that details their gross wages, what deductions have been made, and what their net pay is. Most states require employers to give employees a pay stub showing gross pay, hours worked, and an itemized list of taxes and other deductions made. If you're using payroll software, the program will print a standard pay stub for you.

Chapter 11

Employee Benefits

Virtually every business has to offer some type of monetary compensation to employees. In contrast, you're mostly, but not entirely, free to choose whether to provide other benefits, such as paid time off, health insurance, or a retirement plan, for your employees. There are three good reasons why you might provide employee benefits.

- You have a *legal obligation* to do so. For example, every state has a workers' compensation law that requires employers to compensate employees injured on the job.

- *Other employers competing for the same employees offer benefits* as part of their compensation package, and you need to offer benefits to compete for employees. If other employers offer health care benefits and you can't afford to, for example, you may have to pay more than your competitors, or sell prospective employees on the intangible benefits of working for a small company (less bureaucracy, more flexibility).

- *You want to obtain the benefits for yourself* or your family, but are required to provide them to all employees in order to get them (or at least to get them on a tax-deductible basis).

Work Smart

Use the same techniques you used to obtain competitive salary information (see page 47) to find out about employee benefits offered in your employment market. Get information about employee benefits without regard to the size of the business. You're competing against all businesses that have employees with the same skills that your business needs.

If you can afford it, definitely consider offering some benefits, at least those necessary to match what other employers are providing.

Some benefits require little administration. For example, if you close up shop on major holidays and pay your employees for the day, you're providing benefits. But you don't need a fancy plan or someone to administer it. The other type of benefits almost *requires* a formal plan and plan administrator. If you buy a health insurance contract to provide benefits for employees, you certainly should have a formal plan and plan administrator. You don't want to handle claims yourself, and you don't want the burden of complying with complex federal and state laws.

Warning

There is considerable time and expense involved in administering many types of benefit plans, such as health and insurance benefits, retirement benefits, etc. Complying with regulatory requirements is difficult and the rules aren't always particularly logical, but they are the law. For that reason alone, we strongly urge you to consult with your financial advisors, your attorney and accountant, your insurance agent, and any other appropriate professionals if you're seriously considering providing these benefits. For the same reason, definitely consider outsourcing the administration of these benefits. (See page 218 for more information.)

WHAT WILL IT COST?

There are two types of costs that you can incur when you provide employee benefits. There may be an actual monetary outlay on your part, such as paying some part of health insurance premiums. There can also be indirect costs, such as the decreased productivity your business experiences when someone takes personal time off. This second category of costs should not be overlooked in determining whether it's advisable to offer particular benefits.

Remember that you can take a tax deduction for the cost of many types of benefits, and your employees can exclude their value from taxable income. Because the government is picking up part of the cost, you actually pay less for the benefits than if the employees had to purchase the benefit individually.

Work Smart

When shopping for benefits, keep your employees' wages in mind. If you think that their share of the cost of a certain benefit is going to be more than they can afford, there's no point in offering it.

BENEFITS YOU MUST PROVIDE

As an employer, you're *required* to provide certain benefits for your employees. There can be both state and federal rules with which you must comply, and the terms of those rules can vary. In general, the three types of benefits you must provide involve giving employees time off from work, participating in a workers' compensation program, and withholding FICA and FUTA taxes, thus providing minimal retirement and long-term disability benefits. In a few states, employers must also provide short-term disability or health benefits.

Time Off and Leave

Many benefits that you're required to provide involve allowing employees to take time off under certain circumstances. If you have to allow employees to take time off, you are generally prohibited from taking any type of adverse employment action against them for doing so. In many situations, you even have to give employees their jobs (or similar ones) back when they return from a leave of absence.

Time Off To Vote

There is no federal law that requires you to give employees time off to vote. However, 30 states and Puerto Rico have laws that require private employers to give employees time off to vote, and in some of these states, the employee must be paid for this time. The rules sometimes condition time off to vote on an employee's inability to get to the polling place during non-work hours. And, the employer is frequently free to specify when, during the day, the employee can take time off. The amount of time permitted varies; many states allow between two and four hours away from work.

States Requiring Time Off To Vote

The states that require time off to vote are listed below. The states listed in **bold** have laws prohibiting deductions from pay if employees take time off to vote.

Alaska, **Arizona**, Arkansas, **California**, **Colorado**, Georgia, **Hawaii**, Illinois, **Iowa**, **Kansas**, Kentucky, **Maryland**, Massachusetts, **Minnesota**, **Missouri**, **Nebraska**, **Nevada**, New Mexico, **New York**, North Dakota, Ohio, **Oklahoma**, Puerto Rico, **South Dakota**, **Tennessee**, **Texas**, Utah, **Washington**, **West Virginia**, Wisconsin, and **Wyoming**.

If you're in one of the states that mandate time off to vote, providing this benefit isn't optional. But if you have the choice, seriously consider giving employees time off to vote. The cost is minimal, since it usually involves just a short absence from work. Also, it pays, from a civic perspective, to encourage people to participate in the election process.

Leave for Jury Duty

Employees have the right to take leaves of absence to serve as jurors in *federal* courts, under the Jury Systems Improvement Act.

Example

Federal courts have punished employers for:

- firing an employee the day after returning from jury duty

- terminating an employee after a supervisor commented that an employee could not be at work and on jury duty at the same time

- refusing to pay an employee on jury duty for a paid holiday because she did not work the day after the holiday, while she was still on jury duty

- refusing to pay an employee during jury duty unless financial hardship was shown

- changing policy from one in which the company pays employees during jury service to one in which the company does not, while an employee was serving jury duty

- discharging a night-shift employee for not reporting to work on the night of the day in which he served on a jury

---

Most states, the District of Columbia, and Puerto Rico prohibit an employer from discharging someone who takes leave to serve on a jury in a state court. Some prohibit other forms of reprisal or threats of reprisal. Some treat violations as misdemeanors or as contempt of court; others authorize the employee to bring a court action for reinstatement and damages. Some states specifically say that an employer doesn't have to pay for the lost time or that it may set off from wages any money received by the employee for juror service.

States Requiring Time Off for Jury Duty

The states that have laws protecting employees who serve on state or local juries from negative employment actions are listed below. States in **bold** require employers to pay employees for time spent on jury duty. However, the amount paid is not always what an employee would earn if he or she were at work.

The states are: **Alabama**, Alaska, Arizona, **Arkansas**, California, Colorado, **Connecticut**, Delaware, Florida, Georgia, Hawaii, Idaho, Illinois, Indiana, Iowa, Kansas, Kentucky, **Louisiana**, Maine, **Massachusetts**, Michigan, Minnesota, Mississippi, **Nebraska**, Nevada, New Hampshire, New Jersey, New Mexico, **New York**, North Carolina, North Dakota, Ohio, Oklahoma, Oregon, Pennsylvania, Puerto Rico, Rhode Island, South Carolina, South Dakota, **Tennessee**, Texas, Utah, Vermont, Virginia, Washington, West Virginia, Wisconsin, and Wyoming.

Appearing as a Witness

Two states, Florida and Michigan, require employers to give employees time off to serve as a witness in a court proceeding.

Military Service

Any employee who is called to military service, training, reserve duty, etc., who is not a temporary employee is protected by *federal* law. That includes employees on probationary status and employees who have been employed for only a few days. You *must* grant such employees time off if they are called to active duty, although the leave may be without pay. Further, the employee must be reinstated to the position held before taking military leave upon successful completion of active military duty.

In addition to active duty leave, you must grant annual leave to attend reserve or national guard encampment, maneuvers, drills, training, or any other duty of a short-term nature. Some employers pay reservists the difference between their military pay and their regular pay, but you have no obligation to do so. Employers may *not*, however, charge military leave to annual vacation leave, although an employee may elect to do so if the leave is unpaid.

Some states impose additional restrictions or requirements on employers whose employees are called to militia, National Guard, or other military service. Remember that you're still subject to federal law even if your state has no rules on military leave.

States Requiring Time Off for Military Service

The states that have laws relating to military leave for employees are: Alabama, Alaska, Arizona, California, Colorado, Connecticut, Florida, Georgia, Hawaii, Idaho, Illinois, Indiana, Iowa, Kansas, Kentucky, Louisiana, Maine, Maryland, Massachusetts, Michigan, Minnesota, Mississippi, Missouri, Montana, New Hampshire, New Jersey, New Mexico, New York, North Carolina, Oklahoma, Pennsylvania, Puerto Rico, Rhode Island, South Carolina, South Dakota, Texas, Utah, Vermont, Virginia, Washington, West Virginia, and Wisconsin.

Although many states protect employees who are called to military service with the National Guard or state militia, some states don't. Since people are rarely called up except when there is an emergency, disaster, or other pressing need, you should consider providing time off for this type of service, even if you're not required to do so. You can choose whether or not to pay for the time off.

Family Leave

Only employers with 50 or more employees must provide family leave under the federal Family and Medical Leave Act. It requires that covered employers allow employees to take the equivalent of 12 weeks of unpaid leave each year due either to a birth or adoption of a child, or to attend to the serious health condition of an immediate family member or to the employee's own serious health condition. The leave need not be taken all at once. And, upon returning to work, an employee must be reinstated to the same or a similar job.

In addition to the requirements of the FMLA, six states require employers with fewer than 50 employees to provide family leave. They are: California - 5 employees (maternity leave only); District of Columbia - 20 employees; Maine - 25 employees; Minnesota - 21 employees (maternity and adoption only); Oregon - 25 employees; and Vermont - 10 employees (maternity and adoption leave), -15 employees (family or employee illness). If you meet one of those thresholds, contact your state department of labor.

Pregnancy/Parental Leave

If you have 15 or more employees, you're subject to the federal Pregnancy Discrimination Act (part of Title VII of the Civil Rights Act of 1964). Women affected by pregnancy, childbirth, or related medical conditions must be treated the same as other job applicants or employees on the basis of their ability or inability to perform the required work. Women may not be fired, refused a job, denied a promotion, or forced to go on leave merely because of pregnancy.

Pregnancy leave is a form of medical leave. If your policies permit other employees who take disability leave to return to work, you must treat pregnant women the same way. Parental leave, in contrast, is leave to care for a child. If you're required, or choose, to provide family leave, avoid problems with state or federal antidiscrimination laws by providing both male and female employees the same benefits.

Religious Holidays

No state or federal laws require you to give employees time off to observe religious holidays. However, antidiscrimination laws prohibit you from discriminating against employees based on religion. In general, you must accommodate the religious needs of employees if you can do so without undue hardship to your business.

Work Smart

To avoid problems relating to the observance of religious holidays, you might consider:

- allowing individuals to use vacation or other eligible leave pay when observing religious holidays

- granting leave for religious holidays not otherwise designated as company holidays without pay as an excused absence

- allowing employees to make up the time taken as leave to observe a religious holiday

---

Workers' Compensation

Workers' compensation laws represent an implicit contract between employers who are subject to the system and employees who suffer work-related injury or sickness. Employers are granted immunity from suits by employees injured on the job (barring intentional wrongdoing on the part of the employer); workers' compensation is the sole remedy for the injured employee. In exchange, employers pay money into the state programs that provide the compensation. This helps manage the risk of loss resulting from an employee injury because the costs are predictable. From the employees' perspective, this provides some certainty that they will be compensated for an on-the-job injury regardless of fault or whether the employer is financially capable of paying that compensation.

Every state has enacted workers' compensation laws to protect employees against loss of income and to make medical payments required due to a work-related injury, accident, illness, or disease. In every state except New Jersey and Texas, workers' compensation coverage is mandatory. Before you set up your workers' compensation program, however, discuss it with your attorney to make sure that you're complying with all applicable laws.

State Thresholds for Workers' Compensation Coverage

In most states, *all employers* are subject to workers' compensation laws regardless of the number of employees that they have. In the following states, employers are subject to workers' compensation laws only if they have *at least* the number of employees indicated: Alabama - 3; Arkansas - 3 (2 for repair work and 1 for contractors and subcontractors); Florida - 4 (1 for construction businesses); Georgia - 3; Michigan - 3; Mississippi - 5; Missouri - 5 (1 for construction employers); New Mexico - 3 (1 for state-licensed construction businesses); North Carolina - 3; Rhode Island - 4; South Carolina - 4; Tennessee - 5; and Virginia - 3.

If you're in one of the 48 states that require employers to participate in workers' compensation programs, there are generally three ways to obtain coverage. You may obtain individual insurance, you may self-insure, or you may participate in a state insurance pool.

Save Money

Generally, small employers will find that the state insurance pool is the least expensive choice. Self-insurance is almost always too great a risk for small employers to bear and is a route typically taken only by the largest employers.

Premiums you pay for workers' compensation coverage are tax-deductible business expenses. If you self-insure, the benefit payments that you make are deductible.

Typical Benefits

Each state has its own workers' compensation laws, but these laws share many common elements. Some of these are:

- **Benefits are provided only for accidental job-related injury.** Employees are entitled to benefits when they suffer a "personal injury by accident arising out of and in the course of employment." Benefits aren't available for self-inflicted injuries or those caused by alcohol or substance abuse.

- **Benefits include income replacement, medical, and death benefits.** Wage-loss benefits usually cover about one-half to two-thirds of the employee's average weekly wage. Survivor benefits are provided in the case of a fatal illness or injury

- **Covered employees are defined by law.** States generally exclude independent contractors from their programs.

- **Fault is generally not an issue.** Neither the employee's own negligence in causing the accident nor your complete lack of fault is a factor in deciding whether the worker gets benefits.

- **Employees give up the right to sue you.** In exchange for the assured benefits, employees give up their right to sue you for any injury covered by workers' compensation laws. Although workers' compensation laws protect you from lawsuits for workplace injuries, they don't completely insulate you from being sued. You could be sued by your employees, for example, for failing to provide them with the workers' compensation benefits to which they are entitled.

- **Employees retain the right to sue negligent third parties.** If a third party's negligence contributed to the accident, the employee can still sue the third party. Any proceeds from the suit should be first applied to reimburse you for benefits paid to the employee.

- **The system is administered by a state agency.** The responsibility for administering the system is placed in the hands of a state agency.

- **Most employers are required to participate.** Only Texas and New Jersey have voluntary systems. Penalties for failure to participate are severe. Employers not required to participate may (and probably should) choose to do so, however.

When an Accident Happens

When a job-related accident happens, workers' compensation rules require you to do several things. First is to get prompt, appropriate medical care for the injured employee. After that, you must file an accident report with your state workers' compensation agency. Investigate every accident, but treat every injury as legitimate, even if the circumstances surrounding the injury make you suspicious.

Each state has its own rules setting the time period within which accident reports must be filed. The state agency will decide whether payments should be awarded to your employee. An appeal to a court of law is usually allowed only where the facts are in dispute. Payment of benefits to your employee is usually made after a waiting period, most commonly three to seven days, and is retroactive.

Relationship of injury to work. Even though a workers' compensation agency or an insurance company will determine whether an injury is work-related, you should make your own investigation if the question is in doubt. Gather any facts that you can that support your belief and be prepared to present your arguments to the agency or company. Don't forget that you may be better off if the accident *is* work-related because the workers' compensation laws generally protect you from additional liability. The issue isn't always clear. Consider an employee who is mugged in your parking lot or an employee under stress who commits suicide.

FICA, FUTA, and State Unemployment Taxes

Even though you don't necessarily think of taxes as an employee benefit, you do pick up the tab for certain government-administered benefits. You're obligated to make these payments on behalf of your employees by state and federal laws. (See the discussion of your liability for these taxes beginning at page 231.)

The Federal Insurance Contributions Act (FICA) is a federal law that requires you to pay the employer's portion of two separate taxes: a Social Security tax and a Medicare tax. The law also requires you to withhold the employee's portion of those taxes from each employee's wages.

The Federal Unemployment Tax Act (FUTA) is a federal law that requires you to pay a federal unemployment tax when you have employees. Employees don't pay any part of FUTA taxes.

States also have unemployment taxes that you'll likely have to pay. The amount of those taxes is dependent on your experience rating; that is, how frequently your ex-employees make claims for unemployment benefits. The rules in every state are at least as broad in scope as the federal rules so, if you're paying FUTA, you'll also be paying state unemployment taxes.

State and Federal Disability Programs

Five states (California, Hawaii, New Jersey, New York, and Rhode Island) and Puerto Rico have state disability programs. These jurisdictions require anyone with at least one employee to offer temporary disability benefits to an employee who is unable to work due to illness or injury, but who does *not* qualify for unemployment benefits or workers' compensation.

The funds are financed by deductions from employee pay, and in Hawaii, New Jersey, New York, and Puerto Rico, employers must also contribute. With the exception of Rhode Island's program, an employer may elect out of the state plan and put contributions into a private plan. Private plans must meet state requirements regarding coverage, eligibility, contribution amounts, and employee approval.

Any contributions that you make to a state program are deductible as taxes. Employees may also deduct their contributions. However, if you opt for a private plan, contributions aren't deductible.

Social Security benefits. The Social Security Administration also provides benefits to workers whose disability is of a type that will last at least 12 months. There is a six-month waiting period following the onset of disability before benefits will commence. Monthly cash benefits are paid if the worker is unable to perform any job for which the worker is reasonably qualified. Benefits continue until the individual dies, reaches retirement age, or returns to work for at least three months. Social Security benefits are reduced by any amounts received as workers' compensation. Fortunately, arranging for these benefits is something that a disabled employee will handle directly with the SSA.

Health Benefits

At present, only Hawaii requires employers to make health benefits available to employees.

BENEFITS YOU MAY CHOOSE TO PROVIDE

There are many benefits that small business owners *may* provide, even though they are *not required* to do so. As a practical matter, most businesses have to provide employees with paid holidays and at least two weeks of paid vacation each year. You can set up plans for paid sick leave, retirement saving, health care, insurance, paid vacations, or paid holidays. However, if you decide to offer *employee welfare benefits*, you must do so in accordance with the rules set forth in ERISA (the Employee Retirement Income Security Act).

Over the past few years, health insurance has become an increasingly popular benefit in light of escalating health care costs. Health insurance premiums are tax-deductible by the employer and tax-exempt for the employees. Whatever benefits you choose to offer, be sure that your employees are getting what they need and want. You may find that some workers prefer cash compensation to benefits, while others place more value on particular benefits.

Time Off and Leave

In addition to time off that may be mandated by federal or state law (voting, jury duty, military leave, family leave), many employers also offer paid or unpaid time off. Typically, time off is provided for holidays, vacations, sick leave, personal leave, funeral leave, and maternity or paternity leave.

Work Smart

ERISA's administrative requirements can apply to a time-off plan. To avoid these burdens, it's better to make time off a payroll practice and not a separate plan. If separate vacation pay checks are issued under an organized plan, ERISA will apply. But if employees are paid out of your general assets and vacations are merely a payroll practice, ERISA will not apply.

Holidays

Although many businesses traditionally give employees time off for holidays, such as Christmas, Thanksgiving, Independence Day, etc., there is no requirement that you do so. And, if you choose to give time off, you don't have to pay employees for the time off.

Whether you give time off for holidays, and, if so, which holidays you pick, is strictly up to you. Obviously, you may want to close the business for the day in order to celebrate or just take some time off. On the other hand, the nature of your business may require that you remain open on holidays. If so, many businesses compensate employees who have to work on a holiday at an increased rate.

Did You Know?

The average number of paid holidays for full-time employees is nine. Virtually all companies provide the following as paid holidays: New Year's Day, Memorial Day, Independence Day, Labor Day, Thanksgiving Day, and Christmas Day. Other holidays frequently added to that list include: Martin Luther King, Jr., Day, President's Day, Good Friday, Columbus Day, Veterans' Day, the Friday after Thanksgiving, and Christmas Eve.

Vacations

Most full-time employees expect paid vacation time as part of the compensation and benefits package that they receive. In fact, seven out of eight small businesses (less than 100 employees) provide paid vacation leave for their employees, according to the Bureau of Labor Statistics. Nevertheless, there are no federal or state laws that require an employer to provide paid or unpaid vacation time.

If you do choose to offer vacation benefits (and we strongly suggest that you do), you'll need to decide how much vacation to provide, and what conditions you'll place on taking it.

Did You Know?

A recent survey by Hewitt Associates reveals that employees of 82 percent of all businesses are granted between 10 and 14 paid vacation days. Employees with 15 years or more of service were provided between 20 and 24 days off by 87 percent of employers.

Many businesses use a sliding scale, where vacation time increases the longer an employee works for the business. For example, many employees get two weeks off their first year, with the amount growing incrementally each year up to a certain limit. Whatever you decide to do, make sure that the needs of your business will be met by the remaining staff. If you have just two employees and one goes on vacation, your workforce is reduced by a third.

Another issue is how employees can take their vacation time. Will you permit day-at-a-time vacations? Can employees take half-days off? Are there certain periods during the year when you don't want anyone taking off? Or do you intend to close up shop for some specified period, requiring employees to use some vacation days during that period? As a small business owner, planning and coordination are critical if you choose to provide vacation benefits. It's best to have a written policy that explains how vacation time accrues, how it may be taken, and what type of notice employees must provide prior to taking days off.

Sick Leave

Paid sick leave benefits aren't required by law. Unpaid sick leave may be legally required only if you're subject to state or federal family or medical leave laws. As a practical matter, you don't want sick people coming to work, so the real issue is: are you going to pay people for days when illness keeps them from working?

Did You Know?

A federal survey of businesses with fewer than 100 employees found that half offered some form of paid sick leave.

Again, we strongly suggest that sick leave be a part of your compensation and benefits package. Most of the employers you're competing with for employees will, especially the larger ones. Many plans limit the total number of days that may be taken with pay. Others provide employees with a bank of personal time off which they can take as desired or required for either vacation or sick leave. Whatever you choose to do, incorporate your policy in a document that you can give to employees explaining how your sick leave benefit works. Be sure to address issues such as how you'll treat time off when it is the employee's spouse or family member who is ill, whether unused days may be carried from year to year, and who to notify when an employee can't make it to work.

Personal Time

Some employers recognize that there are situations in which an employee can't reasonably make it to work even though he or she isn't ill or on vacation. Moving, buying a house, having a car break down, and weather emergencies are typical examples. Some employers explicitly provide a limited number of days that can be taken off with pay when these events arise.

Some employers are moving away from classifying each type of paid leave that may be taken and, instead, are providing employees with a set number of days that may be taken off for any reason. Under these "paid time off" plans, employees need not explain why they aren't going to come to work on a particular day. This type of plan is easy to administer, since you don't have to track different types of absences for payroll purposes. However, you must communicate to your employees the terms and conditions that are imposed on the use and scheduling of paid time off (see page 132).

Funeral Leave

It's unrealistic to expect employees to work immediately after the death of a relative, particularly if it's a close family member. You may choose to deal with this situation informally, allowing time off in proportion to the situation. We suggest that the better route is to have a written policy that states the circumstances under which an employee may take funeral or bereavement leave. The policy should indicate how much time can be taken, whether the employee will be paid for the time off, and the relatives whose death will trigger application of the policy.

Health Care

Health care benefits are one of the most important and popular benefits that an employer can provide. Unfortunately, health care is growing more costly every year. The fact that the premiums you pay or contributions you make are tax deductible offers some relief, but health care is expensive. There's also the matter of plan administration. The plan administrator bears the bulk of the responsibilities, but the employer must act as a conduit between the administrator and the employees. And you're exposed to potential liability if the health care provider selected commits malpractice.

Work Smart

Many small business owners forego health insurance during the start-up period, figuring that the risk of ill health is small and the cost of health insurance is prohibitively high. We strongly advise against this. Your business's health is directly tied to your personal health. If you can, use the business as a vehicle to obtain tax-favored health insurance benefits if you don't have coverage through a spouse's plan, COBRA coverage, or other plan.

What Health Insurance Plans Cover

Health plans typically reimburse employees for some or all of the costs associated with their medical care and, if you choose, for the medical care of their dependents. They *don't* cover work-related injuries that are covered by workers' compensation. Beginning July 1, 1997, the federal Health Insurance Portability and Accountability Act of 1996 will prohibit insurers that offer health plans in the small business market from excluding *any* small business from coverage

---

Warning

All 50 states have laws that require insurers to include particular types of health care coverage if they offer health insurance policies at all. Common treatment mandates include mammograms, alcohol and substance abuse, infant care, dependent coverage, and mental health coverage. No two states have the exact same requirements.

However, in some states, insurers have been granted exemption from various mandates in exchange for offering low-cost insurance to small employers, often with guaranteed renewals and no waiting periods.

Whom To Cover

Choosing whom to cover is pretty much up to you. There aren't any laws that require or prohibit you from establishing whatever rules you want regarding who is covered by your health care plan. However, once you establish rules for determining who gets coverage, you *must* apply them consistently. You're free to cover part-time workers or not, and to set thresholds that determine if and when a part-time worker becomes eligible.

Example

You can require that an employee work at least 30 hours a week in order to be eligible to participate in your health care plan.

You have the same discretion regarding coverage for your employees' spouse or dependents. You can choose to provide coverage or not, and you can establish who qualifies as a dependent and who doesn't. You can make health coverage optional to the employee, and ask them to pay some or all of the cost.

Waiting Periods and Eligibility Requirements

There are no laws that restrict or require employers to establish how long after being hired an employee must wait to participate in a health plan. Common practices include immediate eligibility (no waiting period), 30 days, three to six months, or one year of full-time employment. Consider factors such as employee turnover rates, competitive pressure from other employers, whether to provide coverage for part-time employees, and of course, price.

If you have 20 or more employees, restrictions based on age run the risk of violating federal antidiscrimination laws. However, there's no laws directly regulating minimum or maximum ages for health care coverage. Many employers don't have a minimum age. Those that do often choose 18. Age maximums are more common in the area of an employee's dependents. For example, many plans terminate dependent coverage when a child reaches age 22. But health care plans may require employees eligible for Medicare to take advantage of it.

Health Maintenance Organizations (HMOs)

While fee-for-service is still the most popular form of health benefit with small business owners, health maintenance organizations are growing in popularity with employers, in part because they're one of the least expensive health care alternatives. The low cost is possible because of the limits placed on choosing physicians and medical facilities. People who are insured under an HMO must choose a doctor from among those that have contracts with the insurance company or managed care company. A small copayment is required when services are performed.

Warning

If you have at least 25 employees, federal law requires you to offer an HMO as one of your employees' health care options, if there is an HMO in your area.

Preferred Provider Organizations (PPOs)

Preferred provider organizations are a good compromise for those who want more choice than an HMO provides, but don't want to pay a lot more in premiums. Like an HMO, a PPO contracts with a variety of doctors and hospitals. Unlike an HMO, patients are free to go to a PPO physician or not. However, when a PPO doctor or facility is used, the patient pays only a small copayment. Those who obtain treatment from non-PPO care providers generally pay a larger percentage of the total costs than those who use PPO care givers.

Fee-for-Service Plans

Fee-for-service plans are also known as indemnity plans. They are probably the most expensive form of health insurance. These traditional insurance plans give employees complete freedom in choosing doctors and medical facilities. In return, patients usually have to fulfill a yearly deductible (usually $300 to $500 per person) before the plan starts providing reimbursement for expenses. Once the deductible is satisfied, the insurance plan pays for a specified percentage of health care costs (usually 70 to 80 percent).

Dental, Vision, and Hearing Care

Most health insurance excludes dental, vision, and hearing care, so you'll have to purchase coverage for these types of care separately, if you choose. You can obtain both indemnity coverage, which pays for care at the providers your employees choose, and HMO type coverage. If you have a health plan, it's likely that you can add this type of coverage to your plan by paying additional premiums.

Medical Savings Accounts/Flexible Spending Accounts

Flexible spending accounts are, in part, a health benefit that you can provide to your employees at very little cost. Basically, employees are permitted to contribute money to an account, and use that money to pay for medical expenses they incur. A second kind of FSA may be used for dependent care expenses, such as day care center expenses, the care of dependents under 13 by a baby sitter, and expenses of before and after school programs.

Money that employees contribute is *not taxed*, so employees get to pay some expenses with pre-tax dollars, which is much cheaper than paying for it with post-tax dollars. The downside is that money placed in the account each year that isn't spent on qualified expenses in the same year is lost. Employees must choose how much to put into the account at the beginning of the year and you are responsible for making payroll deductions in the amount requested.

Warning

Once an employee designates how much to contribute to a medical FSA for a year, the entire amount must be immediately available. Your cash flow can be adversely affected if an employee incurs substantial medical care expenses early in the year, even though the money will eventually be contributed by the employee over the course of the year.

The most that can be contributed to a medical FSA or a dependent care FSA is $5,000.

Medical Savings Accounts. Congress recently created a new type of FSA called a medical savings account. At present, these MSAs are part of a four-year demonstration project that begins in 1997 and ends in 2000, unless Congress renews it. It's limited to the first 750,000 people who sign up and is open only to the self-employed and to businesses with fewer than 50 workers.

How MSAs work. A business may offer its employees, or a self-employed person may purchase, a high-deductible health insurance plan (often referred to as a catastrophic health plan). The deductible must be a minimum of $1,500 for individual coverage and $3,000 for family coverage, and can be as high as $2,250 for an individual and $4,500 for a family. The employer and employee may then make tax-free contributions to an MSA. Total annual contributions are limited to 65 percent of the deductible for individuals and 75 percent of the deductible for families.

Contributions. Contributions to the account by an individual are deductible from gross income, and contributions that you make are excluded from income (unless made through a cafeteria plan, which is a plan that offers employees the choice to select from a variety of benefits). Contributions may be made for a tax year at any time until the due date of the return for that year (not including extensions). Your contributions must be reported on the employee's W-2. Earnings of the fund are not included in taxable income for the current year.

Withdrawals. Funds may be withdrawn from an MSA, tax-free, to pay for medical expenses, including routine checkups, dental exams, eyeglasses, drugs, even minor surgery. Any funds left in the MSA at the end of the year remain in the account, and can be used in succeeding years, or saved until retirement. Thus, unlike an FSA, there is no "use it or lose it" requirement.

If you have few medical expenses over a period of years, the account may grow to a tidy sum. If funds are withdrawn for non-medical purposes, a 15 percent penalty will be assessed (and the funds will be taxed as ordinary income). However, after age 65, you may use your MSA money for any purpose, just like an IRA, and pay only the regular income tax on withdrawn funds.

In addition to the federal trial program, a number of states permit employers to establish MSAs that are exempt from state taxes.

Disability Benefits

Disability benefits are payments that guarantee income when an employee can't work because of sickness or accident. Disability benefits include paid sick leave (see page 209), short-term disability insurance, and long-term disability insurance. If you decide to provide disability benefits and purchase an insurance policy to provide the benefits, the plan will probably be subject to ERISA.

Short-term disability insurance provides income to employees who become disabled due to sickness or accident. The benefits generally become available after an employee has been absent from work for a short waiting period (usually one to seven days). Benefits continue for the time period specified in the insurance contract. The current industry standard is 26 weeks. Typically, the benefits replace between one-half and two-thirds of an employee's income.

Did You Know?

Amounts received by an employee will be taxable income to the extent that they're attributable to contributions you made that weren't included in the employee's taxable income. Benefits that you pay directly are also included in the employee's taxable income.

Long-term disability policies take up where short-term policies leave off, covering employees who are disabled and unable to work for longer periods of time. Disability payments, which typically amount to 50 to 60 percent of pay, continue for the duration of the disability to retirement age or for a specified number of months. The contracts that provide for disability payments generally define "disability" in one of two ways: the inability to perform the tasks of one's own occupation, or the tasks of any occupation at all. Some plans, for example, may use the former definition for the first 24 months and the latter definition thereafter.

Life Insurance

According to a government survey of small businesses (fewer than 100 employees), 61 percent of employees participated in employer-provided life insurance plans. Group-term life insurance is the most commonly offered form of benefit. Under a group-term policy, an employer typically purchases term life insurance coverage for all employees during the period that they're employed. Each employee is free to designate the beneficiary of the policy. By covering a large group, you can get lower rates and, perhaps, avoid individual medical exams. However, you can cover sub-groups of employees if the distinctions are based on marital status, length of service, compensation, job duties, or other work-related factors.

Premiums you pay for group-term life insurance are tax deductible. Your employees may exclude the premiums from income, except to the extent you pay premiums for coverage in excess of $50,000.

Other types of life insurance are also available, such as accidental death and dismemberment and business travel accident insurance. There are also life insurance policies that have substantial investment elements. As a small business owner, these aren't things you're likely to provide to employees, even if you purchase them for yourself.

Retirement Plans

More and more, employers are expecting their employees to take a more active role in planning for their retirement. Forty years ago, *defined benefit* plans were common. Under a defined benefit plan, an employer set aside however much money was required to fund a specific level of retirement pay for its employees.

Today, employers that offer retirement benefits are far more likely to have some type of *defined contribution* plan, which is somewhat less expensive and provides more flexibility. Defined contribution plans include a wide range of retirement savings arrangements.

Warning

Even with the move toward self-directed retirement savings, you'll *definitely* need professional advice and guidance to establish, fund, and administer any type of retirement arrangement. (A bank or mutual fund company will do the administrative work for you.) That alone should cause you to have serious reservations about providing retirement benefits. In fact, if you don't want or need a retirement plan to arrange for your own retirement, we would advise against retirement plans for most small business owners. There are many other less burdensome benefits that your employees may find more valuable, such as health insurance, time off, or, of course, higher pay.

If you're just looking to provide a low-cost, simple retirement plan for your employees, consider one of the following types of plans:

Profit-sharing plans are a popular type of plan, especially for small businesses. As an employer, you have the discretion to decide, each year, to contribute as little as nothing to as much as 15 percent of the total compensation of all plan participants. You don't have to contribute at all if you have a bad year and don't show a profit. For unincorporated businesses, profit-sharing plans are a subset of Keogh plans, and are available from a wide variety of banks and investment firms.

401(k) plans are probably the most popular type of plan with small businesses, with 20 percent of small business employees participating. A 401(k) plan permits participating employees to make contributions on a before-tax basis. You take deductions from the employees' pay in amounts that they specify and place the funds in a qualified retirement plan. In addition, you have the discretion to make supplemental contributions on behalf of your employees. The amount you can contribute is determined under complex limitations, but whatever you contribute is tax deductible.

Simplified Employee Pensions (SEPs). A simplified employee pension, or SEP, is the simplest, most efficient, and least expensive way for a small business to establish a qualified retirement plan for its owners and any employees. While not as flexible as Keogh plans, they are far easier to set up. They are also more flexible than SIMPLE plans, because you don't have to make contributions every year (for example, if your business didn't meet its profit targets or you simply don't want to contribute).

SEPs are essentially individual retirement accounts (or IRAs). One must be set up for each employee who is over 21, who has worked for you in at least three out of the last five years, and has received at least $400 from you in the current year. You then make contributions directly into the participants' accounts.

Save Time

In the interest of administrative simplicity, we advise you to have all employees set up IRAs with the same institution; for example, the bank that handles your business checking account. Once the contributions have been made, the individual employees can roll them over into other IRAs of their own choosing.

Generally, your SEP contributions must be made in an amount that is the same percentage of total compensation for every employee. Note that this requirement doesn't require you to use the same percentage every year (or even to contribute every year).

As a practical matter, you'll want to wait until you know how much money you have available for SEP contributions (usually after the books are closed at the end of the year) before determining the percentage. After you have determined the percentage and made the contributions, you must give written notice to each participant detailing your contributions to their SEPs, by the later of January 31 of the year following the year for which a contribution is made, or 30 days after the contribution is made.

The maximum contribution you can make to a SEP in a given year is the lower of 15 percent of an employee's pay or $30,000.

As the owner, the limits for your own contributions are slightly lower. You will have to reduce the contribution rate called for in your plan by using the Self-Employed Person's Rate Table found in IRS Publication 560 (you can get a free copy by calling 1-800-TAX-FORM). Under the Rate Table, if, for example, you chose to contribute the maximum 15 percent for each employee, your own contribution is limited to 13.0435 percent of your compensation.

SIMPLE plans are new for 1997. Employers with 100 or fewer employees can now set up a savings incentive match plan. SIMPLE plans trade lower annual contributions for ease of administration.

Your obligation under a SIMPLE plan is to either match each employee's contribution up to 3 percent of pay, or make a 2 percent contribution for all employees, including those not in the plan. Employee contributions are limited to $6,000. Employees acquire a vested interest in your contributions at the time they are made.

Other options. Although there are other types of retirement plans, many, even most, impose restrictions and requirements that the average small business owner is likely to find uncomfortable and burdensome. Nevertheless, if none of the options we've mentioned appeals to you, by all means follow up with a financial planner or other advisor. You should also seek advice if you're interested in using retirement plans as a selective tool to compensate valuable employees. Nonqualified deferred compensation plans offer many options for compensating and retaining special employees.

If you establish a plan, find out about your responsibilities. Even with a plan administrator, you'll have to deal with a few issues like payroll deductions and employee eligibility. But even with respect to the duties undertaken by the administrator, you, as the employer, bear ultimate responsibility for seeing that things are done right.

BENEFIT PROVIDERS AND ADMINISTRATORS

If you offer benefits that involve insurance or investments, plan on spending some time finding both a benefit provider and a benefit administrator. Start by talking to other employers or knowledgeable friends, checking with your insurance agent and other advisors, and looking in the phone book. People are generally happy to share either very good or very bad experiences that they've had. You can also hire a consultant to do the leg work for you, but it can be expensive. You'll have to decide whether you'd rather commit time or money to finding the right benefit provider and administrator.

Benefit Providers

Most benefits that you can offer are likely to be available from more than one source. For example, if you want to offer health insurance, you can check with insurance companies and also with managed care organizations such as HMOs. If you want to offer a retirement plan, you can talk with banks, brokerage firms, or institutional investment firms. The products and services that each offers will generally differ to some extent, but don't exclude any possibilities.

In some communities, there are local, non-profit groups that get small businesses to join together in order to offer them health care at more competitive rates. These purchasing alliances aggregate the employees of a number of businesses in order to increase the size of the risk pool. Check the phone directory in the state government listings or ask the chamber of commerce. Some states permit small businesses to participate in multiple employer welfare arrangements, which are self-funded group health insurance plans. Check with your state department of insurance to see if this is an option.

Once you've identified likely prospects, prepare the information you'll need *before* contacting benefit providers.

Example

If you plan to offer some type of health insurance plan, you'll need demographic data or census information regarding your employees. This involves compiling a list of employees, their birth dates, Social Security numbers, gender, marital status, and addresses. Make sure that anyone you talk to agrees to use this information solely for underwriting purposes, and not for any kind of solicitations.

Also think of what questions you need answered to help you select the best benefit provider. For example, if you're looking for a health plan, ask for a list of participating physicians and medical facilities and statistics on patient satisfaction. You'll also want to know about premiums, and what types of benefits will be provided. Get a copy of any policy that you're interested in to review on your own. If you're looking at retirement plans, ask about the financial performance of the underlying investment vehicles.

If you're uncomfortable with this, don't hesitate to talk to your attorney, insurance agent, broker, or other advisor first. Exercise the same care that you use any time that you enter into a contractual arrangement on behalf of your business. Providing benefits is an expensive proposition to begin with, and you don't want a bad deal or miscommunication to make it even more costly.

Benefit Administrators

Consulting firms, banks, investment brokers, payroll service companies, and insurance companies are among those competing to provide businesses with administrative services for a fee. As a small business owner, this is great news. Compliance, recordkeeping, and reporting rules all eat into your time. The rules are frequently arcane and written in language that can politely be described as "tortured." Plan administration can be frustrating for a small business owner who has other things to deal with, like running a business.

Given the large number of businesses competing to be your administrator, it can be relatively easy to find one that can handle your needs. One way to proceed is to start with the company from whom you buy the plan. For example, an insurance company or investment company will generally administer an insurance plan or manage your pension investments for a small additional charge.

If you outsource the administration of your benefit programs, find a reputable administrator and monitor its performance over time. This involves clearly defining your needs and getting comparable estimates from a number of sources. You may also want to select specific performance criteria that the administrator must meet, such as how quickly claims are to be paid.

Work Smart

Plan administration is becoming increasingly computerized. Select an administrator whose system is easy to understand and is capable of providing the information you need to track the administrator's timeliness and accuracy in administering benefits for your employees.

YOU AND ERISA

The Employment Retirement Income Security Act is a federal law that affects the administrative aspects of employee benefit and retirement plans. While your plan administrator or insurance company may handle most of your ERISA compliance obligations, it's important to know what's required of you as an employer.

Warning

ERISA applies to any plan, program, or fund maintained by an employer to provide: medical, surgical, or hospital care; benefits for sickness, accident, disability, or death; unemployment benefits; vacation benefits; apprenticeship and training programs; day care centers; scholarship funds; prepaid legal services; holiday or severance pay; or retirement plans.

ERISA compliance involves reporting, disclosure, and paying claims. Plan administrators must file information returns, including summary plan descriptions, with the Department of Labor and the IRS. They also must share plan information with plan participants, and the DOL, if it requests it. And every benefit plan must establish a procedure to process claims for benefits. A participant whose claim is denied must be provided information regarding the denial.

If you have a plan subject to ERISA, you'll be responsible for informing employees of the plan's terms and enrolling eligible employees. If you have a welfare plan, such as an HMO or other health insurance contract, you'll have to distribute plan information to employees. If you have a retirement plan, you'll also have to deal with payroll deductions; plan distributions; rollovers; recordkeeping, reporting, and disclosure requirements; plan loans; and other issues.

Warning

If an employee participating in a plan subject to ERISA gets divorced, you may get a court order requiring you to take action if either: (1) the employee is ordered to provide medical benefits for a child living with the former spouse, or (2) part or all of an employee's retirement benefits are ordered to be paid to someone other than the employee. If you receive notice of this type of action, consult your attorney.

What You'll Have To Do

Even if you contract with an administrator, you'll still be faced with some tasks that you'll have to do yourself. These include:

- **Enrolling employees and making changes as required:** You can automatically include someone in your plan when eligibility requirements are met, or provide the employee with information about plan options. Changes in family status or work status can require additional work.

Work Smart

If your employees are going to be paying for some or all of the cost of benefits, it might be a good idea to give them the option to choose not to participate in the benefit plan. If someone chooses not to participate, ask for written confirmation so it can't be alleged later that you didn't allow access to the benefit plan.

- **Deducting premiums from employee wages and remitting them:** Your payroll process must be flexible enough to accommodate accurate deductions and prompt submission of funds to the benefit provider.

- **Acting as liaison between the benefit provider and your employees:** The routine part of this involves tasks like making sure employees have claims forms and complying with disclosure requirements. The other part occurs when employees have difficulty getting claims paid or have some other problem with the plan. Try to get your employees to contact the customer service department of the benefit provider or administrator before coming to you.

- **Terminating benefits and offering COBRA coverage:** When an employee is terminated or leaves, you'll have to take the steps necessary to terminate coverage. If you have at least 20 employees and the plan provides health benefits, COBRA requires you to offer the ex-employee the option to continue participating for a limited period, at his or her own expense.

- **Complying with disclosure and reporting requirements:** These can vary tremendously depending on the type of benefits involved and the number of employees that you have.

- **Plan transactions:** As employees come and go and their financial situations change, you'll be dealing with rollover contributions and plan loans, distributions, and terminations.

Chapter 12

Your Payroll
Tax Obligations

Federal, state, and, perhaps, local taxing authorities all expect you to meet your payroll obligations. And they don't like to be kept waiting. Fortunately, the people who collect the taxes are very helpful and efficient in helping you pay the taxes you owe. The key to keeping your payroll tax obligations under control is to make all required tax payments when they're due. That way, you're just paying taxes, and not costly penalties and interest.

WHAT ARE YOUR PAYROLL TAXES?

The difference between an employee's pay rate and the amount of money that you actually pay the employee each pay period can be fairly substantial. Taxing agencies, such as the IRS and your state's department of revenue, require you to withhold taxes owed by your employee on a "pay-as-you-go" basis. You also have an obligation to deposit the amounts you withhold on time with the appropriate authority. Although withheld taxes represent amounts owed by your employees, *you* are personally liable for those taxes if the government doesn't receive them.

In addition to your obligation to collect and remit the payroll taxes that your employees owe, you have a further obligation to pay your share of certain taxes on your employees' pay. Together, those taxes that you're required to withhold and those that you're required to pay comprise your payroll taxes.

Income Tax Withholding

Whenever you pay wages or other compensation to an employee, the IRS will expect you to collect a portion of the employee's federal income tax on the payment through withholding. In most states, you also have an obligation to withhold state or local income taxes.

Calculating the amount to withhold is fairly straightforward. The IRS and state tax agencies have reduced the rules to simple tax tables that you can use in most cases. The tables show you how much you have to withhold on a payment, given the employee's marital status, your payroll period, and the number of withholding exemptions the employee claims. The tables are included in the IRS's free publication, *Circular E, Employer's Tax Guide*, available by calling 1-800-TAX-FORM.

State Income Taxes

Every state with a personal income tax requires employers to withhold the tax from employees' wages. Nine states don't impose a personal income tax: Alaska, Florida, Nevada, New Hampshire, South Dakota, Tennessee, Texas, Washington, and Wyoming. The listing below provides general information about each state's income tax withholding requirements and identifies the state agency that administers each state's income tax system.

State Income Tax Withholding Requirements

State Agency	Income Tax Withholding Required on:
AL Dept. of Revenue 334-242-1000	Wages paid to residents for services wherever performed and to nonresidents for services performed in Alabama.
AZ Dept. of Revenue 602-255-3381	Wages paid for services performed in Arizona, without regard to the employee's state of residency.
AR Dept. of Finance & Administration 501-682-7290	Wages paid to residents and to nonresidents to the extent paid for services performed in the state.
CA Employment Development Dept. 916-654-8203	Wages paid to residents for services wherever performed and wages paid to nonresidents for services performed in the state.
CO Dept. of Revenue 303-232-2416	Wages paid to residents for services wherever and wages paid to nonresidents for services performed in the state.
CT Dept. of Revenue Services 203-566-8520	Wages paid to residents and nonresidents for services where ever performed. Wages paid to nonresidents who file an exemption certificate only for services performed within the state.

State Agency	Income Tax Withholding Required on:
DE Div. of Revenue 302-577-3300	Wages paid to residents for services wherever performed and wages paid to nonresident for services performed in the state.
DC Dept. of Finance & Revenue 202-727-6104	Wages paid to residents for services performed wherever performed. No withholding on wages paid to nonresidents.
GA Dept. of Revenue 404-656-4181	Wages paid to residents for services wherever performed, and wages paid to nonresidents for services within the state. No withholding on residents working in another state if the employer must withhold and pay income tax to that state.
HI Dept. of Taxation 808-587-4242	Wages paid to residents and nonresidents for services wherever performed. No withholding on wages for services outside the state paid to nonresidents who file statements verifying their nonresidency.
ID State Tax Commission 208-334-7660	Wages paid to residents and nonresidents for services performed within the state. Withholding not required on residents who work outside the state.
IL Dept. of Revenue 217-782-3336	Compensation paid in Illinois to resident and nonresident employees.
IN Dept. of Revenue 317-233-4016	Wages paid to residents for services wherever performed and wages paid to nonresidents for services performed in the state.
IA Dept. of Revenue and Finance 515-281-3114	Wages paid to residents for services wherever performed and wages paid to nonresidents for services performed in the state. Wages of residents subject to another state's withholding tax, only to the extent Iowa tax exceeds the other state's withholding tax on the same wages.
KS Dept. of Revenue 913-296-0222	Wages paid to residents for services wherever performed and wages paid to nonresidents for services performed in the state.
KY Revenue Cabinet 502-564-4580	Wages paid to residents for services wherever performed and wages paid to nonresidents for services performed in the state.
LA Secretary of Revenue 504-925-4611	Wages paid to residents for services wherever performed and wages paid to nonresidents for services performed in the state. No withholding from a resident's wages if the wages have been subjected to another state's income tax withholding.
ME Bureau of Taxation 207-287-3695	Wages paid to residents for services wherever performed and wages paid to nonresidents for services performed in the state.
MD Comptroller of the Treasury 410-974-3981	Wages paid to residents for services wherever performed and wages paid to nonresidents for services performed in the state.
MA Dept. of Revenue 617-727-4545	Wages paid to residents for services wherever performed and wages paid to nonresidents for services performed in the state. No withholding from a resident's wages if the wages have been subjected to another state's income tax withholding.
MI Dept. of Treasury 800-487-7000	Wages paid to residents for services wherever performed and wages paid to nonresidents for services performed in the state.

State Agency	Income Tax Withholding Required on:
MN Dept. of Revenue 612-296-6181	Wages paid to residents for services wherever performed and wages paid to nonresidents for services performed in the state.
MS State Tax Commission 601-359-1141	Wages paid to residents for services wherever performed and wages paid to nonresidents for services performed in the state. No withholding from a resident employee whose wages have been subjected to another state's income tax withholding.
MO Dept. of Revenue 573-751-5752	Wages paid to residents for services wherever performed and wages paid to nonresidents for services performed in the state. No withholding from a resident's wages if at least 50% of the employee's services are performed in another state that imposes a tax on the employee's wages.
MT Dept. of Revenue 406-444-3388	Wages paid to residents for services wherever performed and wages paid to nonresidents for services performed in the state.
NE Dept. of Revenue 800-742-7474	Wages paid to residents for services wherever performed and wages paid to nonresidents for services performed in the state. No withholding from a resident's wages if the wages have been subjected to another state's income tax withholding.
NJ Dept. of Treasury 609-588-2200	Wages paid to residents for services wherever performed and wages paid to nonresidents for services performed in the state. Wages of residents who perform all their services outside the state only to the extent New Jersey tax exceeds the other state's withholding tax on the same wages.
NM Revenue Processing Div. 505-827-0832	Wages paid to residents for services wherever performed and wages paid to nonresidents for services performed in the state.
NY Dept. of Taxation & Finance 518-438-8581	Wages paid to residents for services wherever performed and wages paid to nonresidents for services performed in the state. Wages of residents subject to another state's withholding tax, only to the extent New York tax exceeds the other state's withholding tax on the same wages.
NC Dept. of Revenue 919-733-4626	Wages paid to residents for services wherever performed and wages paid to nonresidents for services performed in the state. No withholding from a resident's wages if the wages have been subjected to another state's income tax withholding.
ND State Tax Commissioner 701-328-3124	Wages paid to residents and nonresidents for services performed in the state.
OH Dept. of Taxation 614-846-6712	Wages paid to residents for services wherever performed and wages paid to nonresidents for services performed in the state.
OK Tax Commission 405-521-3155	Wages paid to residents for services wherever performed and wages paid to nonresidents for services performed in the state. No withholding from a resident's wages if the wages are earned in another state that requires withholding.
OR Dept. of Revenue 503-378-3390	Wages paid to residents for services wherever performed and wages paid to nonresidents for services performed in the state.

State Agency	Income Tax Withholding Required on:
PA Dept. of Revenue 717-787-8201	Wages paid to residents for services wherever performed and wages paid to nonresidents for services performed in the state. No withholding from wages of residents who perform all their services in another state that imposes a withholding tax on their wages.
PR Dept. of Treasury 809-721-2020	Wages paid to residents and nonresidents for services performed in Puerto Rico.
RI Division of Taxation 401-277-2905	Wages paid to residents for services wherever performed and wages paid to nonresidents for services performed in the state. Wages of residents subject to another state's withholding tax, only to the extent Rhode Island tax exceeds the other state's withholding tax on the same wages.
SC Dept. of Revenue & Taxation 803-737-4752	Wages paid to residents for services wherever performed and wages paid to nonresidents for services performed in the state. No withholding from a resident's wages if they're earned in another state that requires withholding.
UT State Tax Commission 801-297-2200	Wages paid to residents for services wherever performed and wages paid to nonresidents for services performed in the state. Wages of residents subject to another state's withholding tax, only to the extent Utah tax exceeds the other state's withholding tax on the wages.
VT Dept. of Taxation 802-828-2551	Wages paid to residents for services wherever performed and wages paid to nonresidents for services performed in the state.
VA Dept. of Taxation 804-367-8038	Wages paid to residents for services wherever performed and wages paid to nonresidents for services performed in the state.
WV State Tax Dept. 304-558-3333	Wages paid to resident's for services wherever performed and wages paid to nonresidents for services performed in the state.
WI Dept. of Revenue 608-266-2776	Wages paid to residents for services wherever performed and wages paid to nonresidents for services performed in the state.

If you have employees who live out of state, the situation is a bit more complicated. Some states require you to withhold state income tax from your employee's income, regardless of where the employee lives. This presents a problem for nonresident employees, who may be required to file for an income tax refund from the state of employment, and owe substantial tax to the state of residence.

To sidestep this problem, some states have entered into "reciprocal agreements" with other states that exempt employers of out-of-state employees from withholding. Under these agreements, you withhold state B taxes from the wages of an employee who is a resident of state B, and remit those taxes to state B, even though your business is in state A. Arizona has no reciprocal agreements in effect, but allows residents of California, District of Columbia, Indiana, Oregon, and Virginia who perform services for an Arizona employer to claim an exemption from withholding if they can claim a credit against Arizona tax for income taxes paid to the state of residency.

States With Reciprocal Agreements

State	Agreements with:	State	Agreements with:
DC	MD	MT	ND
IL	IN, IA, KY, MI, WI	NJ	PA
IN	IL, KY, MI, OH, PA, WI	ND	MN, MT
IA	IL	OH	IN, KY, MI, PA, WV
KY	IL, IN, MI, OH, VA, WV, WI	PA	IN, MD, NJ, OH, VA, WV
MD	DC, PA, VA, WV	VA	DC, KY, PA, WV
MI	IL, IN, KY, MN, OH, WI	WV	KY, MD, OH, PA, VA
MN	MI, ND, WI	WI	IL, IN, KY, MI, MN

Local Taxes

In a few states, cities, counties, and other local governmental units impose their own income tax. If you happen to do business in one of these localities, you may very well have an additional income tax withholding obligation. Apart from local income taxes, you may also find yourself paying local taxes measured by your total payroll (payroll expense taxes) or withholding local occupational fees from your employees' wages.

Local Taxing Jurisdictions

State	Local Tax Jurisdictions
CA	Los Angeles (employer payroll expense tax); San Francisco (employer payroll expense tax)
CO	Aurora (employee occupational privilege tax); Denver (employee occupational privilege tax); Greenwood Village (employee occupational privilege tax)
DE	Wilmington (employee earned income tax; employer business licensing tax)
IL	Chicago (employer expense tax on employers having at least 50 employees)
IN	Most counties impose local income taxes that must be withheld from employees' wages.
KY	Numerous cities and counties impose an occupational license fee that must be withheld from employees' wages.
MI	Numerous cities impose a uniform city income tax that must be withheld from employees' wages.
MO	Kansas City (employees earnings tax); St. Louis (employer payroll expense tax and employees earnings tax)
NJ	Newark (employer payroll tax)
NY	New York City (employee income tax); Yonkers (employee income tax)
OH	Numerous cities impose local income taxes that must be withheld from employees' wages.

State	Local Tax Jurisdictions
OR	Lane County Mass Transit District (employer excise tax); Tri-County Metropolitan Transportation District (employer excise tax)
PA	Numerous cities and boroughs impose local income taxes that must be withheld from employees' wages.

Calculating the Withholding Amount

Your obligation to withhold federal income tax from employees' wages applies to each wage payment that you make. The total tax you withhold from a particular employee's wages over the course of a year should approximate that employee's year-end tax liability.

The amount you must withhold from each employee's wages is determined by the frequency of your payroll period, the employee's marital status, the number of withholding exemptions the employee claims, and the size of the wage payment. You can quickly determine your withholding amounts with easy-to-use IRS tables.

Standard tables. There are two basic types of withholding tables, either of which will likely meet your needs. Tables are available for eight different payroll periods (see page 178). You can use the *wage-bracket tables*, which indicates the amount to withhold based on payroll period and the employee's marital status. You simply find the wage bracket within which the employee's wages fall, and then read the column that reflects the number of withholding exemptions the employee has claimed to find how much you must withhold.

The other standard IRS withholding tables are *percentage method tables*. Use the applicable table for your payroll period and the employee's marital status to find the wage bracket within which the employee's adjusted wages fall. The withholding tax is shown in the table as a dollar amount plus a percentage of the portion of the wages that exceeds the minimum bracket amount.

Alternative methods. There are other methods that you can use to determine how much to withhold. We suggest that you consult with your accountant or other tax professional before employing any of these alternative methods, because of their complexity.

Warning

Keep in mind that no matter what method you select to determine your withholding taxes, you have no discretion to withhold less than the amount of tax prescribed by that method. Nor, as a general rule, may you withhold more than the prescribed amount, unless an employee requests that you do so.

State income taxes. Most states allow employers to use methods that are similar to those used for federal tax purposes in determining their state income tax withholding amounts. With the exception of Arizona and North Dakota, where the state withholding amount is a fixed percentage of the federal withholding amount, and Pennsylvania, where the state withholding amount is a fixed percentage of an employee's gross wages, all of the states provide wage-bracket tables as one of the alternatives for computing state withholding amounts.

Claiming Withholding Exemptions

When your employees prepare their annual tax returns, gross income is reduced by the personal exemptions they can claim. The amounts you withhold reflect this. The more withholding exemptions an employee claims, the less tax you'll be required to withhold.

Form W-4. Your employees claim their withholding exemptions by filing with you federal Form W-4, Employees' Withholding Allowance Certificate. If you don't have a valid W-4 on file for an employee, treat the employee as being single with no exemptions for withholding purposes. It's good practice to remind your employees at the beginning of each year that they should file amended W-4s if their eligibility for claiming withholding exemptions has changed since the filing of their last certificates.

On their W-4, your employees may claim withholding exemptions for themselves, their spouses, and each individual they claim as a dependent on their tax return. In addition, employees who expect to claim large amounts of itemized deductions on their return may be entitled to additional withholding exemptions. Form W-4 includes a worksheet that employees use to determine their eligibility for, and the number of, additional withholding exemptions.

Although your employees may not claim more withholding exemptions than they're entitled to claim, they needn't claim all the exemptions to which they're entitled. Furthermore, employees can request on their W-4 that you withhold additional dollar amounts from their wages. As long as these additional amounts don't exceed the employees' wages, you must comply with the requests.

An employee who anticipates having no federal income tax liability for a year may claim a complete exemption from withholding on Form W-4. This exemption fully relieves you from any obligation to withhold federal income taxes (but not FICA taxes) from the employee's wages. The exemption from withholding lasts only to February 15 of the following year, unless the employee files a new W-4 that renews the exemption claim.

You have no obligation to confirm that your employees are entitled to the withholding exemptions they claim. However, if you learn that an employee has improperly claimed exemptions, you must inform the employee that the W-4 is invalid, request a new W-4, and send the invalid W-4 to the IRS. You should not apply any withholding exemptions that an employee claims on an invalid W-4.

You must also send to the IRS copies of any W-4 on which an employee claims more than 10 withholding exemptions or on which an employee earning more than $200 a week claims complete exemption from withholding.

State exemption certificates. Most states have their own exemption certificate form that serves the equivalent function of the federal Form W-4.

Advance Payment of the Earned Income Credit

Most employees whose family income is less than $25,760 in 1997 and who support a dependent child are eligible for the earned income credit (EIC) against their federal taxes. The IRS permits this credit to be paid in advance, over the course of the year rather than through a tax refund at the end of the year.

How does this affect you? You, the employer, must pay the employee a portion of the credit amount in each of his or her paychecks. The IRS "reimburses" you for the amount of advance EIC you pay, by allowing you to deduct it from the employment taxes you would otherwise have to send to the IRS.

You must make these payments if the employee so requests by giving you a completed IRS Form W-5, Earned Income Credit Advance Payment Certificate. The employee must fill out a new W-5 each year in order to get the advance payments. Also, you must notify the employees that the advance credit is available. The easiest way to do this is by giving the employee the official IRS W-2 form, which includes a notice about advance EIC payments on the back of Copy C.

Directions for figuring out the amount of an employee's EIC that must be added back to the paycheck are included in IRS Publication 15, Employer's Tax Guide, which also contains a more detailed explanation of the EIC.

Social Security and Medicare (FICA) Taxes

The Federal Insurance Contributions Act is a federal law that requires you to *withhold* two separate taxes from the wages you pay your employees: a Social Security tax and a Medicare tax. The law also requires you to *personally pay* an employer portion of these taxes. Unless you have employees who receive tips, your employer portion will be the same as the amount that you're required to withhold from your employees' wages.

Each of the FICA taxes is imposed at a single flat rate. The 1997 Social Security tax rate is 6.2 percent and the Medicare tax rate is 1.45 percent. The taxes are unaffected by the number of income tax withholding exemptions an employee claims. You merely multiply an employee's gross wage payment by the applicable tax rate to determine how much to withhold and how much you must pay.

The Social Security tax is subject to an annual ceiling, which is adjusted annually for inflation. For 1997, your obligation to withhold and to pay Social Security tax for an employee ends once you've paid that employee total wages of $65,400. There is no ceiling on the Medicare tax.

Example

Let's assume you have one employee, to whom you pay gross wages of $500 every two weeks. In 1997, you must withhold from each paycheck $31.00 in Social Security taxes ($500 x 6.2%) and $7.25 in Medicare taxes ($500 x 1.45%). You will also owe equal amounts as your employer portion of the taxes. In other words, each $500 wage payment will create a combined FICA tax liability of $76.50.

Unemployment Taxes

In most cases, once you decide to employ your own workers, you become responsible for paying taxes to fund your state's unemployment insurance program. Because the federal government has retained some say in how each state operates its own program, you probably won't be too shocked to learn that you generally must pay both federal and state unemployment taxes. Fortunately, there is a credit mechanism that limits the overall amount you have to pay.

Federal Unemployment Taxes

The Federal Unemployment Tax Act obliges all employers to pay a federal unemployment tax. You pay this tax yourself; you don't withhold FUTA tax from an employee's wages.

Liability for tax. You must pay the FUTA tax if, during the current or the preceding calendar year, you pay wages totaling at least $1,500 to your employees in any calendar quarter, or you have at least one employee on any given day in each of 20 different calendar weeks (the 20 weeks need not be consecutive and the "one employee" need not be the same individual). Once you meet either of the tests, you become liable for the FUTA tax for the entire calendar year and for the next calendar year as well.

Computing the tax. The FUTA tax is imposed at a single flat rate on the first $7,000 of wages that you pay each employee. Once you've paid an employee that amount in a year, you have no further FUTA liability for that employee for the year. For 1997, the FUTA tax rate is 6.2 percent. However, you can generally claim credits against your gross FUTA tax for a portion of the state unemployment taxes you pay. These credits can effectively reduce the FUTA tax rate to as little as 0.8 percent.

State Unemployment Taxes

Each state operates its own unemployment compensation program that is funded largely by taxes on employers. So, if you have employees, expect to pay some state unemployment taxes. Because you're personally liable for the taxes, you don't withhold the taxes from your employees' wages. Two states also require employees to pay unemployment taxes (Alaska: 0.5% to 1.0%; Pennsylvania: 0.11%), and you have an obligation to withhold those taxes.

Liability for tax. In most states, if you're subject to the federal unemployment tax, you're automatically subject to the state tax. In the remaining states, broader tests for taxability are applied. So, if you happen to be in one of those states, you might end up paying state unemployment taxes even though you're not obligated to pay the federal tax.

Computing the tax. Calculating what you owe in state unemployment taxes is simply a matter of multiplying the wages you pay each of your employees by the applicable tax rate. However, every state limits the tax you must pay with respect to any one employee by specifying a maximum wage amount to which the tax applies. In general, you'll have to pay state unemployment tax regardless of the employee's state of residence.

Experience rating. Every state uses an experience-rating system of some kind to determine each employer's tax rate for the year. The goal is to assign lower tax rates to employers whose workers suffer the least involuntary unemployment and higher rates to employers whose workers suffer the most involuntary unemployment. New employers pay tax at a fixed rate until they've contributed to the unemployment compensation program for a specified period of time (generally one to three years) and established "experience."

Save Money

Minimizing the number of unemployment insurance claims filed by former employees can produce significant payroll tax savings. Monitor all unemployment insurance claims made against your account and be prepared to contest any claims you believe to be improper.

The listing below provides general information about each state's unemployment tax, including the name and phone number of the agency that administers the tax, range of tax rates, rate applicable to businesses with no experience rating, and the maximum wage amount subject to tax.

State Laws on Unemployment Compensation

State Agency	Tax Rates and Taxable Wage Limit
AL Dept. of Industrial Relations 334-242-8025	0.14%—5.4%; 2.7% (no experience) $8,000
AK Dept. of Labor 907-465-2757	0%—6.5%; industry based (no experience) $24,200
AZ Dept. of Economic Security 602-255-4755	0.1%—5.4% (no maximum); 2.7% (no experience) $7,000
AR Director of Labor 501-682-3274	0.5%—6.4%; 3.3% (no experience) $9,000
CA Employment Development Dept. 916-427-4066	1.1%—5.4%; 3.4% (no experience) $7,000
CO Dept. of Labor and Employment 303-866-6045	0%—5.4%; higher of 2.7% or industry average (no experience for construction industry only) $10,000
CT Employment Security Div. 203-566-4288	2%—6.9%; 4.9% (no experience) $12,000
DE Dept. of Labor 302-368-6745	0.8%—8.7%; average of all employers (no experience for other than construction industry) $8,500
DC Unemployment Compensation Board 202-639-2000	1.6%—7.0%; 3% (no experience) $10,000
FL Dept. of Labor & Employment Security 904-488-6093	0.2%—5.4%; 2.7% (no experience) (1996) $7,000 (1996)
GA Dept. of Labor 404-656-3017	0.05%—6.75%; 2.7% (no experience) $8,500
HI Bureau of Employment Security 808-586-8946	0.2%—5.4%; 3% (no experience) $26,000

State Agency	Tax Rates and Taxable Wage Limit
ID Dept. of Employment 208-334-6100	0.5%—5.4%; 2.5% (no experience) $22,800
IL Dept. of Employment Security 312-793-4880	0.2%—8.2%; higher of 2.7% or industry based(no experience) $9,000
IN Dept. of Employment & Training Services 317-232-7670	0.2%—5.5%; 2.7% (no experience) $7,000
IA Dept. of Job Service 515-281-5387	0%—7%; 1% (no experience) $15,200
KS Div. Of Employment Security 913-296-5025	0%—6.0%; 1%, unless reserve fund ratio is less than 2%, then 2% (no experience) $8,000
KY Unemployment Insurance Commission 502-564-2900	0.3%—6%; 3% (no experience) $8,000
LA Office of Employment Security 504-342-3111	0.3%—6.01%; industry based if no experience $7,700
ME Dept. of Labor 207-289-3176	2.3%—7.4%; 4.2% (no experience) $7,000
MD Dept. of Economic & Employment Development 410-333-5600	0.3%—7.4%; industry based if no experience $8,500
MA Dept. of Employment & Training 617-626-5075	0.6%—8.1%; 3% (no experience) (1996) $10,800
MI Employment Security Commission 800-638-3994 (in MI), 313-876-5623	0%—10%; 2.7% (no experience) $9,500
MN Dept. of Economic Security 612-296-6141	0.2%—9.1%; higher of 1% or 5-year state average (subject to 5.4% maximum) if no experience $16,300
MS Employment Security Commission 601-354-8711	0.1%—5.4%; 2.7% (no experience) $7,000
MO Dept. of Labor & Industrial Relations 314-751-3215	0%—7.8%; industry based if no experience (2.7% minimum) $8,000
MT Dept. of Labor & Industry 406-444-3834	0.2%—6.5%; industry based if no experience $16,000
NE Commissioner of Labor 402-471-9000	0.1%—5.4%; 3.5% (no experience) $7,000
NV Employment Security Dept. 702-687-4650	0.25%—5.4%; 2.95% (no experience) $17,200
NH Dept. of Employment Security 603-224-3311	0.1%—6.5%; 2.7% (no experience) $8,000

State Agency	Tax Rates and Taxable Wage Limit
NJ Division of Unemployment & Temporary Disability Insurance 609-292-9626	0.5%—5.8%; 2.8% (no experience) $18,600
NM Employment Security Dept. 505-841-8437	0.3%—5.4%; 2.7% (no experience) $14,200
NY Unemployment Insurance Division 518-457-5718	2.6%—7.1%; 4.4% (no experience) (1996) $7,000
NC Employment Security Commission 919-733-3098	0.1%—5.7%; 1.2% (no experience) $12,100
ND Job Service 701-328-2814	0.1%—5.4%; 2.8% (no experience for other than construction industry) $14,200
OH Bureau of Employment Services 614-466-2578	0.1%—6.5%; industry based if no experience $9,000
OK Employment Security Commission 405-557-7100	0.1%—5.5%; higher of 1% or average rate for second preceding year (no experience) $11,100
OR Dept. of Human Resources 503-378-3162	1%—5.4%; 3% (no experience) $20,000
PA Office of Employment Security 717-787-6868	1.5%—9.2%; 3.5% (no experience) $8,000
PR Bureau of Employment Security 809-754-5262	1.24%—5.4%; 2.7% (no experience) $7,000
RI Dept. of Employment & Training 401-277-3600	2.15%—8.25%; higher of 1% or state's 5-year benefit cost rate, not to exceed 4.2% (no experience) $17,600
SC Employment Security Commission 803-737-2400	1.24%—5.4%; 2.64% (no experience) $7,000
SD Dept. of Labor 605-626-2452	0%—8.5%; 1.2% (no experience) $7,000
TN Dept. of Employment Security 615-741-1948	0%—10%; 2.7% (no experience) $7,000
TX Employment Commission 512-463-2222	0.27%—6.27%; industry based if no experience $9,000
UT Dept. of Employment Security 801-536-7400	0.2%—8%; industry based if no experience $17,800
VT Dept. of Employment & Training 802-229-0311	0.4%—8.4%; 1.1% to 3.2% (no experience) $8,000
VA Employment Commission 800-242-4654 (in Va.); 804-786-1485	0.1%—6.2%; 2.5% (no experience) $8,000

State Agency	Tax Rates and Taxable Wage Limit
WA Employment Security Dept. 360-902-9500	0.36%—5.4%; industry based if no experience $21,300
WV Dept. of Employment Security 304-348-2630	0%—4.5%; 2.7% (no experience) $8,000
WI Unemployment Compensation Div. 608-266-6993	0.2%—9.75%; 3.6% (no experience) $10,500
WY Dept. of Employment 307-235-3200	0.35%—8.85%; industry based if no experience $12,200

Disability Insurance Taxes

If you run your business in one of the handful of states where there are state-mandated temporary disability insurance programs, you can probably add to your payroll tax obligations a duty to withhold and/or pay taxes that fund the state's program. Information about state disability insurance taxes is summarized in the following listing.

State Laws on Disability Insurance Taxes

State Agency	Tax Rates and Taxable Wage Limit
CA Employment Development Dept. 916-427-4066	Employer Tax Rate: None. Withholding Rate: 1%. Taxable Wage Limit: $31,767
HI Dept. of Labor & Industrial Relations 808-586-9188	Employer Tax Rate: None. Withholding Rate: 0.5%. Taxable Wage Limit: $593.94 (weekly)
NJ Div. Of Unemployment & Temporary Disability Insurance 609-292-9626	Employer Tax Rate: 0.1%—1.10%. Withholding Rate: 0.5%. Taxable Wage Limit: $18,000.
NY Worker's Compensation Board 212-348-9002	Employer Tax Rate: Minimum premium rates of 27 to 65 cents per employee for each $100 of covered payroll (limited to $340 per week per employee) Withholding Rate: 0.5%. Taxable Wage Limit: $6,000
PR Bureau of Employment Security 809-754-5262	Employer Tax Rate: 0.3%. Withholding Rate: 0.3%. Taxable Wage Limit: $9,000
RI Dept. of Employment Security 401-277-3600	Employer Tax Rate: None. Withholding Rate: 1.1%. Taxable Wage Limit: $38,000

WORKERS SUBJECT TO PAYROLL WITHHOLDING

In Chapter 2, we looked at the difference between employees and independent contractors. Your payroll tax obligations are directly affected by a worker's status. You must collect and remit taxes on the wages you pay to employees, even if they're minors, or work on a part-time or temporary basis. Workers who are independent contractors are responsible for paying their own payroll taxes.

You might be relieved of some payroll tax withholding obligations if your business isn't a corporation or partnership, and you employ:

- **Family members.** You don't have to pay FUTA taxes with respect to a spouse or parent who works as an employee of your business. For a child who works as an employee of your business, you're relieved from withholding and paying FICA taxes until the child reaches 18 and from paying FUTA taxes until the child reaches age 21.

- **Certain salespersons.** You may be relieved of all federal and most state payroll taxes for real estate agents and direct sellers, even if they are properly classified as being your employees. Direct sellers are persons who sell or solicit the sale of consumer products at a place of business, such as a home, that isn't a permanent retail establishment. You qualify for this relief if substantially all the compensation you pay is directly related to sales or other output, and the services are performed pursuant to written contracts specifying that they will not be treated as employees for payroll tax purposes.

- **Employees who don't expect to earn enough to incur income tax liability for the year.** You don't have to withhold income tax if an employee won't earn enough to have any income tax liability for the year.

Statutory Employees

If you have workers in certain occupations, you're required to withhold and pay certain payroll taxes under specified circumstances even if the workers aren't your employees. These so-called "statutory employees" are:

- **Agent-drivers and commission drivers who deliver specified products.** Agent-drivers and commission drivers are people who (1) operate their own trucks or the trucks of the persons for whom they perform services, (2) serve customers designated by their principals and customers they solicit on their own initiative, (3) make wholesale or retail sales; and (4) are paid commissions on their sales or earn the difference between what they charge their customers and what they pay their principals for the products or services they sell. Such drivers are statutory employees if they distribute beverages (other than milk) or meat, vegetable, fruit, or bakery products or if they pick up and deliver laundry or dry cleaning.

- **Traveling or city salespersons.** Your traveling or city salespersons are statutory employees if they send you orders from customers who are retailers, wholesalers, contractors, or operators of hotels, restaurants, or other businesses whose primary function is the furnishing of food or lodging. The orders must be for items that your customers will resell or will use as supplies in their business operations.

- **Homeworkers.** Homeworkers are individuals who perform work for you, generally on a contract or piecework basis and usually in their own homes or in the homes of others.

When you retain the services of statutory employees who are otherwise independent contractors, you aren't required to withhold income taxes from their compensation. However, you must withhold and pay FICA taxes and, in the case of drivers and salespersons, FUTA and state unemployment taxes, if each of the following conditions is satisfied:

- the service contract contemplates that the worker will personally perform substantially all of the work,

- the worker's investment in required equipment and property, other than for transportation, is insubstantial,

- the worker performs services for you on a regular or frequently recurring basis, and

- with respect to homeworkers, you've paid the workers $100 in cash wages during the year. Once you've reached that threshold, all wages paid during the year are subject to FICA taxes. This includes the initial $100.

Warning

Just to clarify, the "statutory employee" designation becomes relevant only if a worker isn't a common law employee. All the normal payroll tax obligations apply if a statutory employee is in fact a common law employee.

WHAT COMPENSATION IS TAXABLE?

Federal and state payroll tax laws generally identify taxable compensation as being an employee's wages and broadly define "wages" to encompass virtually every payment to an employee for services rendered. Whenever you transfer something of value to an employee as compensation for the employee's services, you've potentially made a taxable wage payment. You should assume that all compensation you pay to employees is taxable wages unless you're aware that the law exempts a given payment from taxation.

Payments for Future Services (Advances)

Payments you make to your employees for services they'll perform or complete in the future are taxable wages for payroll tax purposes. Advances aren't taxable wages if the employees are legally obligated to repay the advanced amounts. Advances to employees to cover expenses they'll incur in performing services for you aren't taxable wages if they're made under an accountable plan (see page 241).

Example

Assume you employ a salesperson and pay him on a monthly commission basis. Each week you advance him $200 against later-earned commissions. If the advances exceed commissions for the month, you carry the excess as an account due from future commissions. The salesperson has no obligation to repay that account if he quits while his account has an outstanding balance. Under these facts, the advances are taxable wages.

Gifts to Employees

Most gifts that you give to your employees are presumed to be compensatory in nature. Unless you can show that a gift is connected with an event that's totally unrelated to your business (for example, an employee's wedding), gifts to your employees are considered taxable wages for payroll tax purposes.

Christmas gifts. Christmas gifts aren't considered taxable wages if the gifts are items of property having nominal value (for example, a turkey or a ham). Small gifts of cash don't qualify for the exception.

Prizes and awards. Employee prizes and awards also are generally considered taxable wages, but a noncash prize or award isn't taxable if the value is no more than $400 and it's given to an employee as a length-of-service or safety-achievement award. If you give a noncash award to a retail commission salesperson whom you ordinarily pay only cash commissions, you can elect not to withhold federal income taxes with respect to the award. However, you'll remain responsible for FICA taxes, unemployment taxes, and possibly state income taxes on the award.

Business Expense Reimbursements

In general, unless you make advances and reimbursements under an accountable plan, they are included in taxable wages. An accountable plan is one that meets three requirements:

- The reimbursements must be for your deductible business expenses that are paid by an employee in the course of performing services for you.

- The employee must be required to substantiate the elements of amount, time, use, and business purpose.

- The employee must be required to return to you any excess of reimbursements over substantiated expenses within a reasonable period of time.

Fringe Benefits

The value of all fringe benefits *not specifically excluded* by the tax laws are considered taxable wages for payroll tax purposes, and you may have to withhold and pay the taxes on the basis of the fringe benefits' fair market value.

However, the law does include a rather lengthy list of fringe benefits that you can provide your employees without incurring any FICA or FUTA tax obligations. For the most part these fringe benefits are also excluded from an employee's income for income tax purposes.

The following benefits are excluded from taxable wages:

- health plan payments, including both insurance premiums and payments from health plans for medical expenses

- long-term care insurance premiums and payments

- any sick pay or disability payments made later than six months after the employee last worked for you

- payments made on account of retirement for disability or death, including wages earned before the employee died but paid to a survivor

- employer's contributions to a qualified pension or retirement plan, including profit sharing, SEP, or SIMPLE plans (employees' elective contributions to retirement plans, such as contributions to 401(k) or SIMPLE plans, are subject to FICA and FUTA taxes but *not* income tax withholding)

- group term life insurance premiums on policies of up to $50,000 per employee

- worker's compensation premiums and benefits

- up to $5,250 in non-graduate-school education assistance, regardless of whether the education is job-related (this exclusion is scheduled to expire in mid-1997 and as the law is now written, doesn't apply to any courses beginning after June 30, 1997; however, it has been extended in the past and may well be extended in the future)

- meals and lodging furnished for the employer's convenience to employees and their dependents

- dependent-care assistance, up to $5,000 per employee

- services that your business provides to an employee at no additional cost to yourself and that you offer for sale to your customers; generally speaking these are "excess capacity" services like free standby air travel for airline employees, free hotel rooms for hotel employees, etc.

- certain employee discounts on the services or products you sell (the discount on services may be up to 20%; the discount on products may be as high as your gross profit percentage)

- property or services that you provide to an employee and for which the employee would have been entitled to a tax deduction had the employee paid you for the property or services (for example, company car used for business purposes; business travel, meals, and entertainment expenses; safety equipment; job training; education expenses to improve or maintain skills needed on the job but not to qualify for a new business or trade)

- benefits that have minimal value, such as occasional parties, occasional supper money or taxi fares when an employee works late, coffee and donuts, occasional tickets to entertainment or sporting events, use of company telephone or copy machines for personal purposes, etc.

- reimbursements for qualified moving expenses

- certain van pooling services, transit passes, and parking privileges

Timing of payment. You have some flexibility in designating when taxable benefits are paid for purposes of determining when your payroll taxes on the benefits are due. You may treat a benefit as having been paid on your regular pay period or on any other periodic basis (monthly, quarterly, etc.), provided you treat them as having been paid at least once a year.

Jury Duty Pay

Amounts you pay your employees while they're serving on jury duty are considered taxable wages for payroll tax purposes, even though the payments may be for periods when the employees are absent from work. However, the taxable amount will differ depending on how you treat your employees' jury duty pay. If you reduce regular wages by jury duty pay, payroll taxes apply to the reduced wage amount. If you pay the regular wage, but require employees to give jury pay to you, payroll taxes apply to the regular wage amount reduced by the jury duty pay. If you pay the regular wage and allow employees to keep jury pay, payroll taxes apply to only the regular wage amount.

Tips and Gratuities

Cash tips that your employees receive from your customers *may* constitute taxable wages for payroll tax purposes. In contrast, non-cash tips, such as theater tickets, are never considered wages. Tips are payments that customers make without compulsion and with the unrestricted right to determine the amount.

Example

You operate a restaurant and include a mandatory gratuity of 17% on the check of parties of eight or more. You distribute these amounts to your employees. This isn't a tip, it's a service charge and it constitutes taxable wages upon its distribution to the employees.

What are your obligations? An employee's cash tips aren't taxable wages unless they amount to $20 or more in a calendar month and the employee reports them to you by the 10th of the month following the month in which they were received. Once the $20 threshold has been reached, however, all cash tips are wages, including the initial $20. You're responsible for paying FICA and FUTA taxes, and withholding income and FICA taxes, on reported tips only to the extent that you have sufficient employee funds under your control.

Credit for FICA tax on tips. Under current law, employees who get $20 or more in tips in a single month must report their tips to their employers. If you have tipped employees, you have to pay Social Security and Medicare (FICA) taxes to the tune of 7.65 percent on tips that are reported to you, even though you don't have any control over the amounts. The purpose of the rule is to make sure that tipped employees are adequately covered by Social Security pension, disability, and survivors' benefits. However, the rule was seen to place a particularly heavy burden on the restaurant industry.

So, if your business is one that provides food or beverages for customers to consume on or off the premises, and if your waiters, waitresses, or delivery personnel are customarily tipped by your patrons, you're entitled to a tax credit for any FICA taxes you pay on the tips.

Note that there's an exception to this general credit rule: if you pay your employees below the minimum wage, with the expectation that tips will bring them up to the minimum, you can't claim the credit for FICA on the portion of the tips that is used to bring them up to the minimum wage.

No double-dipping is allowed: if you are eligible for and decide to claim this credit, you can't deduct the FICA taxes on which the credit is claimed. However, because tax credits are generally worth more than deductions, this is not usually a problem.

Employee reporting. You aren't responsible for verifying the accuracy of the amount of tip income your employees report to you. Your employees may use Form 4070, Employee's Report of Tips to Employer, and Form 4070-A, Employee's Daily Record of Tips and Report to Employer, to report their tips to you. You may want to give employees who receive tip income those two forms and a copy of IRS Publication 1244, which discusses tip reporting requirements.

Employee failure to report tips. When your employees fail to report tips of $20 or more per calendar quarter to you, you're liable only for the employer's portion of FICA and this liability doesn't arise until the IRS provides written notice and demand for payment. Once notice and demand is made, you must make the appropriate adjustment on IRS Form 941, Employer's Quarterly Federal Tax Return, for the calendar quarter in which the notice and demand is made. The liability is calculated using the rates and contribution bases applicable at the time the employee received the tips.

Tip rate alternative agreement commitments. Food service employers can agree to take certain steps to increase tip reporting compliance in exchange for a promise by the IRS not to demand more FICA than you determine to be due after complying with the program. To participate in this program, you have to enter into a Tip Rate Alternative Agreement Commitment with the IRS.

Large food and beverage establishments. Special tip reporting and allocation rules apply to large food and beverage establishments. Among other things, such employers must allocate 8 percent of gross receipts to tipped employees, if reported tips don't reach this level. For tip reporting and allocation purposes, the IRS says a large food or beverage establishment is any trade or business that is a food or beverage operation where tipping is customary and that normally employed more than 10 employees on a typical business day during the preceding calendar year. Fast-food operations, where customers order, pay for, and receive food at a counter and then take it elsewhere to eat are specifically excluded from large establishment classification. And cafeteria-style or self-service restaurants don't qualify because tipping isn't considered customary.

Vacation Pay

If you've extended your employees the benefit of paid vacation time, the amounts you pay them while they are on vacation are considered taxable wages, notwithstanding that the payments are for periods when the employees are absent from work. Furthermore, it shouldn't be at all surprising that the same rule applies to your payments to employees who don't take their vacations and instead receive additional amounts for the time they could have taken off.

Noncash Wages

One of the first issues you'll need to consider if you choose to provide employees with taxable fringe benefits, lodging, equipment, or other noncash items is determining how much you paid. For noncash payments, the amount of taxable wages is the fair market value of the benefits or property at the time of payment. In general, "fair market value" is the amount an individual would pay an unrelated third party to obtain comparable benefits and property.

Perhaps the biggest problem with paying an employee noncash wages is that you must see to it that the income taxes and FICA taxes that you're required to withhold with respect to the payments are available for collection. If you also pay the employee cash wages, you can withhold all the required taxes from the cash remuneration. If you don't pay any cash wages or if the cash wages you pay are insufficient to cover all of the withholding taxes, you must try to get the necessary funds from the employee. Unfortunately, this is frequently easier said than done.

Save Money

If you're going to pay noncash wages to your employees, especially if it's at their request, get a written commitment from them that they'll turn over to you any funds necessary to meet a tax withholding shortfall. Keep in mind that if you use your own funds to make up the shortfall, you've effectively paid additional wages to the employees and will thus incur additional payroll tax liabilities.

Payments for Casual Labor

Occasionally, you may pay workers to do work that doesn't promote or advance your business. For example, during a slow business period you may pay an employee to do some work around your home. Or you may pay one of your computer technicians to set up your personal home computer. Unless certain dollar thresholds are met, your payments to those employees will not constitute taxable wages for payroll tax purposes. Furthermore, noncash payments for casual labor will never be taxable.

Income and unemployment taxes. You're not required to withhold federal and most state income taxes or to pay federal (FUTA) and state unemployment taxes with respect to your cash payments to an employee for casual labor unless the cash payment is $50 or more in a calendar quarter, and the employee was engaged in casual labor for some portion of 24 different days during that quarter or during the preceding calendar quarter.

FICA taxes. You're not required to withhold or pay FICA taxes with respect to cash payments to an employee for casual labor unless the payments amount to $100 or more during the calendar year.

FILING AND PAYMENT DEADLINES

You have to ensure that your taxes are paid and reported in a timely fashion to the appropriate tax agencies. For federal payroll taxes, this usually means depositing the taxes with an authorized financial institution on at least a monthly basis and filing quarterly or annual returns. For most state payroll taxes, you usually send payments with an accompanying return on a quarterly basis directly to the agency that administers the particular tax.

However, your payroll tax obligations don't end when you file your tax returns. You also have reporting obligations to your employees and, in some cases, to your independent contractors. Furthermore, you must maintain, for a specified period, all records pertaining to the payroll taxes and wages you paid. If you stay on top of your payroll tax obligations throughout the year, you're in the clear. But, if you were at all inattentive or simply made some mistakes along the way, you could face some rather unpleasant penalties.

Deposits and Returns

There are two elements to transmitting your payroll taxes to the appropriate tax authorities: paying over the taxes and filing supporting returns that show how you computed the taxes. For federal payroll tax purposes, these two elements generally are done separately. That is, you deposit your taxes on a periodic basis (usually monthly) and you file your returns on a quarterly or annual basis. Although a few states follow the federal model, most require you to pay your state payroll taxes when you file your returns.

Federal tax deposits. You generally pay your federal payroll taxes by depositing them with a bank or other financial institution that is authorized to accept federal tax deposits or with the Federal Reserve bank or branch serving your locality. In most cases, you should use Form 8109, Federal Tax Deposit Coupon, to make the deposit. As for timing, different rules apply to income and FICA taxes and to FUTA taxes.

Income and FICA taxes. Usually, you must deposit these taxes on a monthly basis (deposit due on the 15th day of the following month) or a semiweekly basis. Under semiweekly depositing, you must deposit the taxes that you're required to withhold or pay on wages for a given pay period within the next week. In no event will small employers have less than three banking days to make the deposit.

Toward the end of each year, the IRS informs you of which method you should use during the upcoming calendar year. Whether you must deposit on a monthly or semiweekly basis is determined by the amount of income and FICA taxes you reported during the four-quarter period ending on June 30 of the prior year. If you reported $50,000 or less in taxes during this lookback period, you deposit on a monthly basis. Otherwise, you deposit on a semiweekly basis. However, if your total taxes for a quarter will be less than $500, you can remit the taxes with your quarterly return in lieu of depositing them.

Whenever you deposit less than you're required, you run the risk of being hit with a penalty on the underpaid amount. However, as long as any shortfall doesn't exceed the greater of $100 or 2 percent of the amount you should have deposited, no underpayment penalty will be assessed.

FUTA taxes: Usually, you must deposit your FUTA taxes on a quarterly basis. You must make your quarterly FUTA deposits by the last day of the month that follows the end of each quarter. If your quarterly FUTA tax liability is $100 or less, you don't have to deposit it. Rather, you may carry it forward and add it to your FUTA liability for the next quarter. If your liability for the last quarter of the year (plus any undeposited amounts from prior quarters) is $100 or less, you have the option of either depositing the tax or remitting it with your annual return.

Meeting deposit deadlines. In general, the timeliness of a deposit is determined by the date it's received. However, a mailed deposit received after the due date will be considered timely if you can establish that it was mailed at least two days before the due date. So, if you're planning to rely on the two-day mailing rule, send the deposit by registered or certified mail and request a return receipt.

Using Deposit Coupons

Your federal payroll tax deposits should generally be accompanied by Form 8109, Federal Tax Deposit Coupon. The IRS sends you an initial supply of deposit coupons around the time it assigns you an employer identification number (EIN). The IRS also tracks the number of deposit coupons you use and automatically sends you additional coupons when you need them.

Warning

The fact that you haven't received a supply of deposit coupons doesn't excuse you from making a required deposit. To request deposit coupons, call the IRS at 1-800-829-1040.

Because the IRS uses the information on the deposit coupon to credit your tax account, take the time to ensure that all the information is correct.

Form 8109-B. If you don't have Form 8109, you can make your deposit using Form 8109-B. Form 8109-B is an over-the-counter form that doesn't include your preprinted identifying information. Use Form 8109-B only if you're a new employer and you've been assigned an EIN, but haven't yet received your deposit coupons.

Warning

Don't use Form 8109-B if you've applied for, but not yet received, an EIN. Instead, deposit your taxes directly with the Internal Revenue Service Center for your area. Include your name and address, the type of taxes being deposited, the period covered, and the date you applied for the EIN.

Federal Returns

Part and parcel with your obligation to deposit your federal payroll taxes is your obligation to file periodic returns that show how you computed your tax liabilities. The returns you must file for your income and FICA taxes are different from the returns you file for your FUTA taxes.

Income and FICA taxes. You must file Form 941, Employer's Quarterly Federal Tax Return, to report both the federal income taxes and the FICA taxes you withheld and paid during a calendar quarter. The deadline for filing is the last day of the first month after a quarter ends.

Warning

The IRS can penalize you if you fail to make deposits or file returns when they're due by requiring you to file on a monthly basis.

However, if you've been timely with each of your deposits during the quarter, you're entitled to an automatic 10-day extension. No other extensions are permitted for filing Form 941.

FUTA taxes. You must file an IRS Form 940, Employer's Annual Federal Unemployment Tax Return, by January 31 of the following year. However, if you've been timely with each of your FUTA tax deposits during the year, you're entitled to an automatic 10-day extension. The IRS may allow you a further extension of up to 90 days upon your written request. Many small businesses are likely to be eligible to file a shorter and simpler form (Form 940-EZ). You qualify if you timely paid all your unemployment taxes to a single state, and all wages that were taxable for FUTA tax purposes were also taxable under state unemployment tax law.

Timely filing rules. A mailed return that bears a postmark indicating that it was mailed on or before the due date will be considered to have been timely filed even if it is received after the due date.

State Payments and Returns

States also require employers to periodically remit withheld state income taxes. How frequently you have to remit taxes is tied to the amount of tax you withhold. The greater the amount, the more frequently you have to remit taxes. Monthly or quarterly deposits are common, but some states require you to remit state taxes on the same schedule as federal taxes. Many states have adopted a timely mailed, timely filed rule, similar to the rule regarding IRS filings.

Warning

In addition to periodic returns that accompany your remittance of withheld state income taxes, most states also require you to file an annual reconciliation. Only New Mexico and Pennsylvania don't require annual reports, and Pennsylvania requires quarterly reports. In general, the due date for these annual reconciliations is at the end of February.

However, some states have different due dates: March 15 in Colorado and Nebraska, January 31 in D. C., Kentucky, Mississippi, Missouri, Virginia, and Wisconsin; February 15 in California and New Jersey; January 31 and February 28 in Ohio and Puerto Rico (two filings required); and the same as your federal due date in North Dakota.

Reports to Employees

In addition to your obligation to file payroll tax returns with your taxing authorities, you have a reporting obligation to your employees. If you were ever an employee, you're familiar with Form W-2, Wage and Tax Statement. This form tells employees how much you paid them in taxable compensation and how much you withheld from their wages for payroll taxes. As an employer, it's the form you'll be giving to your employees at each year's end.

Distributing W-2s. You must provide a Form W-2 to each employee who works for you during the calendar year by January 31 of the year following the calendar year covered by the form. However, employees who were terminated during the course of the year may request that you provide their W-2s at an earlier date. When terminated employees request their W-2s at earlier dates, you must furnish the forms within 30 days of the request or, if later, within 30 days of your last payment of wages to the employees. If for any reason you're unable to distribute a W-2 to an employee, you should retain the undelivered form as part of your records.

Filing W-2s. By the end of February, you must file copies of your employees' W-2s with the Social Security Administration (SSA). You must also file Form W-3, Transmittal of Wage and Tax Statements, which summarizes the information on the W-2 forms. If you need to correct or replace a W-2 that you've distributed to an employee or filed with the SSA, use Form W-2c, Statement of Corrected Income and Tax Amounts.

Independent contractors. You don't provide W-2s to your independent contractors, because you generally don't withhold or pay payroll taxes with respect to them. However, you're required to file an information return (Form 1099-MISC) for any independent contractor to whom you've paid at least $600 as compensation for services. Copies of the return must be provided to the contractors by January 31, and to the IRS by February 28.

State reporting. Every state that imposes a personal income tax requires employers to prepare employee reports similar to those required for federal tax purposes. Fortunately, almost every state gives employers the option of satisfying their state reporting obligations by timely furnishing federal Form W-2 (or an equivalent state form) to their employees. Information returns are generally required to be furnished to independent contractors, using either the federal Form 1099 or an equivalent state form. Due dates for the information returns vary, so be sure to check with your state income tax agency if you have worked with independent contractors.

Payroll Tax Records

Once you've paid over your payroll taxes and filed any necessary returns and reports, your last significant obligation is to maintain records that substantiate the payroll taxes you paid. For federal tax purposes, you must retain records for at least four years. A similar recordkeeping requirement exists in each state. (See page 191 for a discussion of the records you need to keep to establish your compliance with federal and state wage and hour laws.) Generally, your payroll records will be sufficient for *payroll tax* purposes if you also retain copies of each employee's Form W-4, records of the dates and amounts of tax deposits you made, copies of returns you filed, and copies of any undeliverable Form W-2.

You're obligated to keep all your required records at a convenient and safe location that is accessible to IRS representatives. And your records must be available at all times for IRS inspections.

Payroll Tax Penalties

There are few opportunities to reduce your obligations to collect, and to pay your share of, payroll taxes. If you hire employees and pay them any kind of compensation, you're going to incur some payroll tax liabilities. Perhaps your biggest opportunity for realizing any kind of real savings is to make sure you tend to each of your obligations and avoid what can be expensive penalties. Many payroll tax penalties are the same ones you'll find when you're dealing with other types of taxes. However, there are two penalties that you should be aware of as you deal with your payroll tax obligations:

- **100-percent penalty tax.** You can be held personally responsible for all income and FICA taxes that you either fail to withhold from your employees' wages or fail to pay to the IRS and your state tax agencies. Once you're aware of your payroll tax obligations and you fail to fulfill them, it's very difficult to avoid the penalty.

- **Form W-2.** If you fail to prepare Form W-2 for your employees, or if you willfully furnish incorrect ones, you'll be subject to a $50 penalty for each statement that should have been sent or that was incorrectly prepared.

Part V

When Employees Leave

No matter how hard you try to pick the best employees available and to manage them well, it's likely that, at some point, you'll have to fire somebody. It's a job most business owners and managers would rather not have to do. Worse, there's a growing body of law that limits your right to fire workers, and more and more workers seem to be filing (and winning) lawsuits against their former employers.

Nevertheless, it's a fact of life that employees come and go, sometimes of their own accord, and sometimes because you no longer require their services. What's important to you as a business owner is taking the steps necessary to minimize the hard feelings that might accompany the termination of the employment relationship.

Chapter 13: Proper Termination Procedures provides insight into the process that you should follow when it becomes necessary to terminate your relationship with an employee. The focus is on avoiding the risks associated with a wrongful termination lawsuit by letting the employee go in a dignified, and legal, manner.

Chapter 14: Your Relationship With Ex-Employees examines some of the obligations and responsibilities you have with respect to former employees, from the benefits you might have to make available to the contentious issue of providing employment references.

Chapter 13

Proper Termination Procedures

There are a variety of reasons why you might have to fire an employee, or terminate a contractual relationship with an independent contractor. It may be that there isn't a good fit between the job and the skills that the worker possesses. Or an employee might do something so bad that it requires the strongest possible disciplinary response you can muster. Even tougher, the worker might be performing well, but your business may no longer be able to support the number of employees you have.

Whatever the reason, be very careful when you fire someone. If you follow the appropriate procedures, you can dramatically reduce your risk of post-employment litigation. Conduct yourself appropriately and keep your cool no matter how difficult it may be. Words spoken in the heat of the moment have a way of sounding very, very bad when repeated in front of a jury. And, remember, the fact that you have to fire someone isn't a judgment on their personal character or fitness. It's merely the recognition that a particular employment relationship isn't working out the way you had hoped.

RESTRICTIONS ON YOUR RIGHT TO FIRE

As we noted in Chapter 5, it's generally best not to enter into employment contracts with your employees. If, for valid reasons, you do enter into a formal agreement with an employee (or a union contract with a group of employees), the contract should specify the proposed length of the employment relationship and the reasons for which either party can end the relationship. In other words, the contract's terms will generally govern your ability to fire the employee, as well as the employee's ability to quit. If either party attempts to terminate the relationship in violation of those terms, a potential breach of contract claim arises.

More likely, however, your relationship with your employees will be based on the principle of employment-at-will. "Employment-at-will" means that there's a presumption that the employee is employed at your will for an indefinite period rather than for a fixed term. In one state, Montana, an employee who has completed a probationary period may be fired only for unsatisfactory job performance, disruption of operations, or other legitimate business reasons.

Traditionally, both the employer and the employee have had the ability to end an at-will relationship at any time and for any reason. However, the freedom to fire at-will employees at any time for good, bad, or no cause has been eroded in recent years by the federal and state governments and the courts. The exceptions that have been carved into the employment-at-will doctrine form the foundation for most wrongful discharge claims, in which employees sue you for lost wages, punitive damages, and, occasionally, reinstatement to their job.

Warning

Don't assume that you're free from a wrongful discharge type lawsuit merely because an employee quits. Courts will frequently treat an employee who quits in order to escape illegal or intolerable employment practices or conditions (for example, sexual harassment or other discriminatory conduct) the same as though he or she were fired.

Federal and state laws that potentially restrict an employer's ability to fire at-will employees fall into two general categories. First, there are laws that make it illegal for employers to discriminate against certain individuals. Second, there are laws that make it illegal for an employer to retaliate against employees who exercise rights conferred by the laws or who take steps to see that the laws are enforced.

Courts, too, have limited employers' ability to fire at-will employees. In doing so, they generally rely on one of the following theories:

- Some statement by or document from the employer effectively created a formal employment contract where none previously existed. This is known as the *implied contract* theory. For example, stating that employees will be fired only for good cause in your employee handbook may form the basis for such an "implied" contract.

- The firing violates a "public policy" by infringing on some right granted employees by federal or state law, or because it is otherwise morally or socially wrong. For example, firing an employee for filing a workers' compensation claim is illegal.

- A few courts have relied on a bad faith limitation to presume that employers are generally obligated to deal fairly and in good faith with all their employees. For example, firing an employee solely to deny a bonus that the employee has earned but not yet received may be unlawful in some states.

Firing Restrictions in Written Laws

One of the easiest ways to find yourself defending a wrongful discharge lawsuit is to fire an employee under circumstances that violate a fair employment law. Numerous federal, state, and even local laws restrict an employer's right to fire an employee for discriminatory or retaliatory reasons.

Warning

Many fair employment laws provide exemptions for employers having some minimum number of employees. However, merely because you qualify for a law's exemption does *not* mean that you're free to fire those employees who the law was designed to protect without any risk of being sued. Courts can, effectively, extend the law to you under the "public policy" theory. The fact that a law protecting a certain class of employees was enacted generally indicates a public policy in favor of that protection.

- Federal fair employment laws protect employees against various forms of discrimination in the workplace. Thus, for example, you could run afoul of federal law if you fire an employee solely on the basis of the employee's race, color, religious preferences, gender, national origin, disabilities (including substance abuse problems), or age.

- Every state has laws that make it unlawful for an employer to fire an employee under certain circumstances. Many states have discrimination laws that give employees protection similar to, or greater than, corresponding federal laws. For example, some states protect employees from discrimination based on sexual orientation or personal appearance. Other frequently encountered limitations bar employee firing in response to filing claims for workers' compensation benefits, reporting an employer's illegal activity, or serving on a jury.

Federal Fair Employment Laws

The table in Chapter 1 includes those federal fair employment laws that are of general application. Normally, the effect of these laws starts with the hiring process and continues through the termination of the employment relationship.

Retaliatory discharge laws. Apart from antidiscrimination laws, a number of federal laws make it unlawful for an employer to fire an employee merely for asserting rights under those laws.

Example

Employees who start legal proceedings or who take other actions to have the law enforced are protected from discharge by the FLSA.

Similar restrictions on so-called "retaliatory" discharges are provided under the Occupational Safety and Health Act, the Vietnam Era Veterans Reemployment Act, the Employee Polygraph Protection Act, various environmental protection laws, and other federal laws.

Firing substance abusers. If an employee's alcohol or drug use caused an accident, endangered another employee, or resulted in excessive absence, you may be tempted to eliminate the "problem" by firing the employee. Federal and state laws that protect disabled employees from discrimination may apply to alcoholics or drug users. It may be unlawful to fire an employee for substance abuse unless you take steps to reasonably accommodate the employee's problem and give him or her a reasonable chance for rehabilitation.

State Firing Restrictions

Many states have civil rights laws that apply to employers with too few employees to be subject to federal antidiscrimination laws. While state laws governing the hiring process also apply to firing and termination, many states also have laws that specifically address firing. These laws generally fall into two categories. First, many laws specifically limit an employer's ability to fire employees merely for exercising or enjoying the rights granted. Second, some laws grant employees rights without specifically limiting an employer's ability to fire. Courts have routinely found that discharging an employee for exercising rights granted under this second type of law is a violation of the employees rights.

Finally, courts in virtually every state have imposed restrictions on an employer's right to fire. These "public policy" limitations arise when courts perceive that a discharge is morally or socially wrong, even if there is no *statutory* authority behind the decision.

Example

In the following situations, employers were found to have illegally violated employee rights protected by statute or by public policy when they took retaliatory action against employees who:

- filed claims for workers' compensation benefits

- filed a workplace safety complaint

- filed a wage claim

- appeared as a witness in response to a subpoena

- served on jury duty

- refused a superior's sexual advances

- was served with a wage assignment order for child support payments

- refused to commit perjury

- reported an employer's illegal acts to appropriate authorities

- filed criminal charges against a fellow employee for acts in the course of employment

- engaged in pro- or anti-union activities

Fired employees have relied on the public policy limitation in winning wrongful discharge lawsuits in a variety of situations. Perhaps most common is the claim that a public policy embodied in a federal or state law was violated when an employee was fired for attempting to exercise a statutory right, such as a right to work in a smoke-free area. Or a firing may involve public policy when it is based on an employee's opposition to illegal conduct. In essence, if a firing is inconsistent with any stated federal or state policy or interest, the fired employee has a potential claim.

Emotional distress claims. A fired employee will frequently accompany a public policy claim with an assertion that the employer's conduct was so improper as to cause the employee mental and emotional anguish. The addition of the emotional distress claim creates the possibility that you may be held liable for monetary damages not only for lost wages and benefits associated with the wrongful discharge, but also for any physical or emotional toll resulting from the discharge that can be translated into money. In addition, if the employer's conduct is found to be particularly offensive, the employee may be entitled to receive punitive damages.

Bad Faith Limitations on Firing

Let's assume an employer fires an employee who is about to close a sale that will entitle her to a substantial commission. Assume also that the firing violates no federal or state statute, public policy, or provision of an express or implied employment contract. Can the fired employee successfully sue for wrongful discharge if the employer's sole reason for firing her was to avoid having to pay the commission? In many states, the answer probably is no. Courts have generally been hesitant to expand the public policy or implied contract theory in wrongful discharge cases to reach every instance when an employer may have acted in bad faith in firing an employee.

State Laws on Dealing in Good Faith With Employees

If you do business in Alaska, Arizona, California, Idaho, or Massachusetts, you should be aware that courts in those states have ruled that employers are generally obligated to deal fairly and in good faith with their employees. In theory, this obligation may cause legal problems not only for employers who fire employees for improper reasons, but also for those who fire employees for no reason at all. So far, however, the courts that have acknowledged a bad faith limitation on firings have primarily applied the limitation to prevent employers from using discharges to deprive employees of compensation or benefits that have already been earned.

Currently, courts in a majority of the states have yet to decide whether a fired employee's argument that the firing was done in bad faith will be sufficient to support a wrongful discharge claim. Accordingly, it's difficult to say what steps, if any, you should take to limit your potential exposure to bad faith claims. Obviously, if you fire an employee in an attempt to retain commissions, bonuses, or other compensation the employee has rightfully earned, you're probably asking for a lawsuit. Beyond that, the best advice for avoiding trouble is to try to be fair and to treat your employees as you yourself would want to be treated.

Implied Employment Contracts

A fired employee may be able to sue you for violating the terms of an employment contract that you didn't even know existed. Employers in virtually every state have incurred tremendous legal costs in defending and paying damage awards in connection with lawsuits brought under so-called "implied" employment contracts.

When you and an employee enter into a formal agreement, whether written or verbal, specifying the terms of the employment relationship, you have an "express" employment contract. In contrast, an "implied" employment contract isn't an agreement that you knowingly enter. Rather, an implied employment contract arises when a court agrees with a fired employee that the employer effectively made some promise that was broken when the employee was fired. Even though the employer may not have intended such a contract to exist, the court finds that the implications of the employment arrangement are such that there is, in fact, a contract.

The promise underlying an implied employment contract is usually found in a statement that you made orally or in an employee handbook or orientation materials. The fired employee claims that the statement defined the duration of employment or established the procedures you would follow before firing the employee.

Example

Statements that may be found to constitute an implied contract:

- "The company's policy is to treat employees in a fair manner and to release employees for just cause only." (Implies that the company must have a reason to fire an employee.)

- "Upon completing a six-month probationary period, an employee can expect to be employed as long as his or her work is performed satisfactorily." (Implies that an employee who has completed the probationary period cannot be fired without some warning that his or her work performance was poor.)

- "An employee will be dismissed following a third warning that the employee has failed to meet performance standards or has violated company policy." (Implies that an employee will not be fired prior to receiving a third warning.)

Be careful about making any employment promises, or statements that can be interpreted as being promises, that you don't intend. Written statements are particularly troublesome, so you should review job application forms, employee handbooks, and any other documents that you may distribute to your employees. Look for any statement that may restrict your right to fire your employees and decide if you really want to live with that restriction. If not, delete the statement. You may even want to include on your job application forms an affirmative statement to the effect that an applicant, if hired, will be subject to employment-at-will.

Your spoken words also can get you into trouble. Although you need to watch what you say at all times, be especially careful during job interviews and performance reviews when statements about an employee's future with your business are likely to come up.

WHEN FAILURE TO FIRE CAN BE EXPENSIVE

Not only can employers be sued for improperly firing employees, they also can be sued for failing to fire employees. This problem arises when an employer becomes aware, or should have become aware, that an employee may cause harm to others, yet fails to take any action to prevent the employee from in fact causing harm.

If the employee should subsequently injure another employee, a customer, or other person, the injured party may sue the employer for negligently retaining the dangerous employee. An employer has a continuing obligation, which first arises during the hiring process, to guard against employing individuals with dangerous propensities. You need to screen people carefully before you hire them to find out if they have a past history of violence or erratic behavior.

Example

A laundromat employee with a known history of drug use, extreme violence, and sexual offenses assaulted a female customer. The employer was liable for negligent retention because it was reasonable for the employer to know that a customer using the laundromat at night might be in danger in the presence of an employee with such a history.

To limit your risk of being sued for negligent retention of a dangerous worker, watch for any signs that an employee is unstable or unfit to remain in his or her position. Danger signals include stress, fatigue, mental illness, carelessness, aggressive or abusive behavior, and drug or alcohol use.

Investigate thoroughly any complaints of employee misconduct. In some situations, you may be able to effectively deal with the problem through training or by changing the employee's responsibilities. In others, however, your safest recourse may be to fire the employee. This is especially true with respect to employees who threaten or harass others.

Warning

Your problems with a potentially dangerous employee do not necessarily end when you fire the employee or the employee quits. You need to be especially careful about what you say about the firing to prospective employers who contact you for an employment reference or to others. An uncertain line exists between what you may be obligated to disclose about the former employee's dangerous propensities, and what you cannot disclose without running the risk of the former employee suing you for defamation. (See the discussion of providing employment references at page 287.)

LIMITING THE RISK OF WRONGFUL TERMINATION

The best way to "win" a lawsuit is to avoid it in the first place. By keeping in mind some basic management and interpersonal rules, you can go a long way toward diffusing the anger of a discharged employee who might otherwise vent his or her wrath in a courtroom. Many of these same rules are also useful in establishing your defense, that you had a good reason to fire your employee, if it turns out that the worker does sue you, after all.

Before Firing for Misconduct or Poor Work

Before you fire somebody for insubordination, breaking a work rule, other misconduct, or poor performance, you should document the problem. Use fair rules and procedures, and thoroughly investigate the "last straw" incident.

First, though, a word about what *not* to do: we recommend that you make a personal commitment that you will *never* fire an employee on the spot. Acting out of anger or frustration is a good way to get yourself in legal hot water. Employees who are fired in this way are the most likely to sue you or to cause other trouble for you and your business. If a worker does something so terrible that you must take immediate action, tell the worker that he or she is suspended, effective immediately, while you investigate (or cool down). Having said that, we realize that even the best-laid plans sometimes go astray, so we've provided a few ideas on damage control if you do fire someone on impulse.

The safest way to fire someone, from a legal standpoint, is to be sure that you have a valid, nondiscriminatory business reason for the action, and that you have enough documentation to prove it. Your documentation must be created in the normal course of business, *before* you fire the person (except, of course, for a record of the actual termination discussion).

Warning

Don't get caught trying to reconstruct documentation (such as warnings or poor performance reviews) after the fact, when you should have been creating them all along. Don't use the documentation process to "build a case" against one worker when other workers in similar situations did not have their actions documented. Selective documentation may be proof that a person was the victim of discrimination.

Playing fair. It's important to remember that workers (and courts) are more likely to perceive a firing as "fair" if your employees had plenty of notice about what conduct and performance you expect from them. It's also important that workers receive regular feedback about their job performance, and that they are warned whenever you find that they aren't living up to expectations.

For that reason, your ability to "fire right" depends on the groundwork you lay, starting as early as the first day you hire somebody. You need to:

- **Establish fair work rules and policies.** Your employees need to know what you expect of them in terms of workplace rules. It's important that you clearly communicate these rules to all employees.

- **Enforce your rules fairly.** You can have the most reasonable rules ever written, but if you don't enforce your rules, they're useless. For legal purposes, *you must apply your rules equally to all your employees,* if you hope to rely on them.

- **Establish a performance feedback system.** Regular performance reviews can help you bring a worker up to par, or document your efforts to do so.

- **Investigate the "last straw" incident thoroughly.** In many cases an investigation can take just a few hours, so don't ignore this important step. Sometimes, after investigating, you may decide that termination isn't appropriate.

Releases and Severance Agreements

Whenever you fire or lay off a worker, there's the possibility that the person will take legal action against you. To avoid this threat, you can negotiate a severance agreement with the employee. As part of the agreement, the worker will sign a release stating that he or she gives up some or all rights to sue you.

Save Money

To make a release contract valid, you must provide the employee with something of value in exchange for the promise not to sue. Courts tend to like to see some dollars changing hands, so you might consider offering a lump-sum payment of at least two weeks' pay. However, you can also offer terms like an agreement not to contest payment of unemployment benefits, or an agreement that you will provide a satisfactory job reference if requested by any prospective employers. These things take little or nothing from your bank account, but can be valuable to the worker.

Employee releases are most often used when you lack proper documentation to fire, but you want to end an employment relationship and avoid the possibility of a lawsuit. They can also be used to offer early retirement to a worker, or when you are seeking to end an employment contract early by "buying out" the worker.

To be effective, the release must be:

- in writing

- signed by the employee who is waiving the right to sue

- a knowing and voluntary waiver

- supported by adequate consideration (You must give the employee something of value in return that he or she would not receive without signing the release.)

Work Smart

Here are a few tips to increase the chances that your release will be "iron-clad" if challenged in court:

- Allow the employee time to think about signing it. The more time the employee has, the more likely that a court will not believe that the employee was forced to sign the release.

- Encourage the employee to review the document with an attorney of his or her choice before signing it.

- Allow the employee a period of several days to change his or her mind after the release is signed.

- Allow the employee to negotiate the terms and conditions of the release (for example, let him or her substitute different benefits for the ones you offered). That way, a court will be more likely to believe that the document was signed willingly.

Make sure that the release uses language and a format that the employee understands. The release should specifically refer to employment laws involved in the waiver of rights. Your object is to ensure that the employee can't claim he or she didn't know what the document said. Under no circumstances should you trick the employee or make it seem that he or she has no choice but to sign. Here's a sample release form.

General Release for Employment Termination

Notice: Various state and federal laws prohibit employment discrimination based on age, sex, race, color, national origin, religion, handicap, or veteran status. These laws are enforced through the Equal Employment Opportunity Commission, Department of Labor, and state human rights agencies. If you feel that your election of ABC Company's severance package was coerced and is discriminatory, you are encouraged to speak with [designated person] at your earliest convenience. You may also want to discuss the release below with an attorney.

In any event, you should thoroughly review and understand the effect of the release before acting on it. Therefore, please take this release home and consider it for at least [pick a number — we recommend at least 21] days before you decide to sign it. If you do sign this release, you will have seven days after signing to reconsider your decision and to rescind your acceptance of the offer if you so desire. [Note: the preceding sentence is required only in the case of workers over 40.]

This release, unless signed by both parties, will expire as of [pick a date that coincides with the number of "consideration days" you chose in paragraph two, above].

General Release

As consideration for the following: [list here the severance pay, extended benefits, or other valuable items you are agreeing to provide] offered to me by ABC Company, Inc., I release and discharge ABC Company, Inc., its successors, subsidiaries, employees, officers, and directors (hereinafter referred to as "the Company") for all claims, liabilities, demands, and causes of action known or unknown, fixed or contingent, which I may have or claim to have against the Company as a result of this termination and do hereby agree not to file a lawsuit to assert such claims.

This includes but is not limited to claims arising under the Age Discrimination in Employment Act or other federal, state, or local laws prohibiting employment discrimination or claims growing out of any legal restrictions on the Company's right to terminate its employees.

This release does not have any effect on any claim I may have against the Company unrelated to this termination.

I have carefully read and fully understand all of the provisions of this agreement and release, which set forth the entire agreement between me and the Company, and I acknowledge that I have not relied on any representation or statement, written or oral, not set forth in this document.

Signed: _____ Date: _____
       (employee)

Signed: _____ Date: _____
       (for the Company)

Releases Under Age Discrimination Law

If the federal Age Discrimination in Employment Act applies to you (generally, if you have 20 or more employees during 20 or more weeks in the year) and if a worker is more than 40 years old, there are special rules that apply. These rules are designed to make sure that the release was signed "knowingly and voluntarily."

- The waiver must be written in language that can be understood by the average worker to which it applies.

- The waiver must specifically mention rights and claims under the ADEA.

- The waiver may not waive rights or claims that may arise after the date it is signed.

- The waiver must be in exchange for valuable consideration in addition to what the individual would already be entitled to receive.

- The individual must be advised in writing to consult with an attorney before signing the waiver.

- Generally, the individual must be given at least 21 days to consider the agreement, but if the waiver is requested in connection with an exit incentive or other employment termination program offered to a group of employees, each worker must be given at least 45 days to consider the agreement.

- The individual must be given at least seven days after signing the waiver to change his or her mind and revoke it, and the waiver may not become effective until the seven-day period has expired.

Early retirement or exit incentives. There are a few other requirements if the waiver is requested as part of any exit incentive or other employment termination program offered to a class of employees. If you are offering such a program to a group of employees, the individuals must be informed in writing about:

- whom the program covers

- what are the eligibility requirements

- what are the time limits for the program

- what are the job titles and ages of all individuals eligible or selected for the program

- what are the ages of all individuals in the same job classification who aren't selected for the program

TERMINATING AN EMPLOYMENT RELATIONSHIP

OK, you've made the decision to fire or lay off one of your employees, and you've done all the groundwork needed to document and justify your actions. What's the best way to break the news? Read on for some time-tested advice on how to conduct the actual termination meeting, minimize your own discomfort, and make things as easy as possible on the departing employee.

Preserving the Employee's Dignity

We can't say it strongly enough: when firing a worker, make every possible effort to maintain the employee's dignity. It's natural for a person being fired to feel resentment toward you and your business. Everything you do in a termination meeting should be designed to minimize, as much as possible, this natural resentment.

We say that not so much out of concern for the worker who is being discharged, but for your own self-protection. It's not good for your business reputation to have ex-employees bad-mouthing you all over town. If customers think that you treat your employees unfairly, they might think that you'll do the same to them.

You'll also want to avoid, as much as you can, the possibility that you might be sued by a disgruntled ex-employee. Most lawsuits in this area are filed because of the employee's feelings, not because the facts of the case are particularly strong. If you can soften the blow to the person's ego, or at least keep from making it worse, your odds of being sued go down dramatically.

Finally, some fired employees become so distraught that they threaten to harm (or actually do harm) their former boss, coworkers, or the business. Treating workers as humanely as possible minimizes the chance that this might happen to you.

Setting Up the Termination Meeting

If you need to fire or lay off someone, it should always be done face-to-face, never by letter or over the phone.

Who should conduct the meeting? In general, the supervisor, manager, or owner who is most familiar with the employee and the reasons for the discharge should conduct the meeting. In many cases, that will be you. If you aren't the immediate supervisor, let him or her handle the meeting.

Who should be at the meeting? In addition to you (or the supervisor) and the worker who's being fired, there are situations where you may want a third party to attend the meeting. If the person being terminated requests a witness, it's probably best that you allow this, so that the person doesn't feel that he or she is being railroaded out the door unfairly. But explain that the person is there as an observer only, not to act as a representative or argue on behalf of the worker.

You may also want to have a witness present if trouble is expected or if an objective third person is needed. Sometimes a second company representative is seen, however, as an attempt to "gang up" on the terminated employee. Use your own judgment in this regard.

Where to conduct the meeting? You'll want to conduct the meeting out of sight and earshot of any other employees, in a quiet place where you won't be interrupted. The meeting room should be in a location that doesn't alert other people to what's taking place. Many advisors suggest that meetings be held on neutral ground, not in your office, and not in the departing worker's office or workplace.

Privacy and neutral territory may be difficult to find in a small business, especially if you work out of your home, so consider holding the meeting in a nearby restaurant or coffee shop. Holding the meeting in a quiet public place has other advantages: it may be easier to avoid emotional outbursts on anyone's part, and it will be easy for you to end the meeting by getting up and walking away (after picking up the tab, of course).

When to hold the meeting? Early in the day and early in the week is generally considered the best time to terminate an employee. Avoid Fridays and the day before a holiday or vacation. An employee who is let go on a Friday has two days to brood about his or her treatment by the company and to look for ways to retaliate.

In contrast, discharging a person early in the week provides an opportunity to focus on the future and begin looking for a new job right away. Also, the person who's doing the firing won't have to leave for the weekend with the bad memory of a distasteful task on his or her mind.

For similar reasons, the discharge should be conducted early in the day. People are fresher, more rested, and better equipped to deal with adversity and stress earlier in the day. People tend to be tired and short-tempered later in the day, which may increase the chance for an unpleasant reaction to bad news. Also, discharging earlier in the day allows you to get back into the work routine and overcome any unwarranted guilt that may exist for having to fire an employee.

What To Do at a Termination Meeting

The actual termination meeting should last 10 to 15 minutes and have the sole purpose of providing a simple and concise statement of the decision to terminate the employment relationship. Have phone numbers ready for medical or security emergencies.

Prepare what you will say ahead of time. It's a good idea to write it out, and have a checklist in front of you so that you don't get sidetracked and forget any important points.

Termination Meeting Checklist

❑ Tell the employee the purpose of the meeting. Give an adequate reason for the termination, but avoid a detailed discussion of the documentation supporting the reason for discharge.

❑ Give the employee an opportunity to have his or her say. Listen for signs that the employee feels that he or she is being forced out as a result of discrimination, harassment, or other illegal conduct on your part.

❑ Advise that the decision is final and cannot be reversed. Tell the employee the effective date of the termination.

❑ Emphasize that all relevant factors were reviewed. Where appropriate, advise that alternative in-house positions were explored. If applicable, stress that everyone involved in management activities agreed to the decision.

❑ Review with the employee a written summary of benefits. This summary should include, where applicable, severance pay, compensation for vacation and sick time, continuation of health and life insurance benefits, other benefits, and re-employment assistance.

❑ Have final paychecks ready. If the employee is to leave immediately, have any final checks, benefits, or vacation payments prepared and inform the employee to collect his or her personal belongings and leave the premises.

❑ Other options: Provide the employee with a written summary of projects to be transferred to ensure a smooth transition of work if the employee will remain as an active employee for a period of time. Outline the next steps in the termination process, such as the last day of work, return of company ID, keys, and credit cards.

❑ Explain your job reference policy (see page 287). Get a release signed, if that's your policy.

❑ End the interview by saying that the employee will be notified of any other matters that must be dealt with, such as COBRA continued health coverage.

❑ Wish the employee good luck and express confidence in his or her future. Stand, extend your hand, and remain standing until the employee has left the meeting site.

WHAT TO DO WHEN YOU HAVE TO DOWNSIZE

When economic reasons demand that you eliminate an employee's job, either temporarily or permanently, you automatically have a sound business reason for the discharge. Few courts will question your judgment in this regard. But if you lay off some but not all of your workers, be sure that your *selection process* does not discriminate on the basis of age, sex, or race, or violate some other public policy.

Seniority or merit? Laying people off in order of seniority (that is, keeping the people with the greatest length of service) is most likely to be seen as fair by your employees. It's also the easiest to defend in court. Generally, if you use this method, you won't have to provide any other evidence as to why certain workers were chosen for layoff.

Given the choice, however, most employers would prefer to keep their best workers and lay off those who are less productive, regardless of seniority. If you have done regular performance reviews you can eliminate the positions of those employees whose performance has been documented as less-than-satisfactory. If there is no documentation, you cannot eliminate that person's position for purely merit reasons without facing possible liability.

Also, if you are choosing between two or more equally qualified candidates for layoff, you should be prepared to show that the "downsized" workers reflect the demographic mix (race, gender, and age) of your workforce as much as possible.

IF YOU FIRE AN EMPLOYEE IN HASTE OR ANGER

If you ignore all the expert advice and fire someone impetuously, perhaps because you had an argument or you caught the worker stealing or damaging property, what should you do?

The answer depends on the worker's previous history with your company. You can start by going through the worker's file to see if you have enough documentation (of previous violations of rules or of poor performance reviews) to justify your action. If you do, you can heave a sigh of relief because you'll have a defense ready in case the worker decides to sue you.

If you have little or no documentation of previous problems with the worker, the safest course of action would be to call him or her, say that you acted too quickly, and offer to reinstate the worker. If he or she refuses, you have just transformed the firing into a voluntary quit, so your possible liability has decreased dramatically. If the worker agrees to come back, you'll naturally keep a watchful eye on him or her. Hopefully things will improve; if not, document any problems before you repeat your hasty conduct.

If you don't want to take the worker back, perhaps because his or her conduct was so appalling that it would justify firing in itself, or because you feel your ability to work together has been destroyed, you should first gather and save any available evidence that supports your version of what happened.

Then, after reviewing the evidence, you have a choice. You can sit tight and hope the whole thing blows over, or you can try to work out a deal with your ex-employee. You might agree to provide some severance benefits to the worker, in exchange for a signed release form that waives his or her right to sue you.

Handling Voluntary Resignations

You can't, of course, stop people from quitting. You may ask employees who resign to give you some advance warning or notice. You can also ask departing employees to participate in an exit interview or fill out a form. If it becomes apparent that the employee felt forced to quit, treat the situation as a firing.

Of course, you can't force a departing employee to follow your procedures any more than you can make him or her stay. However, you can suggest that if the employee follows your procedures, it will allow you to give a good job reference and tell any prospective employers that the worker was responsible and cooperative.

Advance Notice

Whether you want or need advance notice of resignations depends on the nature of your business. If you are in an industry where people commonly come and go, and where it's relatively easy to find good replacements, you may not care about advance notice. If you want exiting employees to train their own replacements, a two-week notice period may be a reasonable request.

In some cases, you may decide that you don't want a "lame duck" employee around. If you have established a notice policy, fairness requires that you pay the person for the remainder of the notice period, if you decide that you don't want him or her to work out the entire period.

How do you establish a notice policy? If high turnover is the norm, include it in the work rules that you give to incoming employees.

Can you threaten to withhold benefits or pay if a resignation procedure isn't followed? Probably not — most states have laws requiring that employees be paid whatever they have earned, and paid on time. Penalties have been imposed even where there were only minor delays in paying the last check.

Handling Prompted Resignations

A "prompted resignation" is a resignation that appears to be voluntary. However, the idea or motivation for the employee to resign comes from somebody else, usually the person's boss.

In some cases, the employee expresses the wish to resign rather than to be fired. In others, you may offer the opportunity to resign, so you don't have to fire the person, so you don't have to document the situation extensively, or so you can avoid additional time and costs.

In general, it's better for you if the employee resigns. An employee who wants a job reference that says he or she resigned, rather than a reference that shows he or she was fired, is less likely to sue you. He or she is also less likely to file for unemployment benefits, since these benefits aren't paid for voluntary resignations. However, it's always possible that the worker could change his or her mind and story sometime in the future, so be sure you treat the prompted resignation as if it were a firing for your own internal records.

In some cases, workers resign because they believe they are being forced out, harassed, or treated unfairly for unlawful reasons. It's important to uncover these situations in advance, so that, if true, you can correct the situation. If not, begin to prepare a defense in case a lawsuit is ultimately filed. For that reason, it's advisable that you conduct an exit interview and/or have the worker fill out an exit questionnaire whenever someone leaves your employ.

Exit Interviews

If one of your employees informs you that he or she is leaving, set up a time to discuss the matter. Follow basically the same procedures that you would if you were the one who was ending the relationship. Topics to discuss include why the employee is leaving, ways that the business could be improved, and information you can use to better understand the position in order to hire a replacement, if required. In addition, it's important to find out the worker's true reason for leaving:

- If there is a legal challenge by any party, you may need the information to prepare a defense.

- In a government investigation, you might have to compare your past record with the action in question, or compare future actions with this one.

- The information may be useful if the employee later files for unemployment benefits, and you want to contest them.

- If more than one employee leaves, you want to know if there is a pattern. Turnover is costly, especially for small business owners who have to take time away from their customers to search for, hire and train a replacement. If possible, you want to get the worker's reasons for leaving in writing and keep them in your permanent records.

Chapter 14

Your Relationship With Ex-Employees

When an employee leaves, you still have a variety of issues to face. The most immediate one is getting the departing employee a final paycheck. You may also have some responsibility to provide continuing health care coverage, at the former employee's expense. When workers are fired, unemployment compensation must be considered. Finally, you can expect to hear from employers seeking references as an ex-employee looks for a new job.

FINAL WAGES

When employment terminates, getting a final paycheck to the employee promptly is important.

Work Smart

When preparing an employee's final check, take all appropriate deductions and reduce the pay of hourly employees by the amount of time not worked in that pay period. Make sure that you don't deduct premiums for benefits if premiums are paid in advance. If the employee wants to continue health benefits, he or she can do so under COBRA.

State laws. Some states require you to deliver the employee's last paycheck within a certain number of days. Many penalize employers for being late by requiring continuation of pay. The list below summarizes each state's rules regarding final paychecks. States omitted from the list have no law on this subject.

State Laws on Final Paychecks

State	Final wages must be paid:
AK	within three working days, to employees who quit or are discharged; on or before the next regular payday, to laid off, locked out, or striking employees.
AZ	to discharged employees, within 3 working days or at the end of the next regular pay period, whichever is sooner; to employees who quit, no later than the next regular payday.
AR	to discharged employees within 7 days; to employees who quit, by the next scheduled payday.
CA	to discharged employees at the time of discharge; to employees who quit, within 72 hours (at the time the employee quits, if 72 hours' notice is given).
CO	immediately, to employees who are discharged or laid off; the next regular payday, to employees who quit.
CT	the next business day, to employees who are discharged; the next regular payday, to employees who resign, are laid off, or are engaged in a labor dispute.
DE	on the next regular payday to employees who quit, resign, are discharged, suspended, laid off, or upon suspension of work due to a labor dispute. Employers who unreasonably fail to pay are liable for liquidated damages in addition to the unpaid wages.
DC	to discharged employees, no later than the day following discharge; to employees who quit, on the next regular payday or within 7 days of quitting, whichever is earlier; to strikers, on the next regular payday. Employers who fail to pay must pay 10 percent of the unpaid wages for each working day the failure continues, or an amount equal to the wages that are due, whichever is smaller.
HI	immediately to discharged employees; by the next regular payday, to employees who quit and strikers.
ID	to employees who are discharged or quit, by the earlier of the next regular payday or within 10 business days of layoff or termination. Employees who request in writing to be paid earlier must be paid within 48 hours of the request, excluding weekends and holidays. Employers who fail to pay are liable for wages on a daily basis for up to 30 days after default.
IL	to employees who are terminated, no later than the next regular payday or, if possible, immediately; to workers on strike or laid off; no later than the next regular payday.
IN	to discharged employees, on the regular payday for the period in which the discharge occurred; to employees who quit and strikers, by the next regular payday.
IA	to employees who quit or are fired, no later than the next regular payday. Employers have 30 days after suspension or termination to pay wages determined on a commission basis.
KS	no later than the next regular payday, to employees who quit or are discharged. Employers that aren't bankrupt must pay 1 percent of pay due for each day payment is late.
KY	to corporate employees who quit or are discharged, no later than the next regular payday or 14 days following severance, whichever occurs last.
LA	to employees who quit, before the next regular payday or no later than 15 days following the resignation, whichever is earlier; to employees who are discharged, within 3 days. Employers who don't pay are liable for wages at the employee's regular rate for up to 90 days from the time of demand until paid.

State	Final wages must be paid:
ME	the earlier of the next regular payday or not more than 2 weeks after demand is made. Manufacturing or mechanical establishments may contract for 1 week's notice of termination; employee to forfeit 1 week's pay or employer to pay 1 week's pay if notice is not given.
MD	to employees who are terminated, on the next regular payday. Discharged mine workers must be paid immediately.
MA	to employees who quit, the following Saturday or next regular payday; to discharged employees, on the day of the discharge.
MI	to employees who quit, as soon as the amount can be determined (no more than 3 days for employees who hand harvest crops); to discharged employees, immediately, or as soon as the amount can be determined; to employees working under contract, at the termination of the contract if the amount due cannot be determined earlier. Pursuant to regulations, employees (other than those engaged in hand harvesting of crops) who quit must be paid on the regular payday; discharged employees must be paid within 4 working days of the termination date. Employees engaged in hand harvesting of crops must be paid within 1 working day of discharge.
MN	to discharged employees, immediately upon demand; to employees who quit, within 5 days (within 24 hours if 5 days' notice is given). If an employer fails to pay, the regular rate of pay continues until paid, up to 15 days. These provisions don't apply to farm laborers, bankrupt employers, receivers, or court-appointed trustees. Transitory workers who quit or are discharged must be paid within 24 hours. An employer who fails to pay must pay the employee's reasonable expenses incurred while living away from home awaiting wages and, if not paid in 3 days, the employee's regular rate of pay continues until paid, up to 15 days.
MO	to corporate employees who are discharged, on the day of discharge or within 7 days if paid by mail at the employee's request. If an employer fails to pay, wages continue to accrue at the employee's regular rate until paid, for up to 60 days
MT	to terminated employees within 3 days (3 extra days if checks originate out of state); to employees discharged for cause, immediately upon separation.
NE	on the next regular payday or within 2 weeks of the termination date, whichever is sooner.
NV	to employees who resign or quit, no later than the next regular payday.
NH	to employees who quit and strikers, on the next regular payday; to discharged employees, within 72 hours after demand (the next regular payday, if working at a field office). If an employer fails to pay, wages continue to accrue for one week.
NJ	no later than the regular payday in cases of discharge, suspension of work due to a labor dispute, layoff, or termination for any reason. An additional 10 days is allowed in the case of a labor dispute involving payroll employees.
NM	to employees who quit and strikers, on the next regular payday; to discharged workers within 5 days when wages are definite in amount, and within 10 days in other cases. If an employer fails to pay, wages continue at the employee's regular rate of pay until paid.
NY	to employees who are terminated, no later than the next regular payday.
NC	to employees whose employment is discontinued for any reason, by the next regular payday.
ND	to discharged workers, within 24 hours at the place of employment, or within 15 days or at the next payday (whichever is sooner) by certified mail; to strikers and employees who resign, no later than the next regular payday.
OK	to terminated employees and to strikers, at the next regular payday.

State	Final wages must be paid:
OR	no later than the end of the first business day after an employee is discharged or terminated by mutual agreement; immediately, to an employee without a contract for a definite period who quits and provides at least 48 hours' notice (within 5 business days, or on the next regular payday, whichever is earlier, if notice isn't provided). Strikers must be paid on the next regular payday or within 30 days of the commencement of the strike. Wages or compensation continue from the due date until paid (up to 30 days) if an employer willfully fails to pay. Financial inability to pay will excuse an employer from this penalty.
PA	to employees who quit or are terminated, or whose work is suspended due to a labor dispute, no later than the next regular payday. Any employer who requires that employees give notice, under penalty of forfeiture of part of wages earned, is liable to pay an equal sum if it discharges an employee without similar notice, except in case of discharge for incapacity or misconduct, or in case of a strike or a general suspension of work.
RI	on the next regular payday. Employees who lose their jobs because an employer leaves the state, merges, liquidates, or is disposed of must be paid within 24 hours of termination.
SC	no later than 48 hours after separation or the next regular payday (no more than 30 days).
SD	to employees without a written contract for a definite period who quit or resign, by the next regular payday or whenever the employee returns all of the employer's property in the employee's possession; to discharged employees within 5 days from the date of separation.
TX	to discharged employees, no later than the 6th day after discharge; to employees who leave employment other than by discharge, no later than the next regular payday.
UT	to discharged employees (excluding commissioned salespeople), within 24 hours; to employees without a contract for a definite period who quit, within 72 hours (immediately, if 72 hours' notice is given). If an employer fails to pay, wages continue to accrue until paid, but not more than for 60 days.
VT	to employees who quit, on the next regular payday or, if there is no regular payday, on the following Friday; to discharged employees, within 72 hours of discharge.
VA	to terminated employees, on or before the next regular payday.
WA	to laborers who are discharged or who withdraw, at the end of the current pay period.
WV	to discharged employees, within 72 hours after demand, or when the wages become due under an employment contract; to employees who quit, are suspended as a result of a labor dispute, or are laid off, no later than the next regular payday. Employees who give at least 1 pay period's notice must be paid at the time of quitting.
WI	to employees who quit or are discharged (excluding commissioned salespeople), no later than the next regular payday or within 31 days of the end of the pay period, whichever is earlier. Businesses that relocate, merge, or shut down must pay employees within 24 hours. Manufacturers that require employees to give notice under penalty of forfeiture are liable for the amount of forfeiture if they discharge an employee without notice, except in cases of misconduct, incapacity, or departmental layoffs.
WY	to employees who quit or are discharged within 5 working days; to employees whose work is suspended as the result of a labor dispute and who request it, at the next regular payday.

BENEFITS FOR FIRED EMPLOYEES

Under federal and state laws, employers have certain legal obligations to the employees they fire with respect to continuing health coverage, unemployment insurance benefits, and vested retirement benefits. Apart from those benefits, employers generally have no legal obligation to provide severance payments or other benefits to the employees they fire. However, many employers provide severance payments or benefits as a matter of company policy or pursuant to a negotiated separation agreement with a fired employee.

Warning

Be careful in discussing with employees the benefits, if any, to which they may be entitled upon leaving your business. More than a few employers have been sued for benefits they didn't intend to provide on the basis of some well-meaning comment about benefits that *might* be available to terminated employees. Refrain from discussing benefits until you know for sure what your obligations will be under applicable law and any policies you adopt.

Continuation of health benefits. Employers with 20 or more employees who maintain group health plans are required by federal law to offer most fired employees who are participants in the plan, as well as their spouses and dependent children, the opportunity to continue to receive health insurance benefits at the employee's own cost. (See the discussion of COBRA requirements at page 282.) Some states have comparable laws that may apply to employers not subject to the federal law.

Unemployment insurance benefits. Employers must notify fired employees of their possible eligibility for unemployment insurance benefits. An employer who fails to provide this notice runs the risk of being sued if an eligible employee fails to timely file a claim. In most states, however, an employer can avoid this obligation by posting state-supplied information about unemployment benefits.

Vested retirement benefits. Fired employees remain eligible to receive any pension or profit-sharing benefits with respect to which they have vested under the terms of the plan.

Vacation pay. Some states specifically require employers to pay terminated employees for earned but unused vacation time.

Warning

Be very careful when you consider firing an employee whose benefits under a retirement plan are about to become vested. Federal law bars firing solely to prevent an employee from qualifying for benefits under most pension, welfare, and deferred compensation plans. If you do, the employee may sue to recover the benefits that were about to vest. The federal government may also hit you with penalties and your retirement plan conceivably could lose tax-favored status. Thoroughly document the reasons for the firing to avoid any appearance that the firing was used to avoid having to pay the employee benefits.

Severance policies. You may decide to voluntarily provide for severance pay and other benefits as a matter of policy, or you may choose to negotiate severance agreements as the need arises. If you provide severance benefits on a case-by-case basis, you're free to negotiate what benefits, if any, you'll provide to each employee. These can include lump-sum or periodic cash payments, temporary health coverage, assistance in finding new employment, or an agreement not to contest unemployment insurance claims.

Warning

We strongly suggest a case-by-case approach rather than a formal, written policy. If you adopt a severance pay policy, you're subject to the recordkeeping and notice requirements of ERISA. Those obligations alone are reason enough to forego a preset plan.

If you choose to have a written plan, clearly define the circumstances under which you'll provide payments and benefits, and the manner in which you'll determine the amount and the method of payment. Specifically reserve the right to withdraw the plan or to change it at any time. Consider requiring employees who accept a severance package to sign a release that protects you and your business from future employment-related lawsuits and claims.

You may have a strong incentive to offer a severance package if an employee is leaving under circumstances that raise a risk of future litigation. For example, you may have concerns about a potential wrongful discharge suit if you fire an employee who has previously complained about being sexually harassed by other employees or being treated unfairly. You can use the offer of a severance package to negotiate a release from the employee of his or her right to sue you for employment-related claims. Be aware, however, that offering severance packages as a means of "buying out" employees isn't without its own risk. The offer could backfire if it alerts an employee to possible claims that the employee didn't realize existed.

COBRA Benefits

If you have 20 or more employees, you are subject to a law known as the Consolidated Omnibus Budget Reconciliation Act of 1985, better known as COBRA. COBRA requires employers to offer individuals who would otherwise lose benefit protection the option of continuing to have group health care plan coverage.

What Events Trigger COBRA?

Events that trigger coverage are called qualifying events. The following are qualifying events:

- an employee's voluntary or involuntary termination of employment, unless it is for gross misconduct. COBRA doesn't define misconduct, but to establish misconduct, you'll need to show that there was a connection between the offense and the employee's job; that the employee is able to understand the gravity of the misconduct; and that the offense was willful. If the departing employee decides to challenge your determination, you're probably going to end up in federal court. Balance the estimated costs of fighting the enforcement suit against the costs of the COBRA coverage.

- an employee's reduction in hours of employment (e.g., from full time to part time)

- a covered spouse's divorce or legal separation from an employee

- an employee's death

- an employee's entitlement to Medicare

- a covered dependent's change in status (for example, reaching an age that no longer qualifies the dependent for coverage under the parent's health plan)

- active military duty when you don't voluntarily maintain health coverage

- failure to return to work at the end of family and medical leave where coverage was in effect at the beginning of the leave but was lost during the leave

- your business's bankruptcy

How long does coverage last? Depending upon the type of event and who the beneficiary is, coverage could continue for 18, 29, or 36 months after the date of the event or the coverage loss.

Your COBRA Communication Duties

COBRA stresses the need to inform employees of the right to continue benefits when a qualifying event occurs. You must notify covered employees and spouses of their initial rights under COBRA when they first join the plan. You have to notify covered persons of their election rights to continue coverage after a qualifying event occurs. And you have 30 days to notify the plan administrator (insurance company) when a loss occurs for any of the reasons listed above, except for divorce or change of status by a dependent. In those two instances, you have 60 days to notify the administrator.

Who Pays for COBRA Coverage?

The employee must pay the full cost of the insurance premiums. In fact, the law allows you to charge 102 percent of the premium, and to use the 2 percent to cover your administrative costs. When an employee gets extended COBRA coverage due to disability, you can charge 150 percent of the premium for months 18 through 29.

Other COBRA Issues

Complying with COBRA can be a pretty taxing job. Even big companies save time and money by outsourcing administration to companies that specialize in doing it. Still, you should know some basics about the administrative side of this important law.

How does the employee sign up for coverage? After you send out the notice to an employee following a qualifying event, the employee has 60 days to notify you that he or she wants coverage. The employee can write you a letter, call you on the phone, or tell you in person. If you don't hear from the employee within 60 days after your notification or 60 days after the event took place (whichever is later), the employee is no longer eligible to sign up.

State law. Most states (all *except* Alabama, Alaska, and Delaware) have laws concerning continuation of benefits. Some of them cover all employers, including small employers, so you might be subject to a state law even if you're exempt from federal law. The laws are complex and differ from state to state. To find out more about your state's laws regarding continuation of coverage, contact your state labor agency or your attorney.

UNEMPLOYMENT COMPENSATION

In general, only workers who "involuntarily" leave their jobs are eligible for unemployment compensation. But that doesn't mean someone who quits won't file a claim. Such people can allege that they were "forced out" due to illegal or discriminatory practices, or misrepresent the circumstances under which they left.

There are two major reasons you should care about whether your ex-workers are collecting unemployment, and why you should try to prevent an improper claim from being paid. First, your state unemployment tax rate is directly affected by the number of ex-employees who collected unemployment after leaving your business. Second, if there's a chance that the worker is going to sue you for discrimination or wrongful discharge, you can discourage the lawsuit. If you establish that your conduct was appropriate in an unemployment compensation hearing, you're more likely to win in a later suit for wrongful termination. However, if you lose in the unemployment matter, you may decide that you should settle with the worker rather than going to trial in the other lawsuit.

How the Unemployment System Works

The benefits paid to jobless workers are financed through federal and state unemployment taxes paid by employers like you. Every state has a system that bases your unemployment tax rate on the amount of benefits that has been paid to your former workers. If you fire or lay off workers only when absolutely necessary, use the proper procedures to do it, and routinely contest unemployment benefit claims when you think the worker is ineligible, you can lower your unemployment tax rate. In some states, you can lower your rate to zero, and pay no unemployment taxes at all. On the other hand, if you don't pay attention to these things, you may well find your unemployment taxes eating into your bottom line. To stay on top of the system, you need to know who's eligible for unemployment benefits and what actions can disqualify an otherwise eligible worker.

Unemployment Benefits Eligibility

To be eligible for unemployment benefits, a person must have some amount of work experience within the last one and one-half years. Most states require that an employee work at least some part of two different calendar quarters within the past one and one-half years, and a large percentage of states also have a specific dollar amount of wages that must have been earned. Your local unemployment office can tell you the minimum in your state. Think about setting up a probationary period for new hires that is shorter than the minimum time that would qualify them for benefits.

Warning

Most states don't count time spent and money earned in self-employment toward the minimums. If you pack up your business, you probably won't be eligible for benefits.

There are a few other requirements that must be met before someone is eligible for benefits. If you think an ex-employee doesn't meet them, consider contesting the payment of benefits.

- The worker must be truly unemployed. A worker who has a part-time job or is self-employed is ineligible for benefits.

- The worker must make a claim for benefits at the local state employment office, and respond to any cards, letters, or requests to appear from the government.

- In most areas, the unemployment office also helps jobless workers find a new position, and the person must cooperate by filing job applications, interviewing, and accepting a suitable position if one turns up. In some states, a worker must report to the agency the number of job applications submitted each week, to prove that a job search is continuing.

- The worker must be ready, willing, and able to work. That means his or her health must be good enough for work in a reasonable number of jobs that are available in your area. If the worker has enrolled in some type of school or training course, it must be approved by the state unemployment agency, or the worker must be willing to leave the course if school hours would conflict with a suitable job offer.

Disqualification Factors

Some people otherwise eligible for benefits can still be disqualified from receiving benefits, based on how and why they lost their jobs. Generally, unemployment benefits are designed for people who are laid off because the employer doesn't have enough work for them, or who lose their jobs because of something the employer did wrong. So, workers will be disqualified if:

- The worker left the job voluntarily, without a good cause connected to the job. In all states, a worker who quits because the employer does something nasty like harassing or discriminating against him or her, or making a significant change in wages, hours, job duties, location, or other working conditions, has "good cause" to quit and won't be denied benefits. States differ in their interpretation of whether "good cause" includes quitting for health-related or personal reasons, such as a spouse's relocation. Consult your attorney for the most up-to-date rules that apply to your area.

- The worker turned down a suitable job offer during the period of unemployment.

- The worker was fired for misconduct. In situations involving misconduct, documenting warnings and disciplinary measures taken will enable you to easily prove what happened and keep the worker from receiving benefits at your expense.

Warning

Poor performance or incompetence isn't usually considered misconduct. Although you have the right to fire a poor performer, he or she will probably be able to collect unemployment compensation.

- The worker is unemployed because of a strike or other work stoppage caused by a labor dispute.

- The worker is receiving workers' compensation payments, Social Security payments, a private pension, or severance pay.

- The worker lied on the benefit claim or omitted some important information, in order to get or increase benefits.

When To Defend Unemployment Claims

There's no point in wasting your time and running up legal bills by contesting the payment of benefits to workers who deserve them. If you have to lay someone off because business isn't booming as you had hoped, or if you fired someone because you want to hire your brother-in-law instead, don't bother to object when your ex-employee makes a claim. On the other hand, if you have to fire someone for stealing or someone quits to start their own business, you can and should contest a claim for unemployment benefits.

What do you do if you're not sure whether the worker deserves benefits or not? Go ahead and contest the claim as discussed below, up to the point where you'd need to hire a lawyer. At that point, if the worker has won, you may want to reevaluate whether the issue is worth pursuing. Your lawyer should be able to estimate your chances of winning.

When not to contest a claim. There may be times when it's not in your interest to prevent your worker from collecting benefits, even if you would probably win if you tried. The most common situation is where you want to get rid of someone but don't have a good (or a legal) reason for doing it, or you suspect the worker is going to sue you. What do you do? You "buy out" the worker by offering a severance package. The package may include an agreement that you won't do anything to prevent the worker from collecting unemployment, along with some severance pay, continuation of health benefits, or other items. If you go this route, have the worker sign an adequate release of liability before he or she leaves. (See the sample release on page 265.)

How To Defend Unemployment Claims

When a former employee files for benefits, you'll get an official report form in the mail from the state unemployment agency. Fill it out and return it *within the deadline* stated on the form. These deadlines are rarely extended, even if you have a good excuse. Fail to respond, or respond too late, and the worker will automatically get benefits in most states.

Work Smart

If you're away from work, have someone check your mail. The person should open letters from the IRS, from the state unemployment agency or any other government office, or from any law office.

Just give the facts. Typically, the report will ask how long the employee worked for you, what his or her earnings were, whether the worker quit voluntarily or was dismissed, and what the facts surrounding the termination were. Don't give just a one-word explanation — but don't write a whole novel either. A few sentences should do it.

Example

If you need to fire somebody because of excessive unexcused absences, don't write "discharged for absenteeism" on the unemployment claim report. Instead, say when the absences occurred, how many there were, and when prior warnings were given. You also need to say something about the final incident that led to dismissal. You might say, "John was absent from work without notice six times within two months. He received oral warnings after the first two absences, and written warnings after the second two. After the fifth absence he was warned in writing that another such absence would lead to being fired. On Feb. 21 he failed to return to work following a scheduled vacation and was dismissed."

Go to the hearing. You should have a presence at any hearings, formal or informal, before the state unemployment insurance officials. This is the only effective way to present your side and to respond to any false or incomplete statements your ex-employee might make. It's up to you to prove your statements, by testifying or presenting documents. The person who actually witnessed the misconduct or other action that led to the termination should be present to testify — in many cases, that means you.

It's a good idea to have an attorney represent you at any hearing, especially the first time you are involved in an unemployment case. Attorney representation becomes a virtual necessity if you lose at the hearing level and decide to appeal to the court.

If you learn new facts, report them to the state. If you later learn of facts that would disqualify the claimant for benefits (for example, turning down a job offer, going on vacation without looking for work, or refusing to take the old job back if you offered to rehire the worker), report these facts to the state unemployment agency.

If you lose, appeal. If an employee is found eligible for benefits despite your objections, follow up with an appeal to the administrative agency, and (if you lose again) to the courts, unless your lawyer tells you this would be fruitless in your particular case.

Don't let a possible claim stop you. Even though a successful unemployment claim may raise your tax rates, don't let the fear of a rate increase keep you from firing an employee who is dragging your business down.

PROVIDING EMPLOYMENT REFERENCES

If you've had employees who left your business, you can expect prospective employers to contact you at some point for information about them. Employment references are one of an employer's most effective tools for verifying an applicant's credentials and qualifications. But as an ex-employer, you want to limit your risk by providing only the appropriate information in the correct manner.

Warning

There's one situation when you may have a legal obligation to provide information about a former employee to a prospective employer. Assume that you know that a former employee has a history of criminal violence or extremely aggressive behavior. An employer approaches you for a reference in connection with a job that would have your former employee working closely with the public. Must you disclose what you know about the employee's conduct? What if you're not sure that the information is true? Your risk in remaining silent is that you could be sued for failing to disclose the information if the former employee subsequently harms someone while on the job. On the other hand, you could be sued for defamation if you disclose the information and it turns out not to be true. Faced with this type of situation, you should consult your attorney.

- **State job reference requirements:** Several states have laws that may require you to provide references to former employees upon their request.

- **Defamation risk:** Certain statements by you or someone connected with your business may form the basis for lawsuits against you. Your primary risk is that former employees may sue for defamation, claiming that your statements are false and damaging to their reputations.

- **Other legal pitfalls:** Unfavorable statements may cause you to incur legal costs in defending suits for invasion of privacy, violations of state blacklisting laws, and similar claims.

However, the bottom line is that the decision is yours to make as to what amount of information, if any, you will provide in response to reference requests.

Employment Verification

The states listed below have laws that may require employers to provide letters concerning past employment services ("service letters") to former employees upon their request. States omitted from the list have no service letter laws. Rules relating to public employers, utilities, governmental units, etc. are excluded.

State Laws on Providing Job References

State	Service Letter Requirements
IN	Former employees are entitled, upon written request, to a letter stating: the nature and character of their services; their employment dates; and for what cause, if any, they quit or were fired. However, the obligation to provide service letters doesn't apply to employers that don't require written recommendations or applications showing an applicant's qualifications or experience. Employers that fail to provide a requested letter may be fined.
KS	Employers must comply with a fired employee's written request for a service letter stating the employee's employment dates; occupational classification; and wage rate. Employers that fail to provide a requested service letter may have their state business licenses suspended.
MN	Fired employees may, within 5 working days following termination, request in writing that their employers specify the reasons for the termination. Employers that fail to provide the reasons in writing within 5 working days of the request may be fined.
MO	Employers having at least 7 employees must provide service letters to ex-employees who worked for at least 90 days. Ex-employees must request the letter in writing within a reasonable period after they've left the business. The letter must be issued within 45 days of the request, and state the nature and character of the services rendered. employment dates, and for what cause, if any, the employee quit or was discharged. Employers that fail to provide a requested service letter may be sued for any damages resulting from that failure.
MT	Employers must furnish fired employees, upon request, a written statement of the reasons for their discharge. Employers who fail to provide the statement within a reasonable period of time are prohibited from furnishing any statement of the reasons for the discharge to any person. Employers who violate these provisions may be sued by the fired employees for damages and may be subject to criminal penalties.
NE	Public service corporations and their contractors are required to provide service letters to their former employees.
NV	Employers must furnish service letters to any former employees who worked for at least 60 days and who make a written request in writing. The letter must state the reasons why the employees left or were fired.
OK	Public service corporations and contractors are required to provide service letters to their former employees.

Employment References and Defamation

Your risk in providing employment references to prospective employers is that former employees may sue you if your references are unfavorable and lead to job rejections. The claim that former employees are most likely to assert is that the references are false and damaging to their reputations and, therefore, defamatory.

An employer may be liable to a former employee for defamation if the employer communicates to a prospective employer or other person a false statement that results in damage to the former employee's reputation. Defamation is commonly referred to as "slander" if the communication is verbal and as "libel" if the communication is written.

Awards in successful defamation suits may include damages for lost earnings, mental anguish, or pain and suffering and, if the employer's conduct was sufficiently egregious, punitive damages.

A successful defamation claim requires more than merely showing that an employer provided an unfavorable employment reference. The law usually protects an employer who in good faith discloses information believed to be true to a prospective employer or other person who has a legitimate interest in asking for the information. This protection may be lost, however, if the information isn't limited in scope to the inquiry being made, is disclosed at an improper time, or is disclosed in an improper manner.

The following are examples of the types of statements that you should avoid in giving employment references:

- **Accusations.** Defamation suits often arise out of accusations that an employee engaged in illegal or improper conduct. Employers have been liable for defamation for making statements to the effect that a former employee was a thief, used illegal drugs, or made "improper" advances to women. If you fired an employee because you suspected that the employee engaged in illegal or improper conduct and you feel compelled to state the reason for the firing, then restrict the statement to your suspicion ("Employee was fired because he was suspected of taking company property," not "Employee was fired because he stole company property"). However, don't even state a suspicion unless you can support it with objective evidence.

- **Exaggerations.** Employers can also get into trouble by exaggerating an employee's misconduct.

Example

A statement that employees were fired for "gross insubordination" was defamatory when the employees' only alleged misconduct was their refusal to adjust their expense accounts.

- **Statements not made in good faith.** The general protection extended to employers giving employment references requires that the statements be made in good faith. An employer's statements aren't made in good faith if the employer knows they are untrue or if the employer makes no effort to determine if they are untrue.

Example

An employer who lied in stating that an employee had admitted falsifying expense records was liable for defamation. Similarly liable was an employer whose manager made negative statements about an employee's work performance solely on the basis of rumors.

- **Statements made to improper parties.** Employers giving employment references are protected only if the statements are made to persons having a legitimate business interest in the information disclosed. For example, you can probably tell an inquiring employer that an employee was fired because the employee was suspected of stealing business property, provided there are objective facts to support your suspicion. In contrast, expressing your suspicion to others, such as other employees or friends who have no real reasons for knowing the specific details why the employee was fired, may be defamatory.

Guarding Against Defamatory Statements

When giving employment references, you can reduce your risk of being sued for defamation if you keep in mind the following key points:

- **Be truthful.** If your statements are true, they aren't defamatory. For this reason, refrain from making any statements that you aren't prepared to back up and substantiate if you are sued. Give objective facts or opinions and conclusions that you can support with objective facts, rather than mere allegations, speculation, or gossip. For example, you can safely state that an employee was fired for missing too many days of work. Don't speculate why the absences occurred.

- **Be clear and unambiguous.** Keep in mind that statements that are technically true may still be defamatory if they are incomplete or misleading. For example, an employer stated that an employee was fired for drug use but neglected to state that the employee's refusal to hire a supervisor's relative also contributed to the firing decision. The incomplete statement was defamatory because it unduly emphasized the employee's improper conduct. If you should decide to discuss why an employee left your business, state the reasons in objective and specific terms. Refrain from stating that an employee was terminated "for cause," "insubordination," "unsatisfactory performance," or other nonspecific reason, because such phrases may be defamatory by implication.

- **Be objective.** The tone of your statement is also important. Your references should not sound petty, vindictive, or accusatory. No matter how trying your relationship with the former employee may have been, you should try to discuss the facts in an objective, non-malicious way.

- **Be responsive.** References should be limited in scope to information that the inquiring employer requests. Don't feel compelled to provide all requested information. Rather, the notion here is that you should not volunteer any unfavorable information that isn't requested.

- **Stick to job-related facts.** Do not provide any information that is irrelevant to the employee's performance or behavior in the workplace. Comments about an employee's personal life are especially hazardous, because even if the comments are true, they may raise invasion of privacy issues.

- **Be selective in choosing your audience.** Limit your disclosure of employee information to those persons who have a legitimate interest in that information.

- **Limit telephone references.** Because you need to be sure that a person to whom you are providing an employment reference has a real business interest in receiving the information, you should use care in providing references over the phone. Unless you are going to limit your references to basic employment data, at a minimum you should arrange to provide the information in a return call. This will give you an opportunity to verify who the caller is. The better alternative is to have the caller make the reference request in writing.

- **Get signed releases or consents.** Your best protection against defamation and other claims that may arise from giving employment references is to get the former employee to consent to your release of information.

Other Risks in Providing References

In addition to defamation, there are other potential claims that should give you further incentive to limit any job references to true and objective facts that are relevant to a former employee's job-performance abilities.

- **Invasion of privacy claims.** Employers who disclose information about an employee's personal life open the door to being sued for invasion of privacy. Accordingly, you should refrain from disclosing information about an employee's private life unless you are absolutely certain that the disclosure will serve legitimate business purposes.

- **Equal employment opportunity claims.** Employers who refuse to provide references or who provide unjustifiably negative references have lost lawsuits because their actions damaged the ex-employees' equal employment opportunities guaranteed by federal or state fair employment laws.

- **Interference with prospective employment claims.** In several states, a former employee can sue an employer who gives false information to prospective employers with the intention of interfering with the former employee's prospects for employment. This type of claim differs slightly from defamation in that it focuses primarily on the employer's intent in providing the unfavorable reference.

- **Blacklisting claims.** In a majority of the states, an employer's "blacklisting" of a former employee is a crime. These blacklisting laws are generally broad enough to cover any communications that are designed to prevent former employees from securing employment.

Limiting Employment Reference Risks

Given the potential lawsuit risks, many employers give no references at all, or provide only basic employment data such as employment dates, job titles, and wage rates. However, such a restrictive policy doesn't foreclose your risk of being sued. For example, if you make exceptions to the policy by giving references for deserving employees, you may open the door to claims of discrimination or unfair treatment. Also, if your refusal to give references compels fired employees to disclose why they left your business, you may become liable for defamation if their disclosures reveal any defamatory comments that you may have made when firing them. Apart from your liability risk, you may even have an incentive to provide references for fired employees, who will be less likely to sue you for claims related to their firing if you help them find new jobs. Accordingly, it's usually in your best interests to have a policy that permits some limited disclosures about employees' work performance.

Using releases. Your best protection against reference-related lawsuits is to obtain in advance the employee's permission to your disclosure of employment information. Make it a practice to discuss with an employee who is leaving your business, either voluntarily or involuntarily, what you are willing to say in response to employment reference inquiries. You should then try to document the employee's consent to your providing information in response to reference requests by having the employee sign a written release authorizing your disclosure.

Sample Employment Reference Release

I acknowledge that I have been informed that it is ABC Company's general policy to disclose in response to a prospective employer's request only the following information about current or former employees: (1) the dates of employment, (2) descriptions of the jobs performed, and (3) salary or wage rates.

By signing this release, I am voluntarily requesting that ABC Company, Inc. depart from this general policy in responding to reference requests from any prospective employer that may be considering me for employment. I authorize ABC Company, Inc. to disclose to such prospective employers any employment-related information that ABC Company, Inc., in its sole discretion and judgment, may determine is appropriate to disclose, including any personal comments, evaluations, or assessments that ABC Company, Inc. may have about my performance or behavior as an employee.

In exchange for ABC Company's agreement to depart from its general policy and to disclose additional employment-related information pursuant to my request, I agree to release and discharge ABC Company, Inc. and ABC Company's successors, employees, officers, and directors from all claims, liabilities, and causes of action, know or unknown, fixed or contingent, that arise from or that are in any manner connected to ABC Company's disclosure of employment-related information to prospective employers. This release includes, but is not limited to, claims of defamation, libel, slander, negligence, or interference with contract or profession.

I acknowledge that I have carefully read and fully understand the provisions of this release. I further acknowledge that I was given the opportunity to consult with an attorney or any other individual of my choosing before signing this release and that I have decided to sign this release voluntarily and without coercion or duress by any person.

This release sets forth the entire agreement between ABC Company, Inc. and me, and I acknowledge that I have not relied upon any representation or statement, written or oral, not set forth in this document.

Signed: _____ Date: _____
    (Employee)

To ensure that any release you obtain will stand up in court, you want to avoid any signs that you forced the former employee to sign the release. Don't try to rush the employee into signing the document. A signed release will serve its purpose as long as you get it back before you provide the reference.

You should also consider adopting a policy of providing detailed references for former employees who have signed written releases and restricted references of only basic employment data for former employees who have not signed releases. This type of flexible policy will help show that the employee had a real choice in deciding whether or not to sign the release.

Finally, you should view a signed release as an insurance policy that will limit your exposure to liability if you accidentally make statements that are incomplete or misleading or that otherwise may be construed as being defamatory. Don't view the release as being a license to say whatever you want without any risk of being held accountable for your statements. Even if you have obtained a written release, your interests are best served if your employment references are made on the basis of true and objective facts that are relevant to a former employee's job-performance abilities and that you are prepared to substantiate if necessary.

Index

Need help running and growing your business?

Try this book. Our award-winning team of small business, accounting, and legal experts gives you everything you need to start, plan, market and grow a successful small business — all in one book. Plus exclusive coverage of:

- *How to minimize your legal and financial risks*
- *How to manage your finances and taxes*
- *STATE and FEDERAL laws that affect you*
- *How to build your personal wealth*

From **CCH** INCORPORATED, the leading source of business and legal information for over 80 years.